I0131762

SELinux System Administration

Second Edition

Ward off traditional security permissions and effectively secure your Linux systems with SELinux

Sven Vermeulen

BIRMINGHAM - MUMBAI

SELinux System Administration

Second Edition

Copyright © 2016 Packt Publishing

All rights reserved. No part of this book may be reproduced, stored in a retrieval system, or transmitted in any form or by any means, without the prior written permission of the publisher, except in the case of brief quotations embedded in critical articles or reviews.

Every effort has been made in the preparation of this book to ensure the accuracy of the information presented. However, the information contained in this book is sold without warranty, either express or implied. Neither the author, nor Packt Publishing, and its dealers and distributors will be held liable for any damages caused or alleged to be caused directly or indirectly by this book.

Packt Publishing has endeavored to provide trademark information about all of the companies and products mentioned in this book by the appropriate use of capitals. However, Packt Publishing cannot guarantee the accuracy of this information.

First published: September 2013

Second edition: December 2016

Production reference: 1131216

Published by Packt Publishing Ltd.
Livery Place
35 Livery Street
Birmingham
B3 2PB, UK.
ISBN 978-1-78712-695-4

www.packtpub.com

Credits

Author
Sven Vermeulen

Reviewers
David Quigley
Sam Wilson

Commissioning Editor
Kartikey Pandey

Acquisition Editor
Namrata Patil

Content Development Editor
Amedh Gemraram Pohad

Technical Editors
Vishal Kamal Mewada
Khushbu Sutar

Copy Editor
Madhusudan Uchil

Project Coordinator
Judie Jose

Proofreader
Safis Editing

Indexer
Pratik Shirodkar

Graphics
Kirk D'Penha

Production Coordinator
Shantanu N. Zagade

About the Author

Sven Vermeulen is a long-term contributor to various free software projects and the author of various online guides and resources. He got his first taste of free software in 1997 and never looked back. In 2003, he joined the ranks of the Gentoo Linux project as a documentation developer and has since worked in several roles, including Gentoo Foundation trustee, council member, project lead for various documentation initiatives, and (his current role) project lead for Gentoo Hardened SELinux integration and the system integrity project.

During this time, Sven gained expertise in several technologies, ranging from OS-level knowledge to application servers. He used his interest in security to guide his projects further in the areas of security guides using SCAP languages, mandatory access controls through SELinux, authentication with PAM, (application) firewalling, and more.

Within SELinux, Sven contributed several policies to the Reference Policy project, and he is an active participant in policy development and user space development projects.

In his daily job, Sven is an IT architect in a European financial institution as well as a self-employed solution engineer and consultant. The secure implementation of infrastructures (and the surrounding architectural integration) is, of course, an important part of this. Prior to this, he graduated with an MSc in computer engineering from Ghent University and MSc in ICT enterprise architecture from `http://inno.com/`, and he worked as a web application infrastructure engineer.

Sven is the main author of the *Gentoo Handbook*, which covers the installation and configuration of Gentoo Linux on several architectures. He also authored the *Linux Sea* online publication, which is a basic introduction to Linux for novice system administrators, and *SELinux System Administration* and *SELinux Cookbook* for Packt Publishing.

I would like to thank the open source / free software community for its never ending drive to create great software, documentation, artwork and services. It is through this drive that companies and organizations around the world are enjoying high quality services with all the freedom that this software provides. Specifically, I would like to thank the Gentoo community as it provides a great meta-distribution and operating system. The people I meet there are all greatly motivated, highly experienced and/or experts in particular fields. Being around in the community makes me eager to learn more.

About the Reviewers

David Quigley started his career as a computer systems researcher for the National Information Assurance Research Lab at the NSA, where he worked as a member of the SELinux team. David lead the design and implementation efforts to provide Labeled-NFS support for SELinux. David has previously contributed to the open source community through maintaining the Unionfs 1.0 code base and through code contributions to various other projects. David has presented at conferences such as the Ottawa Linux Symposium, the StorageSS workshop, LinuxCon, and several local Linux User Group meetings where presentation topics have included storage, file systems, and security. David currently works as a ZFS kernel engineer for the High Performance Data Division at Intel. He previously reviewed *SELinux Cookbook*, published by Packt publishing.

> *I would like to thank my wonderful wife, Kathy, for all she does to make sure I have the time to do things like review this book and travel to give presentations on SELinux. She is the joy of my life and has helped me become the man I am today. I'd also like to thank all my children past and present: Zoe Jane and Caroline, who remind us to love and cherish the time we have as a family.*

Sam Wilson is a senior systems and security engineer with a newly acquired passion for radio hardware and a focus on Red Hat Enterprise Linux. Because of his extensive security knowledge spanning microservices, infrastructure, and SecOps, Sam is approached regularly for SELinux mentorship and advice across the organizations he collaborates and works with. Sam has been active in GNU/Linux communities since early 2007 and has volunteered his time for NTFreenet, Darwin Community Arts, Ansible, and the Fedora project.

More recently, Sam can be found being a cranky neckbeard at `https://www.cycloptivity.net` as well working with the Atlassian Security Intelligence team on visibility, operational security, and controls to support and protect Atlassian customers in the cloud.

www.PacktPub.com

For support files and downloads related to your book, please visit www.PacktPub.com.

Did you know that Packt offers eBook versions of every book published, with PDF and ePub files available? You can upgrade to the eBook version at www.PacktPub.com and as a print book customer, you are entitled to a discount on the eBook copy. Get in touch with us at service@packtpub.com for more details.

At www.PacktPub.com, you can also read a collection of free technical articles, sign up for a range of free newsletters and receive exclusive discounts and offers on Packt books and eBooks.

https://www.packtpub.com/mapt

Get the most in-demand software skills with Mapt. Mapt gives you full access to all Packt books and video courses, as well as industry-leading tools to help you plan your personal development and advance your career.

Why subscribe?

- Fully searchable across every book published by Packt
- Copy and paste, print, and bookmark content
- On demand and accessible via a web browser

Table of Contents

Preface

The secure state of an operating system or service is the result of a layered security approach. Systems can be shielded from the outside world through firewalls, operating systems have to be kept up to date with the latest security patches, services have to be configured properly, separation of duties has to be implemented for end users, and so forth.

Access controls are another layer that administrators have to look into. With Security Enhanced Linux (SELinux), the Linux ecosystem has a robust and established mandatory access control (MAC) system in place. Some distributions enable SELinux by default, others allow administrators to enable SELinux easily. Android, one of the most popular mobile device operating systems, has also embraced SELinux technology under the SEAndroid name.

But unlike Android, where users and applications are tightly controlled and where deviation from the setup and organization of files and resources is not allowed, desktops, workstations, and servers that implement Linux have greater diversity. As a result, configuring and tuning SELinux on these systems requires more knowledge of what SELinux is, how it works, and how it can be configured.

In this book, we discuss what SELinux is and how it is embedded in the Linux operating system. We go through various configuration aspects of SELinux and deal with several use cases that leverage SELinux's strengths to further harden the system and services hosted on it.

What this book covers

`Chapter 1`, *Fundamental SELinux Concepts*, gives administrators insight into what SELinux is and how it is enforced through the Linux kernel. It explains the differences in SELinux implementations between distributions and describes the SELinux-specific terminology that administrators will often read about when diving deeper into the SELinux technology.

`Chapter 2`, *Understanding SELinux Decisions and Logging*, covers the various enforcement states of SELinux and shows where SELinux logs its events. The chapter takes great care to teach administrators how to interpret and analyze those events.

`Chapter 3`, *Managing User Logins*, explains to administrators how to manage Linux users and their permissions and map those users to the various roles that SELinux supports through its own user space support and Linux's pluggable authentication modules.

Furthermore, the chapter deals with SELinux's category support.

`Chapter 4`, *Process Domains and File-Level Access Controls*, introduces administrators to SELinux labels and how these labels are stored on the file system or represented for other resources. It then educates administrators and end users on how to set and update these labels.

`Chapter 5`, *Controlling Network Communications*, further develops the standard network security services, iptables and IPSec, with SELinux features. Administrators are trained to understand and enable SELinux support in those security services and even enable cross-system labeling through Labeled IPSec and NetLabel/CIPSO.

`Chapter 6`, *sVirt and Docker Support*, clarifies how Red Hat has devised the secured virtualization (sVirt) technology and implemented it on both operating system virtualization (through libvirt) and containers (through Docker). The chapter learns how to tune these services with SELinux support and control resources between the guests or containers.

`Chapter 7`, *D-Bus and systemd*, goes into the realms of the mentioned core system services and how they use SELinux rules to further harden their own services and features. With this knowledge at hand, administrators are then shown how to tune the D-Bus service controls as well as handle SELinux's access controls enforced through systemd.

`Chapter 8`, *Working with SELinux Policies*, looks at tuning and controlling the SELinux policies themselves. It shows how custom policy enhancements can be created or even replace the distribution-provided policy.

`Chapter 9`, *Analyzing Policy Behavior*, dives into the analysis tools that allow engineers and administrators to query the SELinux policy more in depth to assert for themselves that the policy is contained and behaves as expected.

`Chapter 10`, *SELinux Use Cases*, covers a number of common server use cases, such as web servers and file servers, and how SELinux can be used to secure those services. It covers how isolation through SELinux is possible, allowing administrators to set up a multi-tenant, hardened environment.

What you need for this book

As SELinux is a core component of a Linux distribution, readers will need to have a Linux system at their disposal that already has SELinux enabled. Converting an installation to SELinux is not in the scope of this book—please consult your distribution's documentation for this.

Furthermore, tuning and configuring the security of a system requires administrative privileges on the system.

Who this book is for

This book targets Linux system administrators who have reasonable experience with maintaining Linux systems and want to understand and work with the SELinux technology. Moreover, this book can be enlightening for IT architects to understand how SELinux can be positioned to enhance the security of Linux systems and Linux-hosted services within their organization.

Conventions

In this book, you will find a number of text styles that distinguish between different kinds of information. Here are some examples of these styles and an explanation of their meaning.

Code words in text, database table names, folder names, filenames, file extensions, pathnames, dummy URLs, user input, and Twitter handles are shown as follows: "We accomplish this through the `semanage login` command."

A block of code is set as follows:

```
dbadm_r
  Dominated roles:
    dbadm_r
  Types:
    qmail_inject_t
    dbadm_t
    ...
    user_mail_t
```

Any command-line input or output is written as follows:

```
# seinfo -amcs_constrained_type -x | grep virt_
```

New terms and **important words** are shown in bold. Words that you see on the screen, for example, in menus or dialog boxes, appear in the text like this: "Once loaded, select **New Analysis** to initiate the policy analysis functions."

Warnings or important notes appear in a box like this.

Tips and tricks appear like this.

Reader feedback

Feedback from our readers is always welcome. Let us know what you think about this book—what you liked or disliked. Reader feedback is important for us as it helps us develop titles that you will really get the most out of.

To send us general feedback, simply e-mail `feedback@packtpub.com`, and mention the book's title in the subject of your message.

If there is a topic that you have expertise in and you are interested in either writing or contributing to a book, see our author guide at `www.packtpub.com/authors`.

Customer support

Now that you are the proud owner of a Packt book, we have a number of things to help you to get the most from your purchase.

Errata

Although we have taken every care to ensure the accuracy of our content, mistakes do happen. If you find a mistake in one of our books—maybe a mistake in the text or the code—we would be grateful if you could report this to us. By doing so, you can save other readers from frustration and help us improve subsequent versions of this book. If you find any errata, please report them by visiting `http://www.packtpub.com/submit-errata`, selecting your book, clicking on the Errata Submission Form link, and entering the details of your errata. Once your errata are verified, your submission will be accepted and the errata will be uploaded to our website or added to any list of existing errata under the Errata section of that title.

To view the previously submitted errata, go to `https://www.packtpub.com/books/content/support` and enter the name of the book in the search field. The required information will appear under the Errata section.

Piracy

Piracy of copyrighted material on the Internet is an ongoing problem across all media. At Packt, we take the protection of our copyright and licenses very seriously. If you come across any illegal copies of our works in any form on the Internet, please provide us with the location address or website name immediately so that we can pursue a remedy.

Please contact us at `copyright@packtpub.com` with a link to the suspected pirated material.

We appreciate your help in protecting our authors and our ability to bring you valuable content.

Questions

If you have a problem with any aspect of this book, you can contact us at `questions@packtpub.com`, and we will do our best to address the problem.

1
Fundamental SELinux Concepts

Security Enhanced Linux (**SELinux**) brings additional security measures to your Linux system to further protect its resources.

In this chapter, we will cover:

- Why SELinux uses labels to identify resources
- How SELinux differs from traditional Linux access controls by enforcing security rules
- How the access control rules enforced by SELinux are provided through policy files

In the end, we will cover an overview of the differences between SELinux implementations across Linux distributions.

Providing more security to Linux

Seasoned Linux administrators and security engineers already know that they need to put some trust in the users and processes on their system in order for the system to remain secure. This is partially because users can attempt to exploit vulnerabilities found in the software running on the system, but a large contribution to this trust level is because the secure state of the system depends on the behavior of the users. A Linux user with access to sensitive information could easily leak that out to the public, manipulate the behavior of the applications he or she launches, and do many other things that affect the security of the system. The default access controls that are active on a regular Linux system are discretionary; it is up to the users how the access controls should behave.

The Linux **discretionary access control** (**DAC**) mechanism is based on the user and/or group information of the process and is matched against the user and/or group information of the file, directory, or other resource being manipulated. Consider the `/etc/shadow` file, which contains the password and account information of the local Linux accounts:

```
$ ls -l /etc/shadow
-rw------- 1 root root 1010 Apr 25 22:05 /etc/shadow
```

Without additional access control mechanisms in place, this file is readable and writable by any process that is owned by the `root` user, regardless of the purpose of the process on the system. The `shadow` file is a typical example of a sensitive file that we don't want to see leaked or abused in any other fashion. Yet the moment someone has access to the file, that user can copy it elsewhere, for example to a home directory, or even mail it to a different computer and attempt to attack the password hashes stored within.

Another example of how Linux DAC requires trust from its users is when a database is hosted on the system. Database files themselves are (hopefully) only accessible to runtime users of the **database management system** (**DBMS**) and the Linux `root` user. Properly secured systems will only grant trusted users access to these files (for instance, through `sudo`) by allowing them to change their effective user ID from their personal user to the database runtime user or even `root` account, and this for a well-defined set of commands. These users too, can analyze the database files and gain access to potentially confidential information in the database without going through the DBMS.

However, regular users are not the only reason for securing a system. Lots of software daemons run as the Linux `root` user or have significant privileges on the system. Errors within those daemons can easily lead to information leakage or might even lead to remotely exploitable vulnerabilities. Backup software, monitoring software, change management software, scheduling software, and so on: they all often run with the highest privileged account possible on a regular Linux system. Even when the administrator does not allow privileged users, their interaction with daemons induces a potential security risk. As such, the users are still trusted to correctly interact with these applications in order for the system to function properly. Through this, the administrator leaves the security of the system to the discretion of its (many) users.

Enter SELinux, which provides an additional access control layer on top of the standard Linux DAC mechanism. SELinux provides a **mandatory access control** (**MAC**) system that, unlike its DAC counterpart, gives the administrator full control over what is allowed on the system and what isn't. It accomplishes this by supporting a policy-driven approach over what processes are and aren't allowed to do and by enforcing this policy through the Linux kernel.

Mandatory means that access control is enforced by the operating system and defined solely by the policy rules that the system administrator (or security administrator) has enabled. Users and processes do not have permission to change the security rules, so they cannot work around the access controls; security is not left to their discretion anymore.

The word *mandatory* here, just like the word *discretionary* before, was not chosen by accident to describe the abilities of the access control system: both are known terms in the security research field and have been described in many other publications, including the **Trusted Computer System Evaluation Criteria** (**TCSEC**) (`http://csrc.nist.gov/publications/history/dod85.pdf`) standard (also known as the *Orange Book*) by the Department of Defense in the United States of America in 1985. This publication has led to the Common Criteria standard for computer security certification (ISO/IEC 15408), available at `http://www.commoncriteriaportal.org/cc/`.

Using Linux security modules

Consider the example of the `shadow` file again. A MAC system can be configured to only allow a limited number of processes to read from and write to the file. On such specifically configured systems, a user logged on as `root` cannot directly access the file or even move it around. He can't even change the attributes of the file:

```
# id
uid=0(root) gid=0(root)
# cat /etc/shadow
cat: /etc/shadow: Permission denied
# chmod a+r /etc/shadow
chmod: changing permissions of '/etc/shadow': Permission denied
```

This is enforced through rules that describe when the contents of a file can be read. With SELinux, these rules are defined in the SELinux policy and are loaded when the system boots. It is the Linux kernel itself that is responsible for enforcing the rules. Mandatory access control systems such as SELinux can be easily integrated into the Linux kernel through its support for **Linux Security Modules** (**LSM**):

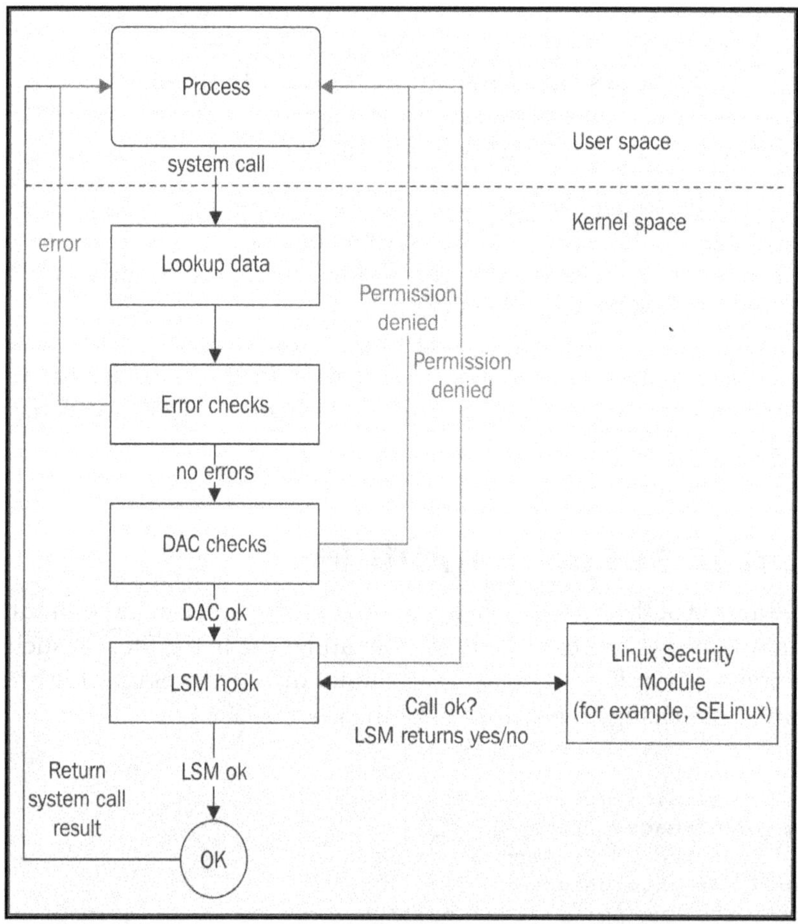

High-level overview of how LSM is integrated into the Linux kernel

LSM has been available in the Linux kernel since version 2.6, released sometime in December 2003. It is a framework that provides **hooks** inside the Linux kernel on various locations, including the system call entry points, and allows a security implementation such as SELinux to provide functions to be called when a hook is triggered. These functions check the policy and other information before returning a go/no-go back. LSM by itself does not provide any security functionality; instead, it relies on security implementations that do the heavy lifting. SELinux is one implementation that uses LSM. There are however, several other implementations: AppArmor, Smack, TOMOYO Linux, and Yama, to name a few.

At the time of writing this book, only one *main* security implementation can be active through the LSM hooks. Although a built kernel can contain multiple security implementations, only one can be active at the same time. Work is underway to enable stacking multiple security implementations, allowing system administrators to have more than one implementation active. Recent work has already allowed multiple implementations to be defined (but not simultaneously active). When supported, this will allow administrators to pick the best features of a number of implementations and activate smaller LSM-implemented security controls on top of the more complete security model implementations, such as SELinux, TOMOYO, Smack, or AppArmor.

Extending regular DAC with SELinux

SELinux does not change the Linux DAC implementation nor can it override denials made by the Linux DAC permissions. If a regular system (without SELinux) prevents a particular access, there is nothing SELinux can do to override this decision. This is because the LSM hooks are triggered *after* the regular DAC permission checks have been executed, which is a conscious design decision from the LSM project.

For instance, if you need to allow an additional user access to a file, you cannot add a SELinux policy to do that for you. Instead, you will need to look into other features of Linux such as the use of POSIX access control lists. Through the `setfacl` and `getfacl` commands (provided by the `acl` package), the user can set additional permissions on files and directories, opening up the selected resource to additional users or groups.

As an example, let's grant user `lisa` read-write access to a file using `setfacl`:

```
$ setfacl -m u:lisa:rw /path/to/file
```

Similarly, to view the current POSIX ACLs applied to the file, use this command:

```
$ getfacl /path/to/file
# file: file
# owner: swift
# group: swift
user::rw-
user:lisa:rw-
group::r--
mask::r--
other::r--
```

Restricting root privileges

The regular Linux DAC allows for an all-powerful user: `root`. Unlike most other users on the system, the logged-on `root` user has all the rights needed to fully manage the entire system, ranging from overriding access controls to controlling audits, changing user IDs, managing the network, and much more. This is supported through a security concept called **capabilities** (for an overview of Linux capabilities, check out the capabilities manual page: `man capabilities`). SELinux is also able to restrict access to these capabilities in a fine-grained manner.

Due to this fine-grained authorization aspect of SELinux, even the `root` user can be confined without impacting the operations on the system. The previous example of accessing `/etc/shadow` is just one example of an activity that a powerful user as `root` still might not be able to perform due to the SELinux access controls being in place.

When SELinux was added to the mainstream Linux kernel, some security projects even went as far as providing public `root` shell access to a SELinux-protected system, asking hackers and other security researchers to compromise the box. The ability to restrict `root` was welcomed by system administrators who sometimes need to pass on the root password or root shell to other users (for example, database administrators) who needed `root` privileges when their software went haywire. Thanks to SELinux, the administrator can now pass on a `root` shell while resting assured that the user only has those rights he needs, and not full system-administration rights.

Reducing the impact of vulnerabilities

If there is one benefit of SELinux that needs to be stressed, while often also being misunderstood, then it is its ability to reduce the impact of vulnerabilities.

A properly written SELinux policy confines applications so that their allowed activities are reduced to a minimum set. This **least-privilege model** ensures that abnormal application behavior is not only detected and audited but also prevented. Many application vulnerabilities can be exploited to execute tasks that an application is not meant to do. When this happens, SELinux will prevent this.

However, there are two misconceptions about SELinux's ability to thwart exploits, namely, the impact of the policy and the exploitation itself.

If the policy is not written in a least-privilege model, then SELinux might consider this nonstandard behavior as normal and allow the actions to continue. For policy writers, this means that their policy rules have to be very fine-grained. Sadly, that makes writing policies very time-consuming: there are more than 80 classes and over 200 permissions known to SELinux, and policy rules need to take into account all these classes and permissions for each interaction between two objects or resources.

As a result, policies tend to become convoluted and harder to maintain. Some policy writers make the policies more permissive than is absolutely necessary, which might result in exploits becoming successful even though the action is not expected behavior from an application's point of view. Some application policies are explicitly marked as *unconfined* (which is discussed later in this chapter), showing that they are very liberal in their allowed permissions. Red Hat Enterprise Linux even starts application policies as completely permissive, and only starts enforcing access controls for those applications after a few releases (and additional testing).

The second misconception is the exploit itself. If an application's vulnerability allows an unauthenticated user to use the application services as if he were authorized, then SELinux will not play a role in reducing the impact of the vulnerability; it only notices the behavior of the application itself and not of the sessions internal to the application. As long as the application itself behaves as expected (such as accessing its own files and not poking around in other file systems), SELinux will happily allow the actions to take place.

It is only when the application starts behaving erratically that SELinux stops the exploit from continuing. Exploits such as **remote command execution** (**RCE**) against applications that should not be executing random commands (such as database management systems or web servers, excluding CGI-like functionality) will be prevented, whereas session hijacking or SQL injection attacks are not controllable through SELinux policies.

Enabling SELinux support

Enabling SELinux on a Linux system is not just a matter of enabling the SELinux LSM module within the Linux kernel.

A SELinux implementation comprises the following:

- The SELinux kernel subsystem, implemented in the Linux kernel through LSM
- Libraries, used by applications that need to interact with SELinux
- Utilities, used by administrators to interact with SELinux
- Policies, which define the access controls themselves

The libraries and utilities are bundled by the SELinux user space project (`https://github.com/SELinuxProject/selinux/wiki`). Next to the user space applications and libraries, various components on a Linux system are updated with SELinux-specific code, including the `init` system and several core utilities.

Because SELinux isn't just a switch that needs to be toggled, Linux distributions that support it usually come with SELinux predefined and loaded: Fedora and Red Hat Enterprise Linux (with its derivatives, such as CentOS and Oracle Linux) are well-known examples. Other supporting distributions might not automatically have SELinux enabled but can easily support it through the installation of additional packages (which is the case with Debian and Ubuntu), and others have a well-documented approach on how to convert a system to SELinux (for example, Gentoo and Arch Linux).

Throughout the book, examples will be shown for Gentoo and **Red Hat Enterprise Linux** (**RHEL**) 7.2. We will use these two because they have different implementation details, allowing us to demonstrate the full potential of SELinux.

Labeling all resources and objects

When SELinux has to decide whether it has to allow or deny a particular action, it makes a decision based on the context of both the **subject** (which is initiating the action) and the **object** (which is the target of the action). These contexts (or parts of the context) are mentioned in the policy rules that SELinux enforces.

The context of a process is what identifies the process to SELinux. SELinux has no notion of Linux process ownership and, once running, does not care how the process is called, which process ID it has, and what account the process runs as. All it wants to know is what the context of that process is, which is represented to users and administrators as a **label**. *Label* and *context* are often used interchangeably, and although there is a technical distinction (one is a representation of the other), we will not dwell on that much.

Let's look at an example label: the context of the current user (try it out yourself if you are on a SELinux-enabled system):

```
$ id -Z
unconfined_u:unconfined_r:unconfined_t:s0-s0:c0.c1023
```

The `id` command, which returns information about the current user, is executed here with the `-Z` switch (a commonly agreed-upon switch for displaying additional security information obtained from the LSM-based security subsystems). It shows us the context of the current user (actually the context of the `id` process itself when it was executing). As we can see, the context has a string representation and looks as if it has five fields (it doesn't; it has four fields–the last field just happens to contain a :).

SELinux developers decided to use labels instead of real process and file (or other resource) metadata for its access controls. This is different to MAC systems such as AppArmor, which uses the path of the binary (and thus the process name) and the paths of the resources to handle permission checks. The decision to make SELinux a label-based mandatory access control was taken for various reasons, which are as follows:

- Using paths might be easier to comprehend for administrators, but this doesn't allow us to keep the context information close to the resource. If a file or directory is moved or remounted or a process has a different namespace view on the files, then the access controls might behave differently as they look at the path instead of the file. With label-based contexts, this information is retained and the system keeps controlling the resource properly.
- Contexts reveal the purpose of the process very well. The same binary application can be launched in different contexts depending on how it got started. The context value (such as the one shown in the `id -Z` output earlier) is exactly what the administrator needs. With it, he knows what the rights are of each of the running instances, but he can also deduce from it how the process might have been launched and what its purpose is.
- Contexts also make abstractions of the object itself. We are used to talking about processes and files, but contexts are also applicable to less tangible resources such as pipes (inter-process communication) or database objects. Path-based identification only works as long as you can write a path.

As an example, consider the following policies:

- Allow the `httpd` processes to bind to TCP port `80`
- Allow the processes labeled with `httpd_t` to bind to TCP ports labeled with `http_port_t`

In the first example, we cannot easily reuse this policy when the web server process isn't using the `httpd` binary (perhaps because it was renamed or it isn't Apache but another web server) or when we want to have HTTP access on a different port. With the labeled approach, the binary can be called `apache2` or `MyWebServer.py`; as long as the process is labeled `httpd_t`, the policy applies. The same happens with the port definition: you can label the port `8080` with `http_port_t` and thus allow the web servers to bind to that port as well.

Dissecting the SELinux context

To come to a context, SELinux uses at least three, and sometimes four, values. Let's look at the context of an Apache web server as an example:

```
$ ps -eZ | grep httpd
system_u:system_r:httpd_t:s0   511  ?   00:00:00 httpd
```

As we can see, the process is assigned a context that contains the following fields:

- `system_u`: This represents the SELinux user
- `system_r`: This represents the SELinux role
- `httpd_t`: This represents the SELinux type (also known as the domain in case of a process)
- `s0`: This represents the sensitivity level

This structure can be depicted as follows:

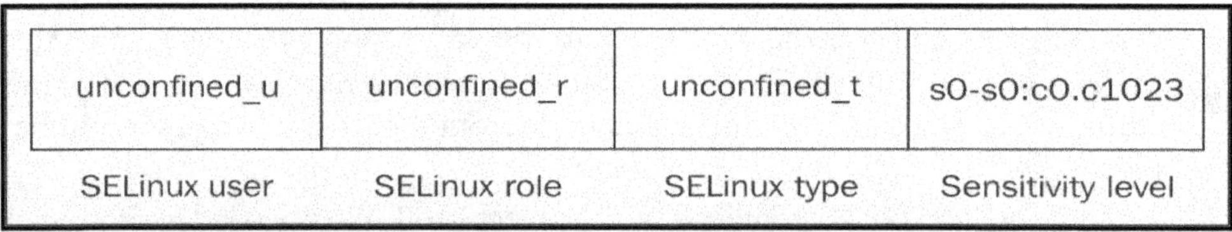

The structure of a SELinux context, using the id -Z output as an example

When we work with SELinux, contexts are all we need. In the majority of cases, it is the third field (called the domain or type) that is most important since the majority of SELinux policy rules (over 99 percent) consists of rules related to the interaction between two types (without mentioning roles, users, or sensitivity levels).

SELinux contexts are aligned with LSM security attributes and exposed to the user space in a standardized manner (compatible with multiple LSM implementations), allowing end users and applications to easily query the contexts. An interesting place where these attributes are presented is within the `/proc` pseudo file system.

Inside each process's `/proc/<pid>` location we find a subdirectory called `attr`, inside of which the following files can be found:

```
$ ls /proc/$$/attr
current    fscreate     prev
exec       keycreate    sockcreate
```

All these files, if read, display either nothing or a SELinux context. If it is empty, then that means the application has not explicitly set a context for that particular purpose, and the SELinux context will be deduced either from the policy or inherited from its parent.

The meaning of the files are as follows:

- The `current` file displays the current SELinux context of the process.
- The `exec` file displays the SELinux context that will be assigned by the next application execution done through this application. It is usually empty.
- The `fscreate` file displays the SELinux context that will be assigned to the next file that is written by the application. It is usually empty.
- The `keycreate` file displays the SELinux context that will be assigned to the keys cached in the kernel by this application. It is usually empty.
- The `prev` file displays the previous SELinux context for this particular process. This is usually the context of its parent application.
- The `sockcreate` file displays the SELinux context that will be assigned to the next socket created by the application. It is usually empty.

If an application has multiple subtasks, then the same information is available in each subtask directory at `/proc/<pid>/task/<taskid>/attr`.

Enforcing access through types

The SELinux type (the third part of an SELinux context) of a process (called the **domain**) is the basis of the fine-grained access controls of that process with respect to itself and other types (which can be processes, files, sockets, network interfaces, and more). In most SELinux literature, SELinux's label-based access control mechanism is fine-tuned to say that SELinux is a **type enforcement** mandatory access control system: when some actions are denied, the (absence of the) fine-grained access controls on the type level are most likely to blame.

With type enforcement, SELinux is able to control what an application is allowed to do based on how it got executed in the first place: a web server that is launched interactively by a user will run with a different type than a web server executed through the `init` system, even though the process binary and path are the same. The web server launched from the `init` system is most likely trusted (and thus allowed to do whatever web servers are supposed to do), whereas a manually launched web server is less likely to be considered *normal behavior* and as such will have different privileges.

The majority of SELinux resources will focus on types. Even though the SELinux type is just the third part of a SELinux context, it is the most important one for most administrators. Most documentation will even just talk about a type such as `httpd_t` rather than a full SELinux context.

Take a look at the following `dbus-daemon` processes:

```
# ps -eZ | grep dbus-daemon
system_u:system_r:system_dbusd_t 4531 ?        00:00:00 dbus-daemon
staff_u:staff_r:staff_dbusd_t    5266 ?        00:00:00 dbus-daemon
```

In this example, one `dbus-daemon` process is the system D-Bus daemon running with the aptly named `system_dbusd_t` type, whereas another one is running with the `staff_dbusd_t` type assigned to it. Even though their binaries are completely the same, they both serve a different purpose on the system and as such have a different type assigned. SELinux then uses this type to govern the actions allowed by the process towards other types, including how `system_dbusd_t` can interact with `staff_dbusd_t`.

SELinux types are by convention suffixed with `_t`, although this is not mandatory.

Granting domain access through roles

SELinux roles (the second part of a SELinux context) allow SELinux to support role-based access controls. Although type enforcement is the most used (and known) part of SELinux, role-based access control is an important method to keep a system secure, especially from malicious user attempts. SELinux roles define the allowed types (domains) processes can run with. These types (domains) on their part define the permissions. As such, SELinux roles help define what a user (which has access to one or more roles) can and cannot do.

By convention, SELinux roles are defined with an `_r` suffix. On most SELinux-enabled systems, the following roles are made available to be assigned to users:

Roles	Description
`user_r`	This role is meant for restricted users: the `user_r` SELinux role is only allowed to have processes with types specific to end-user applications. Privileged types, including those used to switch to another Linux user, are not allowed for this role.
`staff_r`	This role is meant for non-critical operations: the SELinux `staff_r` role is generally restricted to the same applications as the restricted user, but it has the ability to switch roles. It is the default role for operators to be in (so as to keep those users in the least privileged role as long as possible).
`sysadm_r`	This role is meant for system administrators: the `sysadm_r` SELinux role is very privileged, enabling various system administration tasks. However, certain end-user application types might not be supported (especially if those types are used for potentially vulnerable or untrusted software) to keep the system free from infections.
`secadm_r`	This role is meant for security administrators: the `secadm_r` SELinux role is allowed to change the SELinux policy and manipulate the SELinux controls. It is generally used when separation of duties is needed between system administrators and system policy management.
`system_r`	This role is meant for daemons and background processes: the `system_r` SELinux role is quite privileged, supporting the various daemon and system process types. However, end-user application types and other administrative types are not allowed in this role.

`unconfined_r`	This role is meant for end users: the `unconfined_r` role is allowed a limited number of types, but those types are very privileged as it is meant for running any application launched by a user in a more or less unconfined manner (not restricted by SELinux rules). This role as such is only available if the system administrator wants to protect certain processes (mostly daemons) while keeping the rest of the system operations almost untouched by SELinux.

Other roles might be supported as well, such as `guest_r` and `xguest_r`, depending on the distribution. It is wise to consult the distribution documentation for more information about the supported roles. An overview of available roles can be obtained through the `seinfo` command (part of `setools-console` in RHEL or `app-admin/setools` in Gentoo):

```
# seinfo --role
Roles: 14
  auditadm_r
  dbadm_r
  ...
  unconfined_r
```

Limiting roles through users

A SELinux user (the first part of a SELinux context) is different from a Linux user. Unlike Linux user information, which can change while the user is working on the system (through tools such as `sudo` or `su`), the SELinux policy can (and generally will) enforce that the SELinux user remain the same even when the Linux user itself has changed. Because of the immutable state of the SELinux user, specific access controls can be implemented to ensure that users cannot work around the set of permissions granted to them, even when they get privileged access.

An example of such an access control is the **user-based access control** (**UBAC**) feature that some Linux distributions (optionally) enable, which prevents users from accessing files of different SELinux users even when those users try to use the Linux DAC controls to open up access to each other's files.

The most important feature of SELinux users, however, is that SELinux user definitions restrict which roles the (Linux) user is allowed to be in. A Linux user is first assigned to a SELinux user–multiple Linux users can be assigned to the same SELinux user. Once set, that user cannot switch to a SELinux role he isn't meant to be in.

This is the role-based access control implementation of SELinux:

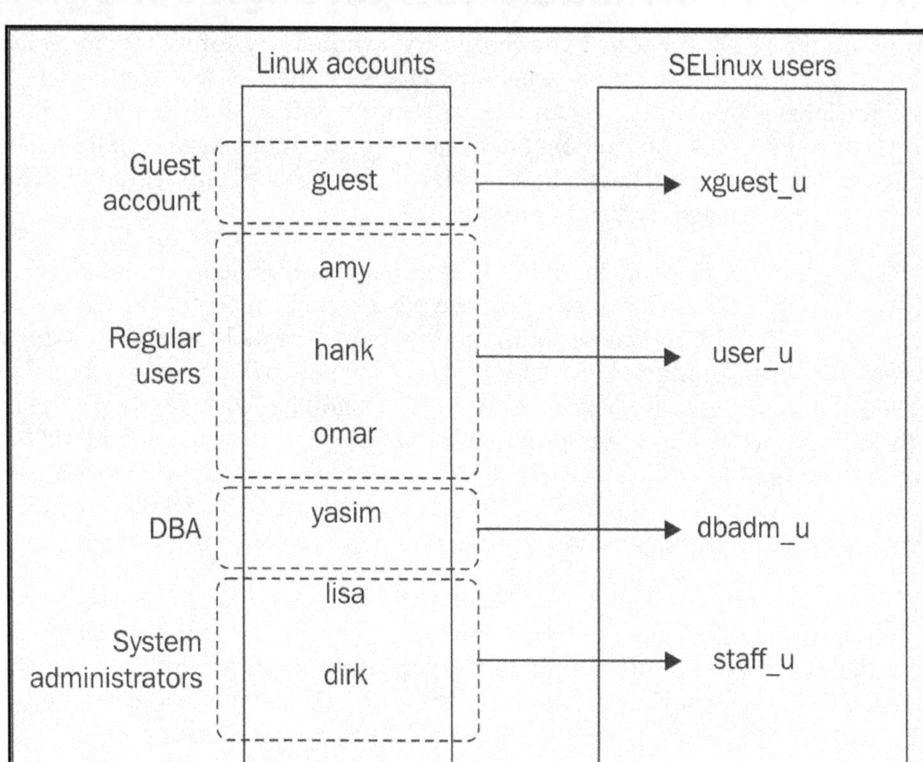

Mapping Linux accounts to SELinux users

SELinux users are, by convention, defined with an `_u` suffix, although this is not mandatory. The SELinux users that most distributions have available are named after the role they represent, but instead of ending with `_r`, they end with `_u`. For instance, for the `sysadm_r` role, there is a `sysadm_u` SELinux user.

Controlling information flow through sensitivities

The fourth part of a SELinux context, the sensitivity, is not always present (some Linux distributions by default do not enable sensitivity labels). If they are present though, then this part of the label is needed for the **multilevel security** (**MLS**) support within SELinux. Sensitivity labels allow classification of resources and restriction of access to those resources based on a security clearance. These labels consist of two parts: a confidentiality value (prefixed with `s`) and a category value (prefixed with `c`).

In many larger organizations and companies, documents are labeled internal, confidential, or strictly confidential. SELinux can assign processes a certain clearance level towards these resources. With MLS, SELinux can be configured to follow the Bell-LaPadula model, a security model that can be characterized by *no read up and no write down*: based on a process' clearance level, that process cannot read anything with a higher confidentiality level nor write to (or communicate otherwise with) any resource with a lower confidentiality level. SELinux does not use the internal, confidential, and other labels. Instead, it uses numbers from `0` (lowest confidentiality) to whatever the system administrator has defined as the highest value (this is configurable and set when the SELinux policy is built).

Categories allow resources to be tagged with one or more categories, on which access controls are also possible. One of the functionalities resulting from using categories is to support multitenancy (for example, systems hosting applications for multiple customers) within a Linux system, by having processes and resources belonging to one tenant be assigned a particular set of categories, whereas the processes and resources of another tenant get a different set of categories. When a process does not have proper categories assigned, it cannot do anything with the resources (or other processes) that have other categories assigned.

An unwritten convention in the SELinux world is that (at least) two categories are used to differentiate between tenants. By having services randomly pick two categories for a tenant out of a predefined set of categories, while ensuring each tenant has a unique combination, these services receive proper isolation. The use of two categories is not mandatory but is implemented by services such as **sVirt** and **Docker**.

In that sense, categories can be seen as tags, allowing access to be granted only when the tags of the process and the target resource match. As multilevel security is not often used, the benefits of only using categories is persisted in what is called **multi-category security** (**MCS**). This is a special MLS case, where only a single confidentiality level is supported (`s0`).

Defining and distributing policies

Enabling SELinux does not automatically start the enforcement of access. If SELinux is enabled and it cannot find a policy, it will refuse to start. That is because the *policy* defines the behavior of the system (what SELinux should allow). SELinux policies are generally distributed in a compiled form (just like with software) as policy modules. These modules are then aggregated into a single policy store and loaded in memory to allow SELinux to enforce the policy rules on the system.

Gentoo, being a source-based meta-distribution, distributes the SELinux policies as (source) code as well, which is compiled and built at install time, just like it does with other software.

The following diagram shows the relationship between **policy rules**, **policy modules**, and a **policy package** (which is often a one-to-one mapping towards a **policy store**):

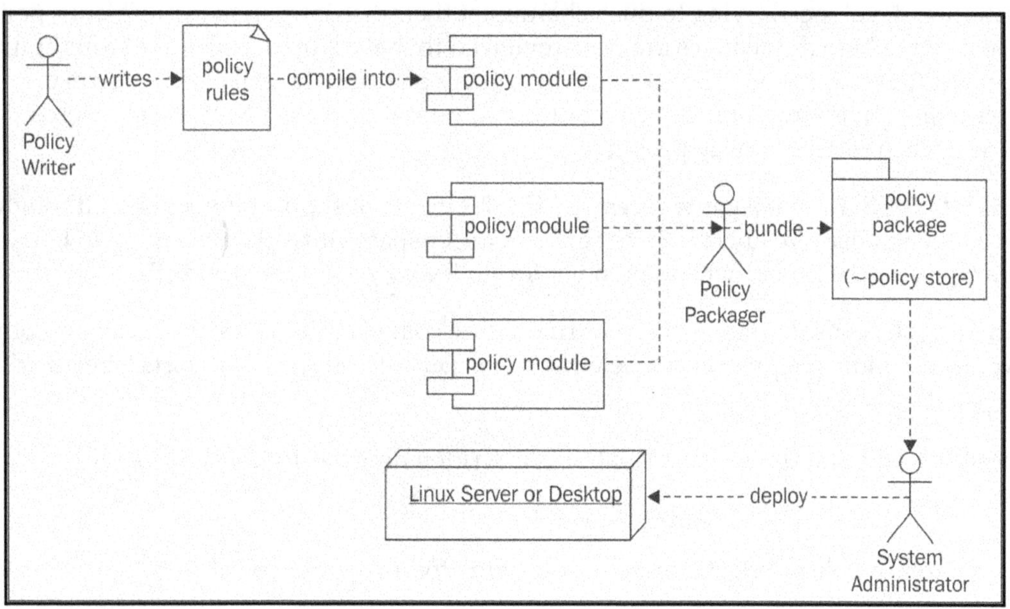

Relationship between policy rules, policy modules, and policy store

Writing SELinux policies

A SELinux policy writer can (currently) write down the policy rules in three possible languages:

- In standard SELinux source format–a human-readable and well-established language for writing SELinux policies
- In reference policy style–this extends the standard SELinux source format with M4 macros to facilitate the development of policies
- In the SELinux **common intermediate language** (**CIL**)–a computer-readable (and with some effort human-readable) format for SELinux policies

Most SELinux supporting distributions base their policy on the reference policy (`https://github.com/TresysTechnology/refpolicy/wiki`), a fully functional SELinux policy set managed as a free software project. This allows distributions to ship with a functional policy set rather than having to write one themselves. Many project contributors are distribution developers, trying to push changes of their distribution to the reference policy project itself, where the changes are peer-reviewed to make sure no rules are brought into the project that might jeopardize the security of any platform. It easily becomes very troublesome to write reusable policy modules without the extensive set of M4 macros offered by the reference policy project.

The SELinux CIL format is quite recent (RHEL 7.2 does not support it yet), and although it is very much in use already (the recent SELinux user space converts everything in CIL in the background), it is not that common yet for policy writers to use it directly.

As an example, consider the web server rule we discussed earlier, repeated here for your convenience: allow the processes labeled with `httpd_t` to bind to TCP ports labeled with `http_port_t`.

In the standard SELinux source format, this is written down as follows:

```
allow httpd_t http_port_t : tcp_socket { name_bind };
```

Using reference policy style, this rule is part of the following macro call:

```
corenet_tcp_bind_http_port(httpd_t)
```

In CIL language, the rule would be expressed as follows:

```
(allow httpd_t http_port_t (tcp_socket (name_bind)))
```

In most representations, we can see what the rule is about:

- The subject (who is taking the action); in this case, this is the set of processes labeled with the `httpd_t` type.
- The target resource or object (the target for the action); in this case, it is the set of TCP sockets (`tcp_socket`) labeled with the `http_port_t` type. In reference policy style, this is implied by the function name.
- The action or permission; in this case, it is the action of binding to a port (`name_bind`). In reference policy style, this is implied by the function name.
- The result that the policy will enforce; in this case, it is that the action is allowed (`allow`). In reference policy style, this is implied by the function name.

A policy is generally written for an application or set of applications. So the preceding example will be part of the policy written for web servers.

Policy writers will generally create three files per application or application set:

- A `.te` file, which contains the type enforcement rules.
- An `.if` file, which contains interface and template definitions, allowing policy writers to easily use the newly-generated policy rules to enhance other policies with. You can compare this to header files in other programming languages.
- An `.fc` file, which contains file context expressions. These are rules that assign labels to resources on the file system.

A finished policy will then be packaged into a SELinux policy module.

Distributing policies through modules

Initially, SELinux used a single, monolithic policy approach: all possible access control rules were maintained in a single policy file. It quickly became clear that this is not manageable in the long term, and the idea of developing a modular policy approach was born.

Within the modular approach, policy developers can write isolated policy sets for a particular application (or set of applications), roles, and so on. These policies then get built and distributed as policy modules. Platforms that need access controls for a particular application load the SELinux policy module that defines the access rules for that application.

The process of building policy modules is shown in the next diagram. It also shows where CIL comes into play, even when the policy rules themselves are not written in CIL. For distributions that do not yet support CIL, `semodule` will directly go from the `.pp` file to the `policy.##` file.

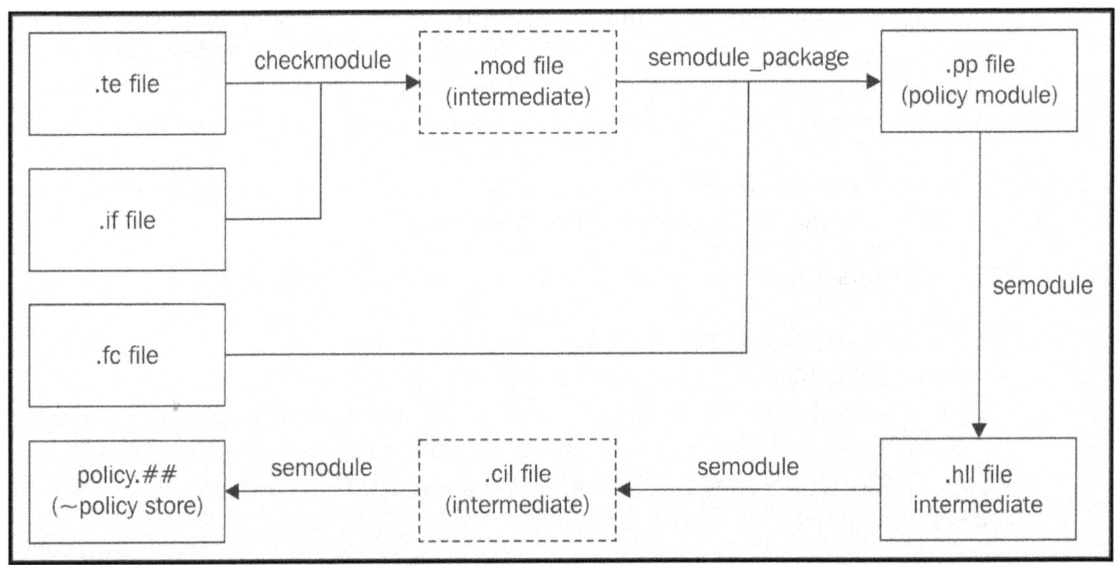

Build process from policy rule to policy store

With the recent SELinux user space, the `*.pp` files (which are the SELinux policy modules) are considered to be written in a **high-level language (HLL)**. Do not assume that this means they are human-readable: these files are binary files. The consideration here is that SELinux wants to support writing SELinux policies in a number of formats, which it calls high-level languages, as long as it has a parser that can convert the files into CIL. Marking the binary module formats as high-level allowed the SELinux project to introduce the distinction between high-level languages and CIL in a backwards-compatible manner.

When distributing SELinux policy modules, most Linux distributions place the `*.pp` SELinux policy modules inside `/usr/share/selinux`, usually within a subdirectory named after the policy store (such as `targeted`). There, these modules are ready for administrators to activate them.

When activating a module, the `semodule` command (part of the `policycoreutils` package) will copy those modules into a dedicated directory: `/etc/selinux/targeted/modules/active/modules` (RHEL) or `/var/lib/selinux/mcs/active/modules` (Gentoo). This location is defined by the version of the SELinux user space–more recent versions use the `/var/lib` location. When all modules are aggregated in a single location, the final policy binary is compiled, resulting in `/etc/selinux/targeted/policy/policy.30` (or some other number) and loaded in memory.

On RHEL, the SELinux policies are provided by the `selinux-policy-targeted` (or `-minimum` or `-mls`) package. On Gentoo, they are provided by the various `sec-policy/selinux-*` packages (Gentoo uses separate packages for each module, reducing the number of SELinux policies that are loaded on an average system).

Bundling modules in a policy store

A **policy store** contains a single comprehensive policy, and only a single policy can be active on a system at any point in time. Administrators can switch policy stores, although this often requires the system to be rebooted and might even require relabeling the entire system (relabeling is the act of resetting the contexts on all files and resources available on that system).

The active policy on the system can be queried using `sestatus` (SELinux status, provided through the `policycoreutils` package), as follows:

```
# sestatus | grep "Loaded policy name"
Loaded policy name:             targeted
```

In this example, the currently loaded policy (store) is named `targeted`. The policy name that SELinux will use upon its next reboot is defined in the `/etc/selinux/config` configuration file as the `SELINUXTYPE` parameter.

It is the system's init system (be it a **SysV-compatible** init system or systemd) that is generally responsible for loading the SELinux policy, effectively activating SELinux support on the system. The init system reads the configuration, locates the policy store, and loads the policy file in memory. If the init system does not support this (in other words, it is not SELinux-aware) then the policy can be loaded through the `load_policy` command, part of the `policycoreutils` package.

Distinguishing between policies

The most common SELinux policy store names are `strict`, `targeted`, `mcs`, and `mls`. None of the names assigned to policy stores are fixed, though, so it is a matter of convention. Hence, it is recommended to consult the distribution documentation to verify what the proper name of the policy should be. Still, the name often provides some information about the SELinux options that are enabled through the policy.

Supporting MLS

One of the options that can be enabled is MLS support. If it is disabled, then the SELinux context will not have a fourth field with sensitivity information in it, making the contexts of processes and files look as follows:

```
staff_u:sysadm_r:sysadm_t
```

To check whether or not MLS is enabled, it is sufficient to see if the context, indeed, doesn't contain such a fourth field, but it can also be acquired from the `Policy MLS status` line in the output of `sestatus`:

```
# sestatus | grep MLS
Policy MLS Status:              disabled
```

Another method would be to look into the pseudo file, `/sys/fs/selinux/mls`. A value of `0` means disabled, whereas a value of `1` means enabled:

```
# cat /sys/fs/selinux/mls
0
```

Policy stores that have MLS enabled are generally `targeted`, `mcs`, and `mls`, whereas `strict` generally has MLS disabled.

Dealing with unknown permissions

Permissions (such as read, open, and lock) are defined both in the Linux kernel and in the policy itself. However, sometimes, newer Linux kernels support permissions that the current policy does not yet understand.

Take the `block_suspend` permission (to be able to block system suspension) as an example. If the Linux kernel supports (and checks) this permission but the loaded SELinux policy does not understand that permission yet, then SELinux has to decide how it should deal with the permission. SELinux can be configured to do one of the following actions:

- `allow`: Assume everything that is not understood is allowed
- `deny`: Assume no one is allowed to perform this action
- `reject`: Stop and halt the system

This is configured through the `deny_unknown` value. To see the state for unknown permissions, look for the `Policy deny_unknown status` line in `sestatus`:

```
# sestatus | grep deny_unknown
Policy deny_unknown status:   denied
```

Administrators can set this for themselves in the `/etc/selinux/semanage.conf` file through the `handle-unknown` variable (with `allow`, `deny`, or `reject`).

RHEL by default allows unknown permissions, whereas Gentoo by default denies them.

Supporting unconfined domains

A SELinux policy can be very strict, limiting applications as close as possible to their actual behavior, but it can also be very liberal in what applications are allowed to do. One of the concepts available in many SELinux policies is the idea of unconfined domains. When enabled, it means that certain SELinux domains (process contexts) are allowed to do almost anything they want (of course, within the boundaries of the regular Linux DAC permissions, which still hold) and only a select number of domains are truly confined (restricted) in their actions.

Unconfined domains have been brought forward to allow SELinux to be active on desktops and servers where administrators do not want to fully restrict the entire system, but only a few of the applications running on it. Generally, these implementations focus on constraining network-facing services (such as web servers and database management systems) while allowing end users and administrators to roam around unrestricted.

With other MAC systems, such as AppArmor, *unconfinement* is inherently part of the design of the system as they only restrict actions for well-defined applications or users. However, SELinux was designed to be a full mandatory access control system and thus needs to provide access control rules even for those applications that shouldn't need any. By marking these applications as unconfined, almost no additional restrictions are imposed by SELinux.

We can see whether or not unconfined domains are enabled on the system through `seinfo`, which we use to query the policy for the `unconfined_t` SELinux type. On a system where unconfined domains are supported, this type will be available:

```
# seinfo -tunconfined_t
  unconfined_t
```

For a system where unconfined domains are not supported, the type will not be part of the policy:

```
# seinfo -tunconfined_t
ERROR: could not find datum for type unconfined_t
```

Most distributions that enable unconfined domains call their policy `targeted`, but this is just a convention that is not always followed. Hence, it is always best to consult the policy using `seinfo`. RHEL enables unconfined domains, whereas with Gentoo, this is a configurable setting through the `unconfined USE` flag.

Limiting cross-user sharing

When UBAC is enabled, certain SELinux types will be protected by additional constraints. This will ensure that one SELinux user cannot access files (or other specific resources) of another user, even when those users are sharing their data through the regular Linux permissions. UBAC provides some additional control over information flow between resources, but it is far from perfect. In essence, it is made to isolate SELinux users from one another.

A constraint in SELinux is an access control rule that uses all parts of a context to make its decision. Unlike type enforcement rules, which are purely based on the type, constraints can take the SELinux user, SELinux role, or sensitivity label into account. Constraints are generally developed once and left untouched, otherwise–most policy writers will not touch constraints during their development efforts.

Many Linux distributions, including RHEL, disable UBAC. Gentoo allows users to select whether or not they want UBAC through the Gentoo `ubac USE` flag (which is enabled by default).

Incrementing policy versions

While checking the output of `sestatus`, we see that there is also a notion of policy versions:

```
# sestatus | grep version
Max kernel policy version:       28
```

This version has nothing to do with the versioning of policy rules but with the SELinux features that the currently running kernel supports. In the preceding output, `28` is the highest policy version the kernel supports. Every time a new feature is added to SELinux, the version number is increased. The policy file itself (which contains all the SELinux rules loaded at boot time by the system) can be found in `/etc/selinux/targeted/policy` (where `targeted` refers to the policy store used, so if the system uses a policy store named `strict`, then the path would be `/etc/selinux/strict/policy`).

If multiple policy files exist, we can use the output of `seinfo` to find out which policy file is used:

```
# seinfo
Statistics for policy file: /etc/selinux/targeted/policy/policy.30
Policy Version & Type: v.30 (binary, mls)
...
```

The next table provides the current list of policy feature enhancements and the Linux kernel version in which that feature is introduced. Many of the features are only of concern to the policy developers, but knowing the evolution of the features gives us a good idea about the evolution of SELinux:

Version	Linux kernel	Description
12		The "old API" for SELinux, now deprecated.
15	2.6.0	Introduced the new API for SELinux.
16	2.6.5	Added support for conditional policy extensions.
17	2.6.6	Added support for IPv6.
18	2.6.8	Added support for fine-grained netlink socket permissions.
19	2.6.12	Added support for MLS.
20	2.6.14	Reduced the size of the access vector table.
21	2.6.19	Added support for MLS range transitions.
22	2.6.25	Introduced policy capabilities.
23	2.6.26	Added support for per-domain permissive mode.
24	2.6.28	Added support for explicit hierarchy (type bounds).
25	2.6.39	Added support for filename-based transitions.
26	3.0	Added support for role transitions for non-process classes. Added support for role attributes.
27	3.5	Added support for flexible inheritance of user and role for newly-created objects.
28	3.5	Added support for flexible inheritance of type for newly-created objects.
29	3.14	Added support for attributes within SELinux constraints.
30	4.3	Added support for extended permissions and implemented first on IOCTL controls. Enhanced SELinux XEN support.

History of SELinux feature evolution

By default, when a SELinux policy is built, the highest supported version as defined by the Linux kernel and `libsepol` (the library responsible for building the SELinux policy binary) is used. Administrators can force a version to be lower using the `policy-version` parameter in `/etc/selinux/semanage.conf`.

Different policy content

Besides the policy capabilities described above, the main difference between policies (and distributions) is the policy content itself. We already covered that most distributions base their policy on the reference policy project. But although that project is considered the *master* for most distributions, each distribution has its own deviation from the main policy set.

Many distributions make extensive additions to the policy without directly passing the policies to the upstream reference policy project. There are several possible reasons why this is not directly done:

- The policy enhancements or additions are still immature: Red Hat initially starts with policies being active but permissive, meaning the policies are not enforced. Instead, SELinux logs what it would have prevented and, based on those logs, the policies are then enhanced. This means that a policy is only ready after a few releases.
- The policy enhancements or additions are too specific to the distribution: If a policy set is not reusable for other distributions, then some distributions will opt to keep those policies to themselves as the act of pushing changes to *upstream* projects takes quite some effort.
- The policy enhancements or additions haven't followed the upstream rules and guidelines: The reference policy has a set of guidelines that policies need to adhere to. If a policy set does not comply with these rules, then it will not be accepted.
- The policy enhancements or additions are not implementing the same security model as the reference policy project wants: As SELinux is a very extensive mandatory access control system, it is possible to write completely different policies.
- The distribution does not have the time or resources to push changes upstream.

This means that SELinux policies between distributions (and even releases of the same distribution) can, content-wise, be quite different. Gentoo for instance aims to follow the reference policy project closely, with changes being merged within a matter of weeks.

Summary

In this chapter, we saw that SELinux offers a more fine-grained access control mechanism on top of the Linux access controls. SELinux is implemented through Linux Security Modules and uses labels to identify its resources and processes based on ownership (user), role, type, and even the security sensitivity and categorization of the resource. We covered how SELinux policies are handled within a SELinux-enabled system and briefly touched upon how policy writers structure policies.

Linux distributions implement SELinux policies, which might be a bit different from each other based on supporting features, such as sensitivity labels, default behavior for unknown permissions, support for confinement levels, or specific constraints put in place such as UBAC. However, most of the policy rules themselves are similar and are even based on the same upstream reference policy project.

Switching between SELinux enforcement modes and understanding the log events that SELinux creates when it prohibits a certain access is the subject of our next chapter. In it, we will also cover how to approach the often-heard requirement of disabling SELinux and why it is the wrong solution to implement.

2

Understanding SELinux Decisions and Logging

Once SELinux is enabled on a system, it starts its access control functionality, as described in the previous chapter. This however might have some unknown side effects, so in this chapter, we will:

- Switch between SELinux in full-enforcement mode (resembling a host-based intrusion prevention system) versus its permissive, logging-only mode (resembling a host-based intrusion detection system)
- Use various methods to toggle the SELinux state (enabled or disabled, permissive or enforcing)
- Disable SELinux's enforcement for a single domain rather than the entire system
- Learn to interpret the SELinux log events that describe which activities SELinux has prevented

We will finish with an overview of common methods for analyzing these logging events in day-to-day operations.

Switching SELinux on and off

This is perhaps a weird section to begin with, but disabling SELinux is a commonly requested activity. Some vendors do not support their application running on a platform that has SELinux enabled. System administrators are generally reluctant to use security controls they do not understand or find too complex to maintain. Luckily, this number is diminishing, and SELinux is also capable of selectively disabling its access controls for a part of the system rather than requiring us to completely disable it.

Setting the global SELinux state

SELinux supports three major states that it can be in: **disabled**, **permissive**, and **enforcing**. These states are set in the `/etc/selinux/config` file, through the `SELINUX` variable. Take a look at the current setting:

```
$ grep ^SELINUX= /etc/selinux/config
SELINUX=enforcing
```

When the system `init` process loads the SELinux policy, the SELinux code checks the state that the administrator has configured. The states are described as follows:

- If the state is `disabled`, then the SELinux code disables further support, booting the system further without activating SELinux.
- If the state is `permissive`, then SELinux is active but will not enforce its policy on the system. Instead, any violation against the policy will be reported but remain allowed. This is sometimes called **host intrusion detection** as it works in a reporting-only mode.
- If the state is `enforcing`, then SELinux is active and will enforce its policy on the system. Violations are reported and also denied. This is sometimes called **host intrusion prevention**, as it enforces the rules while logging the actions it takes.

We can use the `getenforce` command (provided by the `libselinux-utils` package in RHEL or `sys-libs/libselinux` in Gentoo) or the `sestatus` command to get information about the current state of SELinux, like so:

```
# sestatus | grep mode
Current mode: enforcing
# getenforce
Enforcing
```

It is also possible to query the pseudo-file `/sys/fs/selinux/enforce` to get similar information. If the file returns `1`, then SELinux is in the `enforcing` mode. If it returns `0`, then it is in the `permissive` mode:

```
# cat /sys/fs/selinux/enforce
1
```

If the `/etc/selinux/config` file is changed, then the system needs to be rebooted for the changes to take effect. However, if a system has been booted without SELinux support (`disabled`), re-enabling SELinux support alone will not suffice: the administrator will need to make sure that all files on the system are relabeled (the context of all files needs to be set). Without SELinux support, Linux will create and update files without updating or setting the SELinux labels on those files. When the system is later rebooted with SELinux support, SELinux will not have any knowledge of the context of a file unless the labels are reset.

Relabeling the file system is covered in `Chapter 4`, *Process Domains and File-Level Access Controls*.

In many situations, administrators often want to disable SELinux when it starts preventing certain tasks. This is careless to say the least, and here's why:

- SELinux is a security component, part of the operating system. Disabling SELinux is like disabling a firewall completely because it is blocking some communication. It might help because it's a faster way of getting something to work again, but you're removing measures that were enabled to protect you.
- Just like with a firewall, SELinux is configurable by rules. If an application is prevented from working correctly, we need to update the rules for that application, just like the way additional firewall rules can be enabled to allow particular flows.
- In the worst case, when we want to allow every action an application performs unconditionally, we can still leave SELinux on and just run this application without SELinux access controls enabled.

Distributions put a lot of effort into integrating SELinux with their product, and they have awesome support channels to help you out if all things fail.

Switching to permissive (or enforcing) mode

Most distribution-provided kernels allow switching between enforcing and permissive mode through a simple administrative command. This feature is called the **SELinux development mode** and is set through the `CONFIG_SECURITY_SELINUX_DEVELOP` kernel configuration parameter. Although this can be considered a risk (all a malicious person would need to do is switch SELinux to permissive mode to disable its access controls), switching the mode requires strong administrative privileges, which most application domains don't have.

The command to switch between permissive mode and enforcing mode is the `setenforce` command (part of the `libselinux-utils` package in RHEL or `sys-libs/libselinux` in Gentoo). It takes a single argument: `0` (permissive) or `1` (enforcing). The strings `permissive` and `enforcing` are allowed by the command as well.

The change takes effect immediately. For instance, the following command is used to switch to permissive mode:

```
# setenforce 0
```

The effect of `setenforce` is the same as writing the right integer value into the `/sys/fs/selinux/enforce` pseudo file:

```
# echo 0 > /sys/fs/selinux/enforce
```

The ability to switch between permissive and enforcing mode can be of interest for policy developers or system administrators who are modifying the system to use SELinux properly. It can also be used to quickly verify whether an application warning or error is due to SELinux access controls or not–assuming the application is not SELinux-aware, which we will talk about later in this chapter.

On production systems, it might be of interest to disable the ability to switch to permissive mode. Disabling this feature usually requires rebuilding the Linux kernel, but SELinux policy developers have also thought of a different way to disallow users from toggling the SELinux state. The privileges that users need to switch to permissive mode are *conditional*, and system administrators can easily toggle this to disable switching back from enforcing mode to permissive mode. The conditional is implemented through a SELinux boolean called `secure_mode_policyload` whose default value is `off` (meaning switching SELinux state is allowed).

SELinux booleans are configurable options that take on a single value (`on` or `off`, although `true/false` and `1/0` are valid values as well) and manipulate parts of the active SELinux policy. The value of the conditionals can be persisted (meaning they survive reboots) or be kept only during the current boot session. To persist the value across reboots, add `-P` to the `setsebool` command (part of the `policycoreutils` package) used to toggle it:

```
# setsebool -P secure_mode_policyload on
```

To get an overview of the available SELinux booleans along with a small description of what they control, use semanage boolean:

```
# semanage boolean -l
SELinux boolean   State Default Description
ftp_home_dir      (off , off)   Determine whether ftpd can read
                                and write files in user home
                                directories
xdm_sysadm_login (off , off)    Allow the graphical login program
                                to login directly as
                                sysadm_r:sysadm_t
xen_use_nfs       (off , off)   Allow xen to manage nfs files
...
```

The semanage command is part of the policycoreutils-python package in RHEL or sys-apps/policycoreutils in Gentoo. SELinux booleans are covered in more depth in Chapter 8, *Working with SELinux Policies*.

The use of the secure_mode_policyload SELinux boolean allows administrators to restrict switching from enforcing mode back to permissive. However, switching to or from the disabled state is not supported: if SELinux is active (in either permissive or enforcing mode) and its policy is loaded, then only a reboot can effectively disable SELinux again.

Using kernel boot parameters

Using the setenforce command makes sense when we want to switch to the permissive or enforcing mode at a point in time when we have interactive access to the system. But what if we need this on system boot? If the system refuses to boot properly due to SELinux access controls, we cannot edit the /etc/selinux/config file. Luckily, we can change the SELinux state through other means as well.

The solution is to use kernel boot parameters. We can boot a Linux system with one or two parameters that take precedence over the /etc/selinux/config setting, as follows:

- selinux=0: This informs the system to disable SELinux completely, and has the same effect as setting SELINUX=disabled in the config file. When set, the other parameter (enforcing) is not consulted. Please remember that booting a system with SELinux disabled means that to enable it again, the file system must be relabeled completely.

- `enforcing=0`: This informs the system to run SELinux in the `permissive` mode, and has the same effect as setting `SELINUX=permissive` in the `config` file.
- `enforcing=1`: This informs the system to run SELinux in the `enforcing` mode, and has the same effect as setting `SELINUX=enforcing` in the `config` file.

Consider a Linux system that uses GRUB2 as its boot loader. We want to add `enforcing=0` to the boot entry. This can be accomplished during boot as follows:

1. Reboot the system until the GRUB2 boot screen comes up.
2. Navigate with the arrow keys to the boot entry for which the SELinux state has to be altered. This is usually the default boot entry and already selected.
3. Press the *E* key to edit the boot entry line. Do this before the GRUB2 timer reaches zero; otherwise, the system will continue to boot.
4. Use the arrow keys to go to the end of the line that starts with `linux`, `linux16`, or `linuxefi`.
5. Add `enforcing=0` to the end of this line.
6. Press *Ctrl* + X or *F10* to boot the entry.

Other boot loaders have similar approaches to changing the boot line without persisting it for every reboot. Consult your distribution documentation for more details.

Support for the `selinux=` boot parameters is enabled through a kernel configuration parameter, `CONFIG_SECURITY_SELINUX_BOOTPARAM`. The `enforcing=` boot parameter is supported through the `CONFIG_SECURITY_SELINUX_DEVELOP` configuration parameter, which we've already encountered.

When using SELinux in production, it might be wise to either disable the options or properly protect the boot menu, for instance, by password-protecting the menu and regularly verifying the integrity of the boot menu files.

Disabling SELinux protections for a single service

Since policy version 23 (which came with Linux 2.6.26), SELinux also supports a more granular approach to switching between permissive and enforcing mode: the use of permissive domains. As mentioned before, a domain is a term that SELinux uses for types (labels) assigned to processes. With **permissive domains**, we can mark one particular domain as being permissive (and as such not enforcing the SELinux rules) even though the rest of the system is still running in enforcing mode.

Let's say we run a **Digital Living Network Alliance** (**DLNA**) server to serve our holiday pictures to other media devices at our place or to present the latest internal company videos to a distributed set of monitors throughout the campus. Somehow, it fails to show the media recently made available, and we find out it is SELinux that is preventing it. Even though it is strongly recommended to instead resolve the issue or even fine-tune the policy, we might be pushed to fix (read: work around) the problem first and implement the proper fix later. Instead of fully disabling SELinux controls, we can mark the domain in which the DLNA server runs (most likely `minidlna_t`) as a permissive domain.

To make a domain permissive, we use the `semanage` command:

```
# semanage permissive -a minidlna_t
```

With the same `semanage` command, we can list the currently defined permissive domains. On RHEL, a number of domains will, by default, run in the `permissive` mode since that is part of their policy development life cycle approach:

```
# semanage permissive -l
Customized Permissive Types
minidlna_t
Builtin Permissive Types
mon_procd_t
mon_statd_t
...
ptp4l_t
```

Another method for listing the custom permissive types (those not marked as permissive through the distribution) is to use the semodule command. In the previous chapter, we briefly touched on this command when talking about SELinux policy modules. We can use it to list the SELinux policy modules that have permissive_ in their name, because the semanage permissive command will actually generate a small SELinux policy module in which the domain is marked as permissive:

```
# semodule -l | grep permissive_
permissive_minidlna_t          1.0
```

Distributions that have a more recent SELinux user space, such as Gentoo, will not display a version.

To remove the permissive mode from the domain, pass the -d argument to the semanage command. This is only possible for domains that were marked as permissive by the administrator though–distribution-provided permissive domains cannot be switched to enforcing through this approach:

```
# semanage permissive -d minidlna_t
```

When a domain is marked as permissive, the application should behave as if SELinux is not enabled on the system, making it easier for us to find out whether SELinux really is the cause of a permission issue. Note though, that other domains, including those that interact with a permissive domain, are themselves still governed and enforced through the SELinux access controls.

Another use for permissive domains is for policy writers. When an application is running in a permissive domain, every action it takes that is not already allowed by the policy will be logged by SELinux. Policy writers can run the application through various use cases and then use the generated logs to build a policy for it.

There is a significant downside to this approach, which is that some applications will trigger actions (resulting in SELinux logging) that the application does not actually need (such as scanning through all binaries to locate its own helper scripts). Policy writers will need to be careful when updating policies through this approach.

If an application requires SELinux to be disabled, it makes much more sense to make a dummy domain for it and mark its domain as permissive rather than disabling SELinux protections for the entire system.

Understanding SELinux-aware applications

Most applications themselves do not have knowledge that they are running on a SELinux enabled system. When that is the case, permissive mode truly means that the application behaves as if SELinux was not enabled to begin with. However, some applications actively call SELinux code. These applications can be called *SELinux-aware*, because they change their behavior based on the SELinux-related information available.

Such applications change their behavior when SELinux is enabled, for instance, to query the policy or to check for the context that it should run in. Most of these SELinux-aware applications do not properly validate whether they are running in permissive mode or not. As a result, running those applications in a permissive domain (or the entire system in permissive mode) will generally not result in the application running as if SELinux were not active.

Examples of such applications are the SSH daemon, the system login service, the init system, and some cron daemons as well as several core Linux utilities (such as `ls` and `id`). They might show permission failures or different behavior based on the SELinux policy even if SELinux is not in enforcing mode.

We can find out whether or not an application is SELinux-aware by checking if the application is dynamically linked with the `libselinux` library. This can be done with `readelf` or `ldd`, as follows:

```
# readelf -d /bin/ls | grep libselinux
 0x0000000000000001 (NEEDED)     Shared library: [libselinux.so.1]
# ldd /bin/ls | grep selinux
   libselinux.so.1 => /lib64/libselinux.so.1 (0x00007f77702dc000)
```

Knowing whether an application is SELinux-aware or not can help in troubleshooting failures.

SELinux logging and auditing

SELinux developers are well aware that a security-oriented subsystem such as SELinux can only succeed if it is capable of enhanced logging and even debugging. Every action that SELinux takes, as part of the LSM hooks that it implements, should be auditable. Denials (actions that SELinux prevents) should always be logged so that administrators can take due action. SELinux tuning and changes, such as loading new policies or altering SELinux booleans, should always result in an audit message being displayed.

Following audit events

By default, SELinux will send its messages to the Linux audit subsystem (assuming the Linux kernel is configured with the audit subsystem enabled through the `CONFIG_AUDIT` kernel configuration). There, the messages are picked up by the Linux audit daemon (`auditd`) and logged in the `/var/log/audit/audit.log` file. Additional handling rules can be defined through the audit dispatcher process (`audisp`), which picks up audit events and dispatches them to one or more separate processes. This method is used, for instance, for the SELinux troubleshooting daemon (`setroubleshootd`), an optional service to provide help with troubleshooting SELinux events.

The audit event flow is shown in this diagram:

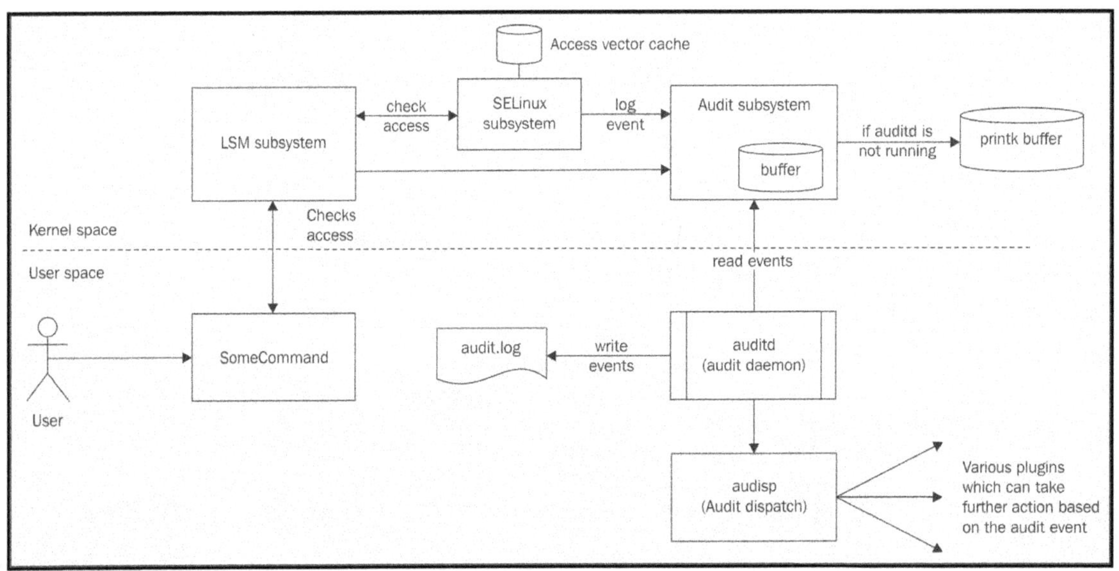

Flow of audit events generated by SELinux

When SELinux is enabled, it will log (almost) every permission check that was denied. When Linux auditing is enabled, these denials are logged by the audit daemon in the `audit.log` file. If not, the events are stored in the Linux kernel message buffer, which can be consulted through the `dmesg` command and is often also captured through the system logger.

If the SELinux troubleshooting daemon is installed (part of the `setroubleshoot-server` package in RHEL), then the audit daemon will, alongside its logging, also dispatch the events through the audit dispatch system towards the `sedispatch` command. This command will further handle the event and send it through D-Bus (a system bus implementation popular on Linux systems) to the SELinux troubleshooting daemon. This daemon will analyze the event and might suggest one or more fixes to the administrator. We will cover the SELinux troubleshooting daemon later in this chapter.

Whenever SELinux verifies a particular access, it does not always go over the entire policy. Instead, it has an **access vector cache** (**AVC**), in which it stores the results of previous access attempts. This cache ensures that SELinux can quickly react to activities without a huge performance impact. The abbreviation of this cache is used as the message type for most SELinux events, as we can see in the following example:

```
type=AVC msg=audit(1470312632.027:4702304): avc: denied { append }
  for  pid=14352 comm="rsyslogd" name="oracle_audit.log" dev="dm-2"
  ino=387512
  scontext=system_u:system_r:syslogd_t:s0
  tcontext=system_u:object_r:usr_t:s0 tclass=file permissive=0
```

The AVC cache can be slightly tuned, by setting the size of the cache. This is handled by the `/sys/fs/selinux/avc/cache_threshold` pseudo-file. For instance, to increase the cache size to `768` (the default is `512`), the following command would be used:

```
# echo 768 > /sys/fs/selinux/avc/cache_threshold
```

The current AVC hash statistics can be read through the `hash_stats` pseudo-file:

```
# cat /sys/fs/selinux/avc/hash_stats
entries: 510
buckets used: 287/512
longest chain: 6
```

If administrators suspect that lower system performance is due to SELinux, it is advised to look at the `longest chain` output in `hash_stats`. If it is longer than 10, then some performance impact can be expected, and updating the cache size might help.

Any permission that needs to be checked is represented as an *access vector*, and the cache is then consulted to see whether that particular permission has been checked before or not. If it has, then the decision is taken from the cache; otherwise, the policy itself is consulted and the cache updated. This inner working of SELinux is less relevant to most administrators, but at least now we know where the term *AVC* comes from.

Uncovering more logging

There is an important SELinux policy directive that also takes part in the AVC, and that is `dontaudit`. A `dontaudit` rule in the SELinux policy tells SELinux that a particular access denial should *not* be logged. This is the only example where SELinux won't log a denial–the SELinux policy writer has explicitly disabled auditing the events. This is usually done to remove clutter from the logs and hide cosmetic denials that have no influence on the security of the system.

The `seinfo` utility can tell us how many of these rules as well as its sibling rule `auditallow` (log events even though they are allowed by the policy) are currently active:

```
# seinfo --stats | grep -i audit
Auditallow:      152  Dontaudit:     8381
```

Luckily, these `dontaudit` rules can be disabled at will. Through the following `semodule` command, these rules are removed from the active policy:

```
# semodule --disable_dontaudit --build
```

The arguments can also be abbreviated to `-D` and `-B` respectively. To re-enable the `dontaudit` rules, just rebuild the policy like so:

```
# semodule -B
```

Disabling the `dontaudit` rules can sometimes help in troubleshooting failures that do not result in any useful audit event being logged. Generally speaking though, audit events that policy writers mark as cosmetic are not the cause of a failure.

Configuring Linux auditing

SELinux will try to use the audit subsystem when available and will fall back to the regular system logging when it isn't. This can either be because the Linux kernel audit subsystem is not configured or because the Linux audit daemon itself is not running.

For the Linux audit, we usually do not need to configure anything as SELinux `AVC` denials are logged by default. The denials will be shown in the audit log file (`/var/log/audit/audit.log`), usually together with the system call that triggered it:

```
time->Thu Aug  4 08:28:57 2016
type=SYSCALL msg=audit(1470313737.195:322): arch=c000003e
  syscall=105 success=yes exit=0 a0=0 a1=7f9c3fdde1d0
  a2=800020 a3=7f9c37ae92e0 items=0 ppid=14542 pid=14544
  auid=1001 uid=1001 gid=1001 euid=0 suid=0 fsuid=0 egid=1001
  sgid=1001 fsgid=1001 tty=pts0 ses=6 comm="su"
  exe="/usr/bin/su" subj=user_u:user_r:user_t:s0 key=(null)
type=AVC msg=audit(1470313737.195:322): avc: denied { setuid }
  for   pid=14544 comm="su" capability=7
  context=user_u:user_r:user_t:s0
  tcontext=user_u:user_r:user_t:s0 tclass=capability
```

The target log file for the audit system can be configured through the `log_file` parameter in `/etc/audit/auditd.conf`.

To enable remote audit logging (to centralize audit events from multiple hosts on a single system), you have the option of either enabling syslog forwarding or enabling the `audisp-remote` plugin.

With syslog forwarding, the audit dispatch daemon is configured to send audit events to the local system logger as well. It is then up to the administrator to configure the local system logger to pass on events towards a remote system.

Edit the `/etc/audisp/plugins.d/syslog.conf` file, and set `active` to `yes`:

```
# vi /etc/audisp/plugins.d/syslog.conf
active = yes
direction = out
path = builtin_syslog
type = builtin
args = LOG_INFO
format = string
```

Using the system logger to centralize audit events might not be the best option though, as system loggers generally use unencrypted, and often not even guaranteed, data delivery. With the `audisp-remote` plugin, audit events can be sent encrypted and with guaranteed delivery to a remote `auditd` server.

First, configure the audit daemon on the target server to accept audit logs from remote hosts by enabling the audit daemon to listen on port `60`:

```
# vi /etc/audit/auditd.conf
tcp_listen_port = 60
```

Next, configure the `audisp-remote` plugin to connect to the target server's audit daemon:

```
# vi /etc/audisp/audisp-remote.conf
remote_server = <targethostname>
port = 60
```

Finally, enable the `audisp-remote` plugin:

```
# vi /etc/audisp/plugins.d/au-remote.conf
active = yes
```

The `audisp-remote` plugin is offered through the `audispd-plugins` package in RHEL or through the standard `sys-process/audit` package in Gentoo.

It is recommended you use the Linux audit subsystem at all times. Not only does it integrate nicely with troubleshooting utilities, it also allows administrators to use the audit tools to query the audit logs or even generate reports, such as with `aureport`:

```
# aureport --avc --start recent
AVC Report
=========================================================
# date time comm subj syscall class permission obj event
=========================================================
...
12. 08/04/2016 09:00:38 su user_u:user_r:user_t:s0 105 capability
setuid user_u:user_r:user_t:s0 denied 376
```

Configuring the local system logger

When auditing is not enabled, or the Linux audit daemon is not running, then the SELinux events will be captured by the system logger through the kernel logging facility (`kern.*`). Most system loggers will save these kernel log events in a general log file, such as `/var/log/messages`.

We can configure the system logger to direct SELinux AVC messages into its own log file, such as `/var/log/avc.log`. For instance, with the `syslog-ng` system logger, the configuration could be as follows:

```
source kernsrc { file("/proc/kmsg"); };
destination avc { file("/var/log/avc.log"); };
filter f_avc { message(".*avc: .*"); };
log { source(kernsrc);  filter(f_avc);  destination(avc); };
```

For the rsyslog system logger, the rule could look like so:

```
:msg, contains, "avc: "     -/var/log/avc.log
```

When SELinux logging is handled through the local system logger, an easy method to quickly obtain the latest AVC denials (or other messages) is through the `dmesg` command:

```
# dmesg | grep avc | tail
```

Be aware though that unlike the audit logs, many systems allow the `dmesg` content to be read by regular users. This might result in some information leakage to untrusted users. For this reason, some SELinux policies do not allow regular users to access the kernel ring buffer (and as such use `dmesg`) unless the `user_dmesg` SELinux boolean is set to `on`:

```
# setsebool user_dmesg on
```

The `user_dmesg` SELinux boolean is not available on RHEL though. There, only the standard unconfined user type as well as the administrative user type have access to the kernel ring buffer. To prevent other users from reading this information, they need to be mapped to non-administrative SELinux users, such as `user_u` or `(x)guest_u`.

Reading SELinux denials

The one thing every one of us will have to do several times with SELinux systems is to read and interpret SELinux denial information. When SELinux prohibits an access and there is no `dontaudit` rule in place to hide it, SELinux will log it. If nothing is logged, it was probably not SELinux that was the culprit of the failure. Remember, SELinux comes after Linux DAC checks, so if a regular permission doesn't allow a certain activity, then SELinux is never consulted.

SELinux denial messages are logged the moment SELinux prevents some access from occurring. When SELinux is in the `enforcing` mode, the application usually returns a **Permission denied** error, although sometimes it might be a bit more obscure. For example, the following attempt of an unprivileged user using `su` to switch to `root` shows a different error:

```
$ su -
Password: (correct password given)
su: incorrect password
```

Most of the time, though, the error is a permission error:

```
$ ls /proc/1
ls: cannot open directory /proc/1: Permission denied
# ls -ldZ /proc/1
dr-xr-xr-x. root root system_u:system_r:init_t:s0       /proc/1
```

So, what does a denial message look like? The following command output shows a denial from the audit subsystem, which we can query through the `ausearch` command:

```
# ausearch -m avc -ts recent
----
time->Thu Aug 4 09:00:38 2016
type=AVC msg=audit(1470315638.218:376): avc:  denied  { search }
  for  pid=5005 comm="dnsmasq" name="net" dev="proc" ino=5403
  scontext=system_u:system_r:dnsmasq_t
  tcontext=system_u:object_r:sysctl_net_t tclass=dir permissive=0
```

Let's break up this denial into its individual components. The following table gives more information about each part of the preceding denials. As an administrator, knowing how to read denials is extremely important, so take enough time for this:

Field name	Description	Example
SELinux action	The action that SELinux took or would take if run in the `enforcing` mode. This is usually `denied`, although some actions are explicitly marked to be audited as well and would result in `granted`.	`denied`

Permissions	The permissions that were checked (action performed by the process). This usually is a single permission, although it can sometimes be a set of permissions (for example, `read write`).	`{ search }`
Process ID	The ID of the process that was performing the action.	for `pid=5005`
Process name	The process name (command). It doesn't display any arguments to the command though.	`comm="dnsmasq"`
Target name	The name of the target (resource) that the process is performing an action on. If the target is a file, then the name is usually the filename or directory.	`name="net"`
Target device	The device on which the target resource resides. Together with the next field (inode number) this allows us to uniquely identify the resource on a system.	`dev="proc"`
Target file inode number	The inode number of the target file or directory. Together with the device, this allows us to find the file on the file system.	`ino=5403`
Source context	The context in which the process resides (the domain of the process).	`scontext=system_u:system_r:dnsmasq_t`

Target context	The context of the target resource.	tcontext=system_u:object_r:sysctl_net_t
Object class	The class of the target object, for instance, a directory, file, socket, node, pipe, file descriptor, file system, or capability.	tclass=dir
Permissive mode	The mode in which the domain was when the action was executed. If set to 0, then SELinux was in the enforcing mode, otherwise it was permissive. This field is available since Linux kernel 3.16.	permissive=0

The previous denial can be read as follows:

SELinux has denied the search operation by the dnsmasq process (with PID 5005) against the net directory (with inode 5403) within the proc device. The dnsmasq process ran with the system_u:system_r:dnsmasq_t label, and the net directory had the system_u:object_r:sysctl_net_t label. SELinux was in the enforcing mode when it happened.

Some denials have different fields, such as this one:

```
avc: denied { send_msg } for msgtype=method_call
  interface=org.gnome.DisplayManager.Settings
  member=GetValue dest=org.gnome.DisplayManager
  spid=3705 tpid=2864
  scontext=unconfined_u:unconfined_r:unconfined_t:s0-s0:c0.c1023
  tcontext=system_u:system_r:xdm_t:s0-s0:c0.c1023
  tclass=dbus permissive=0
```

Although it has a few different fields, it is still readable and can be interpreted as follows:

SELinux has denied the process with PID `3705` to invoke a D-Bus remote method call (the `GetValue` method of the `org.gnome.DisplayManager.Settings` interface) against the `org.gnome.DisplayManager` implementation offered by the process with PID `2864`. The source process ran with the `unconfined_u:unconfined_r:unconfined_t:s0-s0.c0.c1023` label, and the target process with the `system_u:system_r:xdm_t:s0-s0:c0.c1023` label.

Depending on the action and the target class, SELinux uses different fields to give all the information we need to troubleshoot a problem. Consider the following denial:

```
avc: denied  { name_bind } for  pid=23849
  comm="postgres" src=6030
  scontext=system_u:system_r:postgresql_t
  tcontext=system_u:object_r:unreserved_port_t
  tclass=tcp_socket permissive=0
```

The preceding denial came up because the PostgreSQL database was configured to listen on a non-default port (`6030` instead of the default `5432`).

Identifying the problem is a matter of understanding how the operations work, and properly reading the denials. The preceding D-Bus denial is difficult to troubleshoot if we do not know how D-Bus works (or how it uses message types, members, and interfaces in its underlying protocols). For troubleshooting, the denial logs give us enough to get us started. It gives a clear idea what was denied.

It is wrong to immediately consider allowing the specific action (by adding an allow rule to the SELinux policy as described in `Chapter 8`, *Working with SELinux Policies*) because other options exist and are usually better, such as these:

- Providing the right label on the target resource (usually the case when the target is a non-default port, non-default location, and so on)
- Switching booleans (flags that manipulate the SELinux policy) to allow additional privileges
- Providing the right label on the source process (often the case when the acting application is not installed by the distribution package manager)
- Using the application as intended instead of through other means (as SELinux only allows expected behavior), such as starting a daemon through a service (init script or systemd unit) instead of through a command-line operation

Other SELinux-related event types

Although most of the SELinux log events are AVC related, they aren't the sole event types an administrator will have to deal with. Most audit events will show SELinux information as part of the event even though SELinux has little to do with the event itself. But a few audit event types are directly concerned with SELinux.

Looking through all possible audit event types:
A full list of all possible audit events can be found in the `linux/audit.h` header file available in `/usr/include` (installed through the `kernel-headers` package in RHEL).

USER_AVC

The `USER_AVC` event is similar to the regular `AVC` audit events, but now the source is a user space object manager. These are applications that use SELinux policy rules, but they enforce these rules themselves rather than through the kernel.

The following example is such an event, generated by D-Bus:

```
type=USER_AVC msg=audit(1467890899.875:266): pid=693 uid=81
  auid=4294967295 ses=4294967295
  subj=system_u:system_r:system_dbusd_t:s0-s0:c0.c1023
  msg='avc:  denied  { acquire_svc }
    for service=org.freedesktop.resolve1 spid=1434
    scontext=system_u:system_r:systemd_resolved_t:s0
    tcontext=system_u:system_r:system_dbusd_t:s0-s0:c0.c1023
    tclass=dbus  exe="/usr/bin/dbus-daemon" sauid=81
    hostname=? addr=? terminal=?'
```

The event has two parts. Everything up to the `msg=` string is information about the user space object manager that generated the event. The true event itself is stored within the `msg=` part and includes similar fields as we already know from regular AVCs.

SELINUX_ERR

The SELINUX_ERR event comes up when SELinux is asked to do something that not just violates an access control, but actually violates the policy. It cannot be resolved by SELinux policy writers by just *allowing* the operation. These events usually point to a misuse of applications and services that the policy is not tailored to accomplish:

```
type=SELINUX_ERR msg=audit(1387729595.732:156): security_compute_sid:
  invalid context unconfined_u:system_r:hddtemp_t:s0-s0:c0.c1023 for
  scontext=unconfined_u:unconfined_r:unconfined_t:s0-s0:c0.c1023
  tcontext=system_u:object_r:hddtemp_exec_t:s0 tclass=process
```

In the preceding example, a user (running in the unconfined_t domain) was executing hddtemp (with hddtemp_exec_t as the label), and the policy wanted to transition to the hddtemp_t domain. However, that resulted in a full context of unconfined_u:system_r:hddtemp_t:s0-s0:c0.c1023, which is not a valid context. The unconfined_u SELinux user is not meant to use the system_r role.

MAC_POLICY_LOAD

The MAC_POLICY_LOAD event occurs whenever the system loads a new SELinux policy in memory. This occurs when the administrator loads a new or updated SELinux policy module, rebuilds the policy with the dontaudit rules disabled, or toggles a SELinux boolean that needs to be persisted across reboots:

```
type=MAC_POLICY_LOAD msg=audit(1470381810.215:178): policy loaded
  auid=1001 ses=2
```

When a MAC_POLICY_LOAD event occurs, it might be followed by a USER_MAC_POLICY_LOAD event. This is when a user space object manager detects that the policy was updated and has taken action. Note that not all user space object managers will send out this event: some object managers will query the *live* policy and as such do not need to take any action when a new policy is loaded.

MAC_CONFIG_CHANGE

When a SELinux boolean is changed but not persisted, then a `MAC_CONFIG_CHANGE` event will be dispatched. This tells the administrator that the active policy has been instructed to change its behavior slightly, but within the bounds of the existing loaded policy:

```
type=MAC_CONFIG_CHANGE msg=audit(1470381810.200:177):
  bool=user_ping val=0 old_val=1 auid=1001 ses=2
```

In the preceding example, the `user_ping` SELinux boolean was changed from the value `1` (on) to `0` (off).

MAC_STATUS

The `MAC_STATUS` event is displayed when the state of SELinux has been changed. For instance, when an administrator uses `setenforce 0` to put SELinux in the `permissive` mode, then the following event occurs:

```
type=SYSCALL msg=audit(1470383274.576:74): arch=c000003e syscall=1
  success=yes exit=1 a0=3 a1=7ffe4d5ee270 a2=1 a3=7ffe4d5edff0
  items=0 ppid=8977 pid=9226 auid=0 uid=0 gid=0 euid=0 suid=0
  fsuid=0 egid=0 sgid=0 fsgid=0 tty=tty1 ses=1 comm="setenforce"
  exe="/usr/sbin/setenforce"
  subj=unconfined_u:unconfined_r:unconfined_t:s0-s0:c0.c1023
  key=(null)
type=MAC_STATUS msg=audit(1470383274.576:74): enforcing=0
  old_enforcing=1 auid=0 ses=1
```

Here, the `SYSCALL` event is displayed alongside the event as it offers more detail about the action: who changed the state, through which command, and so on. When available, the `ausearch` command will group all related events (including the `SYSCALL` event) to give the administrator a full view of what has happened.

NetLabel events

NetLabel is a Linux kernel project to support labeled network packets, allowing security contexts such as SELinux contexts to be passed on between hosts. One of the protocols that the NetLabel implementation supports in Linux is **Common IP Security Option** (**CIPSO**) labeling, which we will cover in `Chapter 5`, *Controlling Network Communications*.

The following audit events are related to the NetLabel capability:

- The `MAC_UNLBL_STCADD` and `MAC_UNLBL_STCDEL` events are triggered when a static label is added or removed, respectively. Static labeling means that if a packet is received or sent and it does not have a label, then this static label is assigned as a sort of default.
- The `MAC_MAP_ADD` and `MAC_MAP_DEL` events are triggered when a mapping between a labeling protocol (such as CIPSO) and its parameters against a LSM (SELinux) domain is added or removed from the configuration, respectively.
- The `MAC_CIPSOV4_ADD` and `MAC_CIPSOV4_DEL` events are triggered when a CIPSO (IPv4) configuration is added or removed, respectively.

Labeled IPsec events

Another labeled network protocol that Linux supports is **labeled IPsec**. Through this, the SELinux context of the source process (which is communicating over the IPsec tunnel towards a target resource) is known by the IPsec daemons on both ends of the tunnel. Furthermore, SELinux will contain rules about which domains can communicate over an IPsec tunnel and which domains are allowed to communicate with each other network-wise.

The following audit events are related to IPsec:

- The `MAC_IPSEC_ADDSA` and `MAC_IPSEC_DELSA` events are used when a security association is added or removed (new IPsec tunnels are defined or deleted), respectively.
- The `MAC_IPSEC_ADDSPD` and `MAC_IPSEC_DELSPD` events are used when a security policy definition is added or removed, respectively. Security policies generally describe whether network packets need to be handled by IPsec and, if so, through which security association.
- The `MAC_IPSEC_EVENT` event is a generic event for IPsec audit messages.

SELinux support for labeled IPsec is described in `Chapter 5`, *Controlling Network Communications*.

Using ausearch

The `ausearch` command, which is part of the `audit` package, is a frequently used command for querying the audit events stored on the system. We already briefly covered it when taking a first look at an AVC denial, but only briefly mentioning it won't do it justice.

With `ausearch`, we can search for events that originated after a particular time period. We used the `-ts recent` (time start) option in the past, which displays events that occurred during the past 10 minutes. The argument can also be a timestamp. Other supported shorthand values are:

- `today`: This means starting at 1 second past midnight on the current day
- `yesterday`: This means starting at 1 second past midnight the previous day
- `this-week`, `this-month` or `this-year`: These mean starting at 1 second past midnight on the first day of the current week, current month, or current year, respectively
- `checkpoint`: This uses the timestamp mentioned in a `checkpoint.txt` file

The use of `checkpoint` is particularly useful when troubleshooting SELinux issues as it allows us to show the denials (and other SELinux events) since the last invocation of the `ausearch` command:

```
# ausearch --checkpoint /root/ausearch-checkpoint.txt -ts checkpoint
```

This allows administrators to perform minor tweaks and reproduce the problem and only see the events since then, instead of going through all events over and over again.

By default, the `ausearch` command displays all the events that occur in the audit log. On busy systems, this can be very verbose and result in unwanted events to be displayed as well. Luckily, users can limit the type of events that are queried through the `ausearch` command.

For SELinux troubleshooting, using `avc`, `user_avc`, and `selinux_err` limits the events nicely to those needed for the job:

```
# ausearch -m avc,user_avc,selinux_err -ts recent
```

If the numeric display of fields such as the user IDs and timestamps is too confusing, then it is possible for `ausearch` to look up and translate user IDs to usernames and timestamps to formatted time fields. Add the `-i` option to `ausearch` to have it interpret these fields and display the interpreted values instead.

Getting help with denials

On some distributions, additional support tools are available that help us identify the cause of a denial. These tools have some knowledge of the common mistakes (for instance, setting the right context on application files in order for the web server to be able to read them). Other distributions require us to use our experience to make proper decisions, supporting us through the distribution mailing lists, bug tracking sites, and other cooperation locations, for example, IRC.

Troubleshooting with setroubleshoot

In Fedora and RHEL, additional tools are present that help us troubleshoot denials. The tools work together to catch a denial, look for a plausible solution, and inform the administrator about the denial and its suggested resolutions.

When used on a graphical workstation, denials can even result in popups that ask the administrator to review them immediately. Install the `setroubleshoot` package to get this support. On servers without a graphical environment, administrators can see the information in the system logs or can even configure the system to send out SELinux denial messages via e-mail. Install the `setroubleshoot-server` package to get this support.

Under the hood, it is the audit daemon that triggers its audit event dispatcher application (`audispd`). This application supports plugins, something the SELinux folks gratefully implemented. They built an application called `sedispatch` that will act as a plugin for `audispd`. The `sedispatch` application checks whether the audit event is a SELinux denial and, if so, forwards the event to D-Bus. D-Bus then forwards the event to the `setroubleshootd` application (or launches the application if it isn't running yet), which analyzes the denial and prepares feedback for the administrator.

When running on a workstation, `seapplet` is triggered to show a popup on the administrator workstation:

Example popup when a SELinux security alert comes up

The administrator can then select **Show** to view more details. But the information is readily available even without graphical support. The analyzed feedback is stored on the file system, and a message is displayed in the system logs:

```
Jun 03 10:41:48 localhost setroubleshoot: SELinux is preventing
  /usr/sbin/httpd from 'getattr' accesses on the directory
  /var/www/html/infocenter. For complete SELinux messages, run
  sealert -l 26d2a1c3-a134-452e-c69b-4ef233e20909
```

We can then look at the complete explanation through the `sealert` command as mentioned in the log:

```
# sealert -l 26d2a1c3-a134-452e-c69b-4ef233e20909
SELinux is preventing /usr/sbin/httpd from getattr access on the
directory infocenter
*****  Plugin restorecon (99.5 confidence) suggests  *****
If you want to fix the label.
/var/www/html/infocenter default label should be httpd_sys_content_t.
Then you can run restorecon.
Do
# /sbin/restorecon -v /var/www/html/infocenter
Additional Information:
Source Context                system_u:system_r:httpd_t:s0
Target Context                unconfined_u:object_r:user_home_t:s0
Target Objects                infocenter [ dir ]
Source                        httpd
Source Path                   /usr/sbin/httpd
Port                          <Unknown>
Host                          <Unknown>
Source RPM Packages           httpd-2.4.6-40.el7.x86_64
Target RPM Packages
Policy RPM                    selinux-policy-3.13.1-23.el7.noarch
Selinux Enabled               True
```

```
    Policy Type                   targeted
    Enforcing Mode                Enforcing
    Host Name                     localhost.localdomain
    Platform                      Linux localhost.localdomain
                                  3.10.0-327.13.1.el7.x86_64 #1
                                  SMP Fri Jun 3 11:36:42 UTC 2016 x86_64
x86_64
    Alert Count                   2
    First Seen                    2016-06-03 10:33:21 EDT
    Last Seen                     2016-06-03 10:41:48 EDT
```

The `sealert` application is a command-line application that parses the information stored by the `setroubleshoot` daemon (in `/var/lib/setroubleshoot`).

It will provide us with a set of options to resolve the denial. In case of the Apache-related denial shown earlier, `sealert` gives us one option with a certain confidence score. Depending on the problem, multiple options can be shown.

As we can see from this example, the `setroubleshoot` application itself uses plugins to analyze denials. These plugins (offered through the `setroubleshoot-plugins` package) look at a denial to check whether they match a particular, well-known use case (for example, when booleans need to be changed or when a target context is wrong) and give feedback to `setroubleshoot` about how *certain* the plugin is so that this denial can be resolved through its recommended method.

Sending e-mails when SELinux denials occur

Once a system is fine-tuned and denials no longer occur regularly, administrators can opt to have `setroubleshootd` send e-mails whenever a new denial comes up. This truly brings SELinux's host intrusion-detection/prevention capabilities on top, as administrators do not need to constantly watch their logs for information.

Open `/etc/setroubleshoot/setroubleshoot.conf` in a text editor such as `vi` and locate the `[email]` section. Update the parameters to match the local mailing infrastructure:

```
# vi /etc/setroubleshoot/setroubleshoot.conf
...
[email]
recipients_filepath = /var/lib/setroubleshoot/email_alert_recipients
smtp_port = 25
smtp_host = localhost
from_address = selinux@infra.example.com
subject = [infra] SELinux Alert for host infra.example.com
```

Next, edit the `email_alert_recipients` file (as referenced through the `recipients_filepath` variable), and add the e-mail addresses that need to be notified when a SELinux alert comes up.

Finally, restart the D-Bus daemon (as `setroubleshootd` is handled through D-Bus):

```
# systemctl restart dbus
```

When working on a non-systemd system, use this instead:

```
# service dbus restart
```

Using audit2why

If `setroubleshoot` and `sealert` are not available in the Linux distribution, we can still get some information about a denial. Although it isn't as extensible as the plugins offered by `setroubleshoot`, the `audit2why` utility (which is short for `audit2allow -w` and is provided by the `policycoreutils-python` package in RHEL) does provide some feedback on a denial. Sadly, it isn't always right in its deduction.

Let us try it out against the same denial for which we used `sealert`:

```
# ausearch -m avc -ts today | audit2why
type=AVC msg=audit(1371204434.608:475): avc:  denied { getattr }
  for  pid=1376 comm="httpd" path="/var/www/html/infocenter"
  dev="dm-1" ino=1183070 scontext=system_u:system_r:httpd_t:s0
  tcontext=unconfined_u:object_r:user_home_t:s0 tclass=dir

Was caused by:
The boolean httpd_read_user_content was set incorrectly.
Description:
Determine whether httpd can read generic user home content files.
Allow access by executing:
# setsebool -P httpd_read_user_content 1
```

The `audit2why` utility here didn't consider that the context of the target location was wrong, and it suggests us to enable the web server to read user content.

Interacting with systemd-journal

Alongside the Linux audit system, which is used for most of the SELinux logging and events, information can also be gathered through other logging systems. Systemd's journal, for instance, captures SELinux context information with the events and allows administrators to use this information while querying the journal.

For instance, to see the events in `systemd-journal` that are generated by an application associated with the `user_u:user_r:user_t:s0` context, the following command can be used:

```
# journalctl _SELINUX_CONTEXT="user_u:user_r:user_t:s0"
-- Logs begin at Fri 2016-08-05 03:12:39 EDT, end at Fri
2016-08-05 05:46:36 EDT. --
Aug 05 04:31:25 selinuxtest su[11586]: pam_unix(su-l:auth):
  authentication failure; logname=lisa uid=1001 euid=0 tty=pts/0
  ruser=lisa rhost=  user=root
Aug 05 04:31:25 selinuxtest su[11586]: pam_succeed_if(su-l:auth):
  requirement "uid >= 1000" not met by user "root"
Aug 05 04:31:27 selinuxtest su[11586]: FAILED SU (to root)
  lisa on pts/0
```

Because `systemd-journal` adds the SELinux context of the originating application, it is harder for malicious applications to generate fake events. Whereas regular system loggers just capture string events, `systemd-journal` retrieves the SELinux context from the system.

Making fake events (such as authentication events originating from a service that does not have any authentication services) might still be possible, but through the use of the SELinux context, it is easy to group events across applications and have a higher guarantee that events come from a particular application.

When the `bash-completion` application is installed, we can even use it to see which SELinux contexts are already present in the `systemd-journal` logs, which makes querying the journal logs much easier:

```
# journalctl _SELINUX_CONTEXT=<tab><tab>
system_u:system_r:audisp_t:s0 system_u:system_r:rpcd_t:s0
system_u:system_r:auditd_t:s0 system_u:system_r:sshd_t:s0-s0:c0.c1023
...
system_u:system_r:rhnsd_t:s0  user_u:user_r:user_t:s0
```

But `systemd-journal` goes further than just capturing the SELinux contexts. There is decent integration between `systemd-journal` and `setroubleshoot` (which we talked about previously). When debugging an issue with, say, Apache, we can ask `journalctl` to show all events related to the `httpd` binary–and it will include the SELinux events captured by `setroubleshoot` as well.

Using common sense

Common sense is not easy to document, but reading a denial often leads to the right solution when we have some experience with file labels (and what they are used for). If we look at the previous denial example (the one about `/var/www/html/infocenter`), then seeing that its context is `user_home_t` should ring a bell. The `user_home_t` context is used for end-user home files, not system files inside `/var`.

One way to make sure that the context of the target resource is correct is to verify it with `matchpathcon` (provided through the `libselinux-utils` package in RHEL or `sys-libs/libselinux` in Gentoo). This utility returns the context as it should be according to the SELinux policy:

```
# matchpathcon /var/www/html/infocenter
/var/www/html/infocenter
system_u:object_r:httpd_sys_content_t:s0
```

Performing this for denials related to files and directories might help in finding a proper solution quickly.

Furthermore, many domains have specific manual pages that inform the reader about types that are commonly used for each domain as well as how to deal with the domain in more detail (for example, the available booleans, common mistakes made, and so on). These manual pages start with the main service and are suffixed with `_selinux`:

```
$ man ftpd_selinux
```

In most cases, the approach to handling denials can be best described as follows:

- Is the target resource label (such as the file label) the right one? Verify this with `matchpathcon`, or compare with labels of similar resources that do not result in denials.
- Is the source label (the domain) the expected one? An SSH daemon should run in the `sshd_t` domain, not the `init_t` domain. If this is not the case, make sure that the labels of the application itself (such as its executable binary) are correct (again, use `matchpathcon` for this).
- Is the denial one that might be optional? There might be a SELinux boolean to allow the rule. This will be reported by `setroubleshootd` if it is the case, and usually, the manual page of the domain (such as `httpd_selinux`) will also cover the available SELinux booleans. Querying SELinux booleans is covered in `Chapter 8`, *Working with SELinux Policies*.

Changing file labels will be discussed in more detail in `Chapter 4`, *Process Domains and File-Level Access Controls*.

Summary

In this chapter, we saw how to enable and disable SELinux both on a complete system level as well as a per-service level using various methods: kernel boot options, SELinux configuration file, or plain commands. One of the commands is `semanage permissive`, which can disable SELinux protections for a single service.

Next, we saw where SELinux logs its events and how to interpret them, which is one of the most important capabilities of an administrator dealing with SELinux. To assist us with this interpretation, there are tools such as `setroubleshoot`, `sealert`, and `audit2why`. We also dived into several utilities related to Linux auditing to help us sift through various events.

In the next chapter, we will look at the first administrative task on SELinux systems: managing user accounts, their associated SELinux roles, and security clearances for the resources on the system.

3
Managing User Logins

When we log in to a SELinux-enabled system, we are assigned a default context to work in. This context contains a SELinux user, a SELinux role, a domain, and optionally, a sensitivity range.

In this chapter, we will:

- Define users that have sufficient rights to do their jobs, ranging from regular users with strict SELinux protections to fully privileged, administrative users with few SELinux protections
- Create and assign categories and sensitivities
- Assign roles to users and use various tools to switch roles

We will end the chapter by learning how SELinux integrates with the Linux authentication process.

User-oriented SELinux contexts

Once logged in to a system, our user will run inside a certain context. This user context defines the rights and privileges that we, as a user, have on the system. The command to obtain current user information, `id`, also supports SELinux context information:

```
$ id -Z
unconfined_u:unconfined_r:unconfined_t
```

On SELinux systems with a targeted policy type, chances are very high that all users are logged in as `unconfined_u` (the first part of the context). On more restricted systems, the user can be `user_u` (regular restricted users), `staff_u` (operators), `sysadm_u` (system administrators), or any of the other SELinux user types.

The SELinux user defines the roles that the user can switch to. SELinux roles define the application domains that the user can use. By default, a fixed number of SELinux users are available on the system, but administrators can create additional SELinux users. It is also the administrator's task to assign Linux logins to SELinux users.

SELinux roles on the other hand cannot be created through administrative commands. For this, the SELinux policy needs to be enhanced with additional rules that create the role. To view the currently available roles, use `seinfo`:

```
# seinfo --role
Roles: 14
  auditadm_r
  dbadm_r
  ...
  unconfined_r
```

Before looking at SELinux users and roles, let's look at the various complexity levels that policies can reflect since they will direct our choice of the right SELinux user and role later on. For instance, they will guide us in differentiating between a coarse-grained user (such as `sysadm_u`) and a functionality-oriented user (such as `dbadm_u`).

Understanding domain complexity

SELinux is able to provide full system confinement: each and every application runs in its own restricted environment that it cannot break out of. But that requires fine-grained policies that are developed as quickly as the new releases of all the applications that they confine.

The following diagram shows this relation between the policies, the domain scope towards multiple processes, and the development effort. As an example, `postfix_cleanup_t` is shown as a very fine-grained policy domain (which is used for the cleanup process involved in the Postfix mail infrastructure) whereas the `unconfined_t` domain is shown in the example as a very broad, almost unlimited access domain:

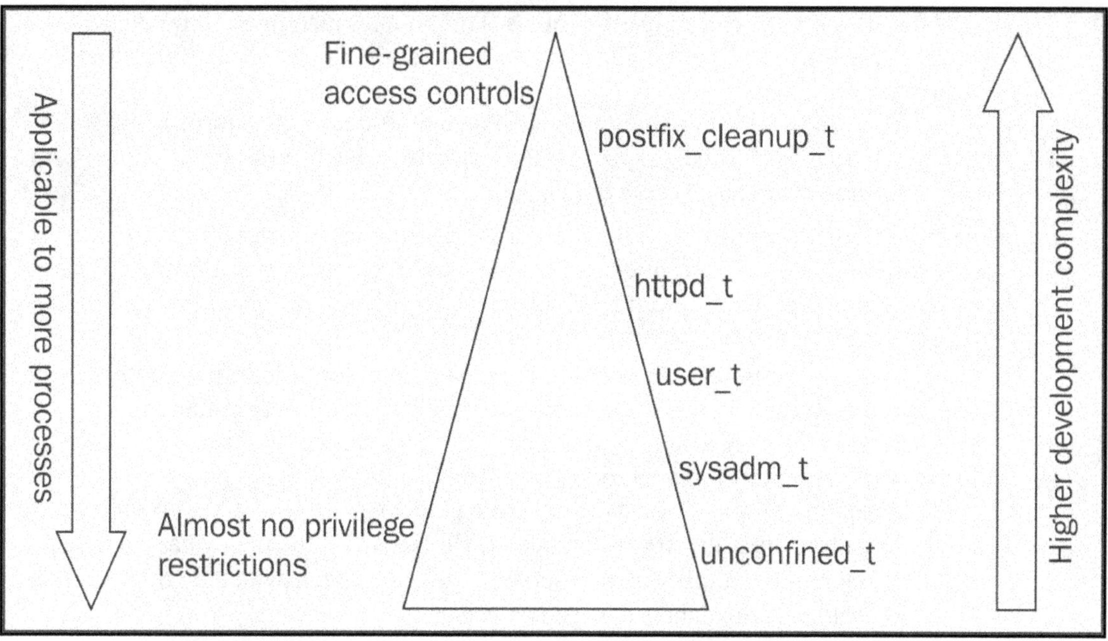

Relationship between domain development complexity and the associated SELinux access controls

Policy complexity can be roughly categorized as follows:

- Fine-grained policy, with separate domains for individual applications and commands
- Policy on application level
- Category-wide policy, reusable for multiple applications implementing similar functionality
- Coarse-grained policy sets, including unconfined system access

Let's discuss policy complexity in depth:

- **Fine-grained policies**: These policies have the advantage that they really attempt to restrict applications as much as possible. And through that, roles developed with users and administrators in mind become fine grained as well. The disadvantage of such policies is that they are hard to maintain, requiring frequent updates as the application itself evolves. The policies also need to take into account the impact of the various configuration options that the application supports:

  Such fine-grained policies are not frequently found. An example is the policy set provided for the Postfix mail infrastructure. Each sub-service of the Postfix infrastructure has its own domain.
- **Application-level policies**: These use a single domain for an application, regardless of its sub-components. This balances the requirement for application confinement versus the maintainability of the application. Such application-level policies are the most common in most distribution policies.
- **Category-wide policies**: These policies use a single domain definition for a set of applications that implement the same functionality. This is popular for services that act very similarly and whose user-role definitions can be described without really thinking about the specific application:

  A popular example of a category-wide policy is the policy for web servers. Initially written just for the Apache HTTP daemon, the policy has become reusable for a number of web servers, such as those provided by the Cherokee, Hiawatha, Nginx, and Lighttpd projects.
- **Coarse-grained policies**: These policies are used for applications or services whose behavior is very hard to define. End user domains are a good example of this, as is the unconfined domain, which puts almost no restrictions on what a domain can do.

Querying for unconfined domains

The freedom in policy complexity results in different policy models being implemented and supported by different Linux distributions. RHEL for instance focuses its attention on the targeted policy store, where network-facing services are confined but user activities are generally not. This is handled by assigning the `unconfined_u` SELinux user, `unconfined_r` SELinux role, and `unconfined_t` SELinux type to the end users.

Moving on from the user domains, we also have unconfined process domains for daemons and other applications. Some of these run in the `unconfined_t` domain as well, but most of them run in their own domain even though they are still unconfined.

To find out whether a domain is unconfined, we can query the SELinux policy to show us those domains that have a SELinux attribute associated with unconfined domains. SELinux attributes enable us to group multiple SELinux types and assign permissions to them. A common unconfined attribute type is the `unconfined_domain_type` attribute. We can query which SELinux types have this attribute assigned through the `seinfo` tool:

```
# seinfo -aunconfined_domain_type -x
  unconfined_domain_type
    sosreport_t
    bootloader_t
...
```

Administrators cannot switch individual unconfined domains to confined ones.

SELinux users and roles

Within SELinux systems, the moment a user logs in, the login system checks which SELinux user his or her login is mapped to. Then, when a SELinux user is found, the system looks up the role and domain that the user should be in and sets that as the user's context.

Listing SELinux user mappings

When logged in to the system, we can use `id -Z` to obtain the current SELinux context. For many users, this context will be `unconfined_u:unconfined_r:unconfined_t:s0-s0:c0.c1023`, regardless of their username. If not that, it will be a context based on one of `sysadm_u`, `staff_u`, or `user_u`. This is because the majority of Linux distributions will only provide a limited set of SELinux users by default, aligned with the SELinux roles that they support.

When the login process is triggered, a local definition file will be checked to see which SELinux user is mapped to the Linux account. Let's take a look at the existing login mappings using `semanage login -l`. The following output is the default output on a RHEL system:

```
# semanage login -l
Login Name           SELinux User         MLS/MCS Range        Service
__default__          unconfined_u          s0-s0:c0.c1023         *
root                 unconfined_u          s0-s0:c0.c1023         *
system_u             system_u              s0-s0:c0.c1023         *
```

In the output, one mapping is shown per line. Each mapping consists of:

- The `Login Name` for which the mapping is applicable
- The `SELinux User` to which the login is mapped
- The `MLS/MCS Range` to which the login is mapped
- The `Service` for which the mapping applies (this is used for local customizations, which we will tackle later)

The login name can contain a few special values that do not map directly to a single Linux account:

- `__default__` is a catchall rule. If none of the other rules match, then the users are mapped to the SELinux user identified through this line. In the given example, all users are mapped to the `unconfined_u` SELinux user, meaning regular Linux users are hardly confined in their actions. When this isn't meant to happen, administrators usually map regular logins to restricted SELinux users, while administrative logins are mapped to the `staff_u` or `sysadm_u` SELinux users.
- Login names starting with `%` will map to groups. This allows administrators to map a group of people directly to a SELinux user rather than having to manage the mappings individually.
- The `system_u` line is meant for system processes (non-interactively logged in Linux accounts). It should never be assigned to end user logins.

When both an individual user mapping and group mapping match, then the individual user mapping takes precedence. When multiple group definitions exist, then the first group mapping (in the order that the `semanage login` command shows) that matches the user is used.

In case of an MLS- or MCS-enabled system, the mapping contains information about the sensitivity range in which the user is allowed to work (MLS/MCS range). This way, two users might both be mapped to the same restricted SELinux user, but one might only be allowed to access the low sensitivity (`s0`) whereas another user might also have access to higher sensitivities (for example, `s1`) or different categories.

Mapping logins to SELinux users

Let's use a few examples to show how these mappings work. We'll assume we have a Linux user called `lisa`, and we want her account to be mapped to the `staff_u` SELinux user, whereas all other users in the `users` group are mapped to the `user_u` SELinux user.

We can accomplish this through the `semanage login` command, using the `-a` (add) option:

```
# semanage login -a -s staff_u lisa
# semanage login -a -s user_u %users
```

The `-s` parameter is used to assign the SELinux user, whereas the sensitivity (and categories) can be handled with the `-r` parameter. For instance, let's modify (using `-m` instead of `-a`) the recently-created group-based mapping by mapping to the `staff_u` user instead and limiting these users to the `s0-s0` sensitivity range and `c0` to `c4` categories:

```
# semanage login -m -s staff_u -r "s0-s0:c0.c4" %users
```

The sensitivity range of a login mapping may not exceed the range that is assigned to the SELinux user. For example, if the `staff_u` SELinux user itself would only be granted access to `s0-s0:c0.c3`, then the previous command will fail as it is trying to assign a broader access range. We'll discuss how to define SELinux users and their range later in this chapter.

The changes take effect when a new login occurs, so we should force a logout for these users. The following command kills all the processes of a user, forcing a logout for that user:

```
# pkill -KILL -u lisa
```

Also, when a user is modified, we should also reset the contexts of that user's home directory (while that user is not logged in). To accomplish this, use `restorecon` with the `-F` (force reset) and `-R` (recursively) options, as follows:

```
# restorecon -RF /home/lisa
```

Running this command will also reset file contexts that the user has manually set using tools such as `chcon`. Define SELinux user mappings up front, or recursively change only the SELinux user using `chcon -R -u`. The `chcon` application and file contexts are discussed in the next chapter.

To remove a login mapping, use the `-d` (delete) option. Don't forget to run the `restorecon` command afterward:

```
# semanage login -d lisa
# restorecon -RF /home/lisa
```

Customizing logins towards services

When login mappings are added using `semanage login`, they apply to all services. There is no option in `semanage` to allow customizing the mappings based on the service. However, that does not mean it is not possible.

The SELinux user space tools and libraries will consult two configuration files to know what the mappings are:

- The `/etc/selinux/targeted/seusers` file contains the standard, service-agnostic mappings. This file is managed by `semanage login` and should not be updated through any other means.
- The `/etc/selinux/targeted/logins` directory contains customized mappings, one file per Linux account. So the custom mapping for the `root` user will be in `/etc/selinux/targeted/logins/root`.

Inside the files for customized mappings, administrators can define, per service, a different SELinux user to map to. The services are the **pluggable authentication module** (**PAM**) services through which a user can log on.

For instance, to have the `root` user through SSH be mapped to the `user_u` SELinux user rather than his default `unconfined_u` user, the `root` file would contain the following:

```
sshd:user_u:s0
```

When querying the current mapping, semanage login will show this customization as follows:

```
# semanage login -l
Login Name          SELinux User         MLS/MCS Range        Service
%users              staff_u              s0-s0:c0.c4          *
__default__         unconfined_u         s0-s0:c0.c1023       *
root                unconfined_u         s0-s0:c0.c1023       *
system_u            system_u             s0-s0:c0.c1023       *
Local customization in /etc/selinux/targeted/logins
root                user_u               s0                   sshd
```

Of course, this customization does not need to be as drastic. It can also be used to limit the MLS/MCS Range through which the user is logged on. For instance, to limit the categories to c0.c8 (rather than the default c0.c1023 range) you'd use this:

```
sshd:unconfined_u:s0-s0:c0.c8
```

Creating SELinux users

By default, only a small number of SELinux users are available to which logins can be mapped. If we want more control over the Linux accounts and their mappings, we need to create additional SELinux users.

First, list the current known SELinux users using the semanage user -l command, as follows:

```
# semanage user -l
SELinux      Labeling MLS/    MLS/
User         Prefix   MCS     MCS            SELinux Roles
                      Level   Range
guest_u       user    s0      s0             guest_r
root          user    s0      s0-s0:c0.c1023 staff_r sysadm_r system_r
                                             unconfined_r
staff_u       user    s0      s0-s0:c0.c1023 staff_r sysadm_r system_r
                                             unconfined_r
sysadm_u      user    s0      s0-s0:c0.c1023 sysadm_r
system_u      user    s0      s0-s0:c0.c1023 system_r unconfined_r
unconfined_u user     s0      s0-s0:c0.c1023 system_r unconfined_r
user_u        user    s0      s0             user_r
xguest_u      user    s0      s0             xguest_r
```

Next, create a new SELinux user with `semanage user`, using the `-a` (add) option. We need to give SELinux additional information about this SELinux user, such as:

- The default sensitivity (using the `-L` option) for the SELinux user. This is the sensitivity that the user starts with.
- The security clearance (using the `-r` option) applicable to the SELinux user. This is the range that is valid for the user.
- The role or roles (using the `-R` option) that the SELinux user is allowed to have.

In the following example, we're configuring the SELinux user `finance_u`:

```
# semanage user -a -L s0 -r "s0-s0:c0.c127" -R user_r finance_u
```

SELinux roles are enabled through the SELinux user that a Linux account is mapped to. When an administrator wants to introduce support for additional roles, he either updates existing SELinux mappings to include the new role(s) or creates a new SELinux user that has access to the new role(s).

When the SELinux user is created, its information is made part of the SELinux policy. From this point onwards, Linux accounts can be mapped to use this SELinux user.

Just like with login mappings, `semanage user` also accepts the `-m` option to modify an existing entry or `-d` to delete one. For instance, the following command deletes the `finance_u` SELinux user:

```
# semanage user -d finance_u
```

Separate SELinux users enhance the audit information since SELinux users do not change during a user's session, whereas the Linux effective user ID can. If the user creates files or other resources, these resources also inherit the SELinux-user part in their security context.

Listing accessible domains

When creating SELinux users, one of the parameters that needs to be provided is the role or roles for a SELinux user. Most of the roles are self-explanatory: the `dbadm_r` role is for DBAs, while the `webadm_r` role is for web application infrastructure administrators. If a role is not clear or an administrator is not certain which accesses are part of a role, he can still query the SELinux policy for more information.

As documented earlier, roles define which domains are accessible for the users associated with the role. We saw that `seinfo` can show us the available roles, but it can do more. It can list the domains that are accessible for a role as well, using the `-x` option:

```
# seinfo -rdbadm_r -x
dbadm_r
  Dominated Roles:
    dbadm_r
  Types:
    qmail_inject_t
    dbadm_t
    ...
    user_mail_t
```

In this example, users that are running with the `dbadm_r` role as part of their security context will be able to transition to, for instance, the `qmail_inject_t` (the domain used to read e-mail messages and pass those on to the `qmail` queue) and `user_mail_t` (the domain used for generic e-mail-sending command-line applications) domains.

The information provided through the **dominated roles** is usually not of concern to administrators. Role dominance, although supported in SELinux core, is not used by Linux distribution policies. It signifies which (other) roles types are inherited from, but it will always just show the queried role.

Managing categories

Sensitivity labels and their associated categories are identified through numeric values, which is great for computers but not that obvious for users. Luckily, the SELinux utilities support translating the levels and categories to human-readable values, even though they are still stored as numbers. As a result, almost all tools that are capable of showing contexts will show the translated rather than numerical values.

The translations are managed through the `setrans.conf` file, located in `/etc/selinux/targeted`. Inside this file, we can name specific values (for example, `s0:c102`) or ranges (similar to `s0-s0:c1.c127`) with a string that is much easier for administrators to use. However, for translations to be performed, `mcstransd`—the MCS translation daemon—needs to run. Not all Linux distributions have it installed by default though. For RHEL, the `mcstrans` package needs to be installed first. Don't forget to have it launched automatically after installation:

```
# yum install mcstrans
# systemctl enable mcstransd
# systemctl start mcstransd
```

Consider our example of the `finance_u` SELinux user who was allowed access to the `c0.c127` category range. Two of the categories within that range are `c102`, which we will tag as `Contracts`, and `c103`, which we will tag as `Salaries`. The `c1.c127` range will be labeled as `FinanceData`. The following diagram shows the relationship between these various categories:

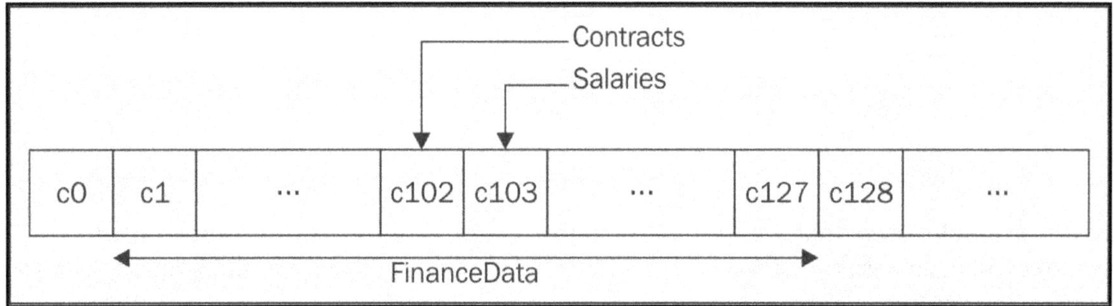

Relationship of the example categories and category ranges

To accomplish this, the following should be placed in the `setrans.conf` file:

```
s0:c102=Contracts
s0:c103=Salaries
s0-s0:c1.c127=FinanceData
```

After editing the `setrans.conf` file, the `mcstransd` application will need to be restarted.

These translations are handled by the SELinux utilities, which connect to the `mcstransd` daemon through the `.setrans-unix` socket located in `/var/run/setrans` to query the `setrans.conf` file. If the daemon is not running or the communication with the daemon fails, the numeric sensitivity and category values are displayed.

For instance, with the daemon running, the output of `id -Z` is now as follows:

```
# id -Z
unconfined_u:unconfined_r:unconfined_t:SystemLow-SystemHigh
```

We can view the available sensitivities and their human-readable counterparts using the `chcat` tool (part of the `policycoreutils` Python package in RHEL or `sys-apps/policycoreutils` in Gentoo). The following example displays the translations after adding the finance-related ones:

```
$ chcat -L
s0                     SystemLow
s0-s0:c0.c1023         SystemLow-SystemHigh
s0:c0.c1023            SystemHigh
s0:c102                Contracts
s0:c103                Salaries
s0:c1.c127             FinanceData
```

The same `chcat` utility can be used to assign categories to users. For instance, to grant the `Salaries` category (assuming it is defined in `setrans.conf`) to the `lisa` Linux user, we'd use the following command:

```
# chcat -l -- +Salaries lisa
```

If no SELinux user mapping exists for the given Linux user yet, one will be added automatically.

Using the preceding command, the `Salaries` category (`c103`) is granted to the Linux user `lisa`. The user mapping is immediately updated with this information. Again, the `lisa` user needs to log out for the changes to take effect.

Handling SELinux roles

We saw how SELinux users define the role(s) that a user can be in. But how does SELinux enforce which role a user logs on through? And when logged on, how can a user switch his active role?

Defining allowed SELinux contexts

To select the context that a successfully authenticated user is assigned to, SELinux introduces the notion of a default context. Based on the context of the tool through which a user is logged in (or through which it executes commands), the right user context is selected.

Inside the /etc/selinux/targeted/contexts directory, a file called default_contexts exists. Each line in this file starts with the SELinux context information of the parent process and is then followed by an ordered list of all the contexts that could be picked based on the role(s) that the user is allowed to be in.

Consider the following line of code for the sshd_t context:

```
system_r:sshd_t:s0    user_r:user_t:s0 staff_r:staff_t:s0 \
                      sysadm_r:sysadm_t:s0 \
                      unconfined_r:unconfined_t:s0
```

This line of code mentions that when a user logs in through a process running in the sshd_t domain, the listed roles are checked against the roles of the user. The first role that a user is assigned that is mentioned in the list is the role (and related domain) that the user is transitioned to.

For instance, assume we are mapped to a SELinux user that is assigned the staff_r and sysadm_r roles. In that case, we will log in as staff_r:staff_t since that is the first match.

However, like the seusers file for the Linux account mappings, the default_contexts file is a default file that can be overruled through specific customizations. These customizations are stored in the /etc/selinux/targeted/contexts/users/ subdirectory. These files are named after the SELinux user for which they take effect. This allows us to assign different contexts for particular SELinux users even if they share the same roles with other SELinux users. And because SELinux checks the entries per line, we do not need to copy the entire content of the default_contexts file; only the lines for those services that we want to implement a deviating configuration for need to be listed.

Let's modify the default contexts so that the dbadm_u SELinux user logs in with the dbadm_r role (with the dbadm_t type) when logged in through SSH. To do so, use the sshd_t line, but set dbadm_r:dbadm_t:s0 as the only possible context, and save the result as /etc/selinux/targeted/contexts/users/dbadm_u:

```
system_r:sshd_t:s0    dbadm_r:dbadm_t:s0
```

Validating contexts with getseuser

To validate whether our change succeeded, we can ask SELinux what the result of a context choice will be without having to parse the files ourselves. This is accomplished through the getseuser command, which takes two arguments: the Linux user account and the context of the process that switches the user context.

The getseuser command is a helper utility offered by the SELinux user space project, but is not made available on all distributions. RHEL users for instance will search in vain for the getseuser command.

Here's an example that checks what the context would be for the lisa user when she logs in through a process running in the sshd_t domain:

```
# getseuser lisa system_u:system_r:sshd_t
seuser:  dbadm_u, level (null)
Context 0        dbadm_u:dbadm_r:dbadm_t
```

One of the advantages of the getseuser command is that it asks the SELinux code what the context would be, which not only looks through the default_contexts and customized files, but also checks whether the target context can be reached or not and that there are no other constraints that prohibit the change to the context.

Switching roles with newrole

After being successfully authenticated and logged in, users will be assigned the context through the configuration mentioned previously. If the SELinux user however, has access to multiple roles, then the Linux user can use the newrole application to transition from one role to another.

Consider a SELinux system without unconfined domains and where we are, by default, logged in as the staff_r role. In order to perform administrative tasks, we need to switch to the sysadm_r administrative role, which we can do with the newrole command (part of the policycoreutils-newrole package in RHEL or the sys-apps/policycoreutils package in Gentoo). This command only works when working through a secure terminal, listed in /etc/securetty:

```
$ id -Z
staff_u:staff_r:staff_t
$ newrole -r sysadm_r
Password:
$ id -Z
staff_u:sysadm_r:sysadm_t
```

Notice how the SELinux user remains constant, but the role and domain have changed.

The `newrole` command can also be used to transition to a specific sensitivity, as follows:

```
$ newrole -l s0-s0:c0.c100
```

When we switch toward another role or sensitivity, a new session is used (with a new shell). It does not change the context of the current session, nor does it exit from the current session. We can return from our assigned role and go back to the first session by exiting (through exit, logout, or *Ctrl* + *D*).

Managing role access through sudo

Most administrators use `sudo` for privilege delegation: allowing users to run certain commands in a more privileged context than the user is otherwise allowed. The `sudo` application is also capable of handling SELinux roles and types.

We can pass the target role and type to `sudo` directly. For instance, we can tell `sudo` to switch to the database administrative role when we edit a PostgreSQL configuration file:

```
$ sudo -r dbadm_r -t dbadm_t vim /etc/postgresql/pg_hba.conf
```

However, we can also configure `sudo` through the `/etc/sudoers` file to allow users to run particular commands within a certain role or type or get a shell within a certain context. Consider a user that has access to both the `user_r` and `dbadm_r` roles (with the `dbadm_r` role being a role designated for database administrators). Within the `sudoers` file, the following line allows the `myuser` user to run any command through `sudo` which, when triggered, will run with the `dbadm_r` role and within the `dbadm_t` domain:

```
myuser ALL=(ALL) TYPE=dbadm_t ROLE=dbadm_r ALL
```

Often, `sudo` is preferred over `newrole` as most operations that we need another role for require switching effective user IDs (toward `root` or a service-specific runtime account) anyway. The `sudo` application also has great logging capabilities, and we can even have commands switching roles without requiring the end user to explicitly mention the target role and type. Sadly, it does not support changing sensitivities.

Reaching other domains using runcon

Another application that can switch roles and sensitivities is the `runcon` application. The `runcon` command is available for all users and is used to launch a specific command as a different role, type, and/or sensitivity. It even supports changing the SELinux user—assuming the SELinux policy lets you.

The `runcon` command does not have its own domain—it runs in the context of the user executing the command, so any change in role, type, sensitivity, or even SELinux user is governed by the privileges of the user domain itself.

Most of the time, `runcon` is used to launch applications with a particular category. This allows users to take advantage of the MCS approach in SELinux without requiring their applications to be MCS-enabled.

For instance, to run a shell session with the `Salaries` category (prohibiting it from accessing resources that do not have the same or fewer categories set), enter the following:

```
$ runcon -l Salaries bash
$ id -Z
unconfined_u:unconfined_r:unconfined_t:Salaries
```

Switching to the system role

Sometimes, administrators will need to invoke applications that should not run under their current SELinux user context but instead as the `system_u` SELinux user with the `system_r` SELinux role. This is acknowledged by the SELinux policy administrators, who allow a very limited set of domains to switch the SELinux user to a different user—perhaps contrary to the purpose of the immutability of SELinux users mentioned earlier. Yet, as there are cases where this is needed, SELinux will need to accommodate this. One of the applications that is allowed to switch the SELinux user is `run_init`.

The `run_init` application is used mainly (almost exclusively) to start background system services on a Linux system. Using this application, the daemons do not run under the user's SELinux context but the system's, as required by SELinux policies.

As this is only needed on systems where launching additional services is done through service scripts, distributions that use `systemd` do not require the use of `run_init`. `systemd` already runs as the `system_r` role and is responsible for starting additional services. As such, no role transition is needed. Other init systems, such as Gentoo's OpenRC, integrate `run_init` so that administrators do not generally need to invoke `run_init` manually.

Still, there might be a situation it is needed in, so let's launch a service script with `run_init` and validate that it indeed is running with the `system_u` SELinux user:

```
# run_init /etc/rc.d/init.d/mcstrans start
# ps -Z $(pidof mcstransd)
system_u:system_r:setrans_t  7972  ?  Ss  0:00  mcstransd
```

Most SELinux policies enable role-managed support for selective service management (for non `systemd` distributions). This allows users that do not have complete system administration rights to still manipulate particular services on a Linux system if allowed by the SELinux policy. These users are to be granted the `system_r` role, but once that has been accomplished, they do not need to call `run_init` to manipulate specific services anymore. The transitions happen automatically and only for the services that are assigned to the user-other services cannot be launched by these users.

To grant the `finance_u` SELinux user access to the `system_r` role, first look at the currently assigned roles, and then modify the role set to include `system_r`:

```
# semanage user -l
...
finance_u      user      s0        s0     user_r
# semanage user -m -R user_r -R system_r finance_u
```

Granting a SELinux user access to the `system_r` role does not mean that that user is capable of always transitioning to this role—it will only be allowed through a limited, well-defined set of domains governed by the SELinux policy.

With the `system_r` role granted to the SELinux user, and assuming that the SELinux user is granted the permissions to handle the PostgreSQL service, the user can now directly execute the `postgresql` service (preferably through `sudo`), as follows:

```
$ sudo /etc/rc.d/init.d/postgresql stop
```

If users have access to `run_init` (more precisely, the `run_init_t` domain), then they can launch any service they want. For this reason, it is preferred to grant the necessary power users the right to use the `system_r` role and transition through specific accesses rather than granting them the privilege to use the `run_init` tool.

SELinux and PAM

With all the information about SELinux users and roles, we have not touched upon how exactly applications are able to create and assign a SELinux context to a user.

Assigning contexts through PAM

End users log in to a Linux system through either a login process (triggered through a `getty` process), a networked service (for example, the OpenSSH daemon), or through a graphical login manager (`xdm`, `kdm`, `gdm`, `slim`, and so on).

These services are responsible for switching our effective user ID (upon successful authentication, of course) so that we are not logged on to the system as the `root` user. In the case of SELinux systems, these processes also need to switch the SELinux user (and role) accordingly, as otherwise, the context will be inherited from the service, which is obviously wrong for any interactive session.

In theory, all these applications can be made fully SELinux aware, linking with the SELinux user space libraries to get information about Linux mappings and SELinux users. But instead of converting all these applications, the developers decided to take the authentication route to the next level using the PAM services that Linux systems provide.

PAM offers a very flexible interface for handling different authentication methods on a Linux (and Unix) system. All applications mentioned earlier use PAM for their authentication steps. To enable SELinux support for these applications, we need to update their PAM configuration files to include the `pam_selinux.so` library.

The following code listing is an excerpt from the Gentoo /etc/pam.d/system-login file, limited to PAM's session service directives. It triggers the pam_selinux.so library code as part of the authentication process, as follows:

```
session         required        pam_selinux.so close
session         optional        pam_loginuid.so
session         required        pam_env.so
session         optional        pam_lastlog.so
session         include         system-auth
session         optional        pam_ck_connector.so nox11
# Note: modules that run in the user's context must come after this
line.
session         required        pam_selinux.so multiple open
session         optional        pam_motd.so motd=/etc/motd
session         optional        pam_mail.so
```

The arguments supported by the pam_selinux code are described in the pam_selinux manual page. In the preceding example, the close option clears the current context (if any), whereas the open option sets the context of the user. The pam_selinux module takes care of querying the SELinux configuration and finding the right mappings and context based on the service name used by the daemon.

Prohibiting access during permissive mode

Having SELinux active and enforcing on a system improves its resilience against successful exploits and other malicious activities, especially when the system is used as a shell server (or provides other interactive services) and the users are confined—meaning they are mapped to user_u or other confined SELinux users.

But some administrators might want to temporarily switch the system to permissive mode. This could be to troubleshoot issues or to support some changes on the system. When using permissive mode, it would be a good idea to ensure that the interactive services are not usable for regular users.

With pam_sepermit, this can be enforced on the system. The PAM module will deny a set of documented users access to a system if the system is in permissive mode. By default, these users are mentioned in /etc/security/sepermit.conf, but a different file can be configured through the conf= option inside the PAM configuration itself.

In the sepermit.conf file, there are three approaches to document which users are to be denied access when the system is in permissive mode:

- Regular usernames
- Group names, prefixed with the @ sign
- SELinux usernames, prefixed with the % sign

Each is mentioned on a single line and can be enhanced with one or two options. These options are documented in the sepermit.conf manual page.

To enable pam_sepermit, it's sufficient to enable the module in the auth PAM service:

```
auth  required pam_sepermit.so
```

Of course, don't forget to remove all active user sessions when switching to permissive mode as any running session is otherwise left untouched.

Polyinstantiating directories

The last PAM module we'll look at is pam_namespace.so. Before diving in how to configure this module, let's first look at what polyinstantiation is about.

Polyinstantiation is an approach where, when a user logs on to a system, he gets a view on file system resources specific to his session, while hiding the resources of other users. This differs from regular access controls, where the other resources are still visible, but might just be inaccessible.

This session-specific view however does not just use regular mounts. The module uses the Linux kernel namespace technology to force a particular view on the file system isolated and specific to the user session. Other users have a different view on the file system.

Let's use a common example. Assume that all users, except root, should not have access to the home directories of other users, nor should they have access to the temporary files generated by those users. With standard access controls, these resources would still be visible (perhaps not readable, but their existence would be visible). Instead, with polyinstantiation, a user will only see his own /home based home directory, with his own /tmp and /var/tmp view.

The following setting in /etc/security/namespace.conf will remap these three locations:

```
/tmp        /tmp-inst/             level     root
/var/tmp    /var/tmp/tmp-inst/     level     root
$HOME       $HOME/$USER.inst/      level     root
```

On the real file system, those locations will be remapped to a subdirectory inside /tmp-inst, /var/tmp/tmp-inst and /home/<user>/<user>.inst. The end users do not know or see the remapped locations—for them, /tmp, /var/tmp and their HOME directory are as they would expect.

In the previous example, only the root user is exempt from these namespace changes. Additional users can be listed (comma-separated), or an explicit list of users can be given for which polyinstantiation needs to be enabled (if the user list is preceded by the ~ character). To allow the namespace changes to take place, the target locations need to be available on the system with the 000 permission:

```
# mkdir /tmp-inst && chmod 000 /tmp-inst
```

Next, enable pam_namespace.so in the PAM configuration files at the session service:

```
session    required      pam_namespace.so
```

Finally, make sure that SELinux allows polyinstantiated directories. On RHEL, this is governed through the polyinstantiation_enabled SELinux boolean. Other distributions will have it through the allow_polyinstantiation SELinux boolean:

```
# setsebool polyinstantiation_enabled on
```

Summary

SELinux maps Linux users onto SELinux users and defines the roles that a user is allowed to be in through the SELinux user definitions. We learned how to manage those mappings and SELinux users with the semanage application and were able to grant the right roles to the right people.

We also saw how the same commands are used to grant the proper sensitivity to the user and how we can describe these levels in the setrans.conf file. We used the chcat tool to do most of the category-related management activities.

After assigning roles to the users, we saw how to jump from one role to another using `newrole`, `sudo`, `runcon`, and `run_init`. We ended this chapter with important insight into how SELinux integrates in the Linux authentication process and how to tune a Linux system further using a couple of SELinux-aware PAM modules.

In the next chapter, we will learn to manage the labels on files and processes and see how we can query the SELinux policy rules.

4

Process Domains and File-Level Access Controls

When we work on a SELinux-enabled system, gathering information about the contexts associated with files and processes is a necessary basic capability. We need to understand how these contexts are used in policies and what the applicable security rules and access controls are for a specific process.

In this chapter, we will:

- Work with file contexts and learn where they are stored
- Understand how contexts are assigned
- Learn and obtain information about how and when processes get into their current context
- Get a first taste of a SELinux policy and how to query it

We will end with another SELinux feature called constraints and learn how they are used to provide the user-based access control feature.

About SELinux file contexts

Throughout this chapter, we will be using a web-based application deployment as an example: DokuWiki. This is a popular PHP wiki that uses files rather than a database as its backend system and is easy to install and manage.

Getting context information

Let's assume that the DokuWiki application is hosted at `/srv/web/localhost/htdocs/dokuwiki` and stores its wiki pages (user content) in subdirectories of the `data/` directory. This can be accomplished by downloading the latest DokuWiki tarball from the project site and extracting it in this location. Some distributions might have a different location for the DokuWiki application (such as `/var/lib/dokuwiki`) which is correctly labeled already. The example here generally follows the same labeling regardless of the distribution, allowing us to show various context related actions.

The contexts of files can easily be acquired using the `-Z` option of the `ls` command. Most utilities that are able to provide feedback on contexts will try to do so using the `-Z` option, as we saw with the `id` utility.

Let's look at the current context of the `dokuwiki` directory itself:

```
# ls -dZ /srv/web/localhost/htdocs/dokuwiki
drwxr-xr-x. root root system_u:object_r:var_t:s0 dokuwiki
```

The context displayed here is `var_t`. Later, we will change this to the correct context (as `var_t` is too generic and not meant for hosting web content).

File and directory contexts are stored in the file system as extended attributes when the file system supports this. An **extended attribute** (often abbreviated to **xattr**) is a key/value combination associated with a resource's **inode** (an information block that represents a file, directory, or symbolic link on a file system). Each resource can have multiple extended attributes, but only one value per unique key. Also, by convention, extended attributes on Linux use the following syntax:

```
<namespace>.<attribute>=<value>
```

The namespace of an extended attribute allows for additional access controls or features. Of the currently supported extended attribute namespaces (`security`, `system`, `trusted`, and `user`), the `security` namespace enforces specific restrictions on manipulating the attribute: if no security module is loaded (for instance, SELinux is not enabled) then only processes with the `CAP_SYS_ADMIN` capability (basically `root` or similarly privileged processes) are able to modify this parameter.

We can query the existing extended attributes using the `getfattr` application (provided through the `attr` package in RHEL or `sys-apps/attr` in Gentoo), as shown in the following example:

```
$ getfattr -m . -d dokuwiki
# file: dokuwiki
security.selinux="system_u:object_r:var_t:s0"
```

As we can see, a SELinux context is defined through the `security.selinux` extended attribute. This ensures that the SELinux context of a file cannot be altered by non-administrative users when SELinux is disabled and that manipulating contexts is controlled through the SELinux policy when SELinux is enabled.

The `stat` application can also be used to show SELinux contexts:

```
$ stat dokuwiki
  File: 'dokuwiki'
  Size: 4096           Blocks: 8          IO Block: 4096    directory
Device: fd01h/64769d   Inode: 8570035     Links: 8
Access: (0755/drwxr-xr-x) Uid: (    0/     root) Gid: (    0/    root)
Context: system_u:object_r:var_t:s0
Access: 2016-08-16 13:46:44.573764039 -0400
Modify: 2016-08-16 13:36:59.698275931 -0400
Change: 2016-08-16 13:36: 59.698275931 -0400
Birth: -
```

Getting context information from a file or directory should be as common to an administrator as getting regular access control information (read (`r`), write (`w`), and execute (`x`) flags).

Interpreting SELinux context types

After using SELinux for a while, the motive behind using file labels becomes somewhat clearer. File contexts are named after their purpose, allowing administrators to more easily see whether a context is correctly assigned or not.

Consider the contexts of a user file in its home directory (`user_home_t`), a temporary directory in `/tmp` for a Java application (`java_tmp_t`), and a socket of `rpcbind` (`rpcbind_var_run_t`). All these files or directories have considerably different purposes on the file system, and this is reflected in their assigned contexts.

Policy writers will always try to name the context consistently, making it easier for us to understand the purpose of the file, but also to make the policy almost self-explanatory.

For the regular file system, for instance, files are labeled with a context resembling their `root` location. For example, we find binaries in the `/bin` folder (and `/usr/bin`) to be labeled with `bin_t`, boot files in `/boot` labeled `boot_t`, generic system resources in `/usr` labeled `usr_t`, and so on.

The more interesting labels are those for a particular application. For instance, for the MySQL database server (or compatible databases such as MariaDB), we have:

- The `mysqld_t` context, meant for the application itself (process type or domain)
- The `mysqld_port_t` context, meant for the TCP port on which the MySQL daemon listens
- The `mysqld_server_packet_t` and `mysqld_client_packet_t` contexts, which are types associated with network packets received (`server`) or sent to (`client`) the MySQL port
- The `mysql_exec_t` type, which is assigned to the `mysqld` binary
- The various `mysql_*` types for specific file system locations related to the daemon, such as `mysqld_var_run_t` (for in `/var/run`), `mysqld_etc_t` (for in `/etc`), `mysqld_log_t` (for in `/var/log`), and `mysqld_tmp_t` (for in `/tmp`)
- The `mysqld_home_t` type for end user (administrator) files specific to MySQL management (such as the `~/.my.cnf` file)

Based on the context of a file or resource, administrators can easily detect anomalies in the system setup. An example of an anomaly is when a file is moved from the user's `home` directory to the web server location. When this occurs, it retains the `user_home_t` context as extended attributes are moved with it. As the web server process isn't allowed to access `user_home_t` by default, it will not be able to serve this file to its users.

Keeping or ignoring contexts

Now that we are aware that file contexts are stored as extended attributes, how do we ensure that files receive the correct label when they are written or modified? For that, a number of guidelines exist, ranging from inheritance rules to explicit commands, to set a SELinux context on a file system resource.

Inheriting the default context

By default, the SELinux security subsystem uses context inheritance to identify which context should be assigned to a file (or directory, socket, and so on) when it is created. A file created in a directory with a `var_t` context will be assigned the `var_t` context as well. This means that inheritance is based on the parent directory and not on the context of the executing process.

There are a few exceptions to this though:

- In the case of SELinux-aware applications, the application can force the context of a file to be different (assuming the SELinux policy allows it, of course). As this is completely within the realm of the software itself, this behavior cannot be generally configured.
- An application called `restorecond` can be used that enforces contexts on a number of paths/files based on SELinux's context rules. We will cover these rules and the `restorecond` application later in this chapter.
- The SELinux policy allows for transition rules that take into account the context of the process that is creating new files or directories.

It is these transition rules we will cover next.

Querying transition rules

Type transition rules are policy rules that force the use of a different type upon certain conditions. In the case of file contexts, such a type transition rule can be as follows: if a process running in the `httpd_t` domain creates a file in a directory labeled `var_log_t`, then the `type` identifier of the file becomes `httpd_log_t` instead of `var_log_t`.

Basically, this rule ensures that any file placed in a log directory by web servers is assigned the `httpd_log_t` web server log context rather than the default `var_log_t`, which would be the case when standard inheritance was used.

We can query these type transition rules using `sesearch`, part of the `setools-console` package in RHEL or `app-admin/setools` in Gentoo. The `sesearch` application is one of the most important tools available to query the current SELinux policy. For the previous example, we need the (source) domain and the (target) context of the directory: `httpd_t` and `var_log_t`. In the following example, we use `sesearch` to find the type transition declaration related to the `httpd_t` domain for the `var_log_t` context:

```
$ sesearch -T -s httpd_t -t var_log_t
Found 1 semantic te rules:
   type_transition httpd_t var_log_t : file httpd_log_t;
```

The `type_transition` line is a SELinux policy rule, which maps perfectly to the description. Let's look at another set of type transition rules for the `tmp_t` label (assigned to the top directory of temporary file locations, such as `/tmp` and `/var/tmp`):

```
$ sesearch -T -s httpd_t -t tmp_t
Found 4 semantic te rules:
   type_transition httpd_t tmp_t : file httpd_tmp_t;
   type_transition httpd_t tmp_t : dir httpd_tmp_t;
   type_transition httpd_t tmp_t : lnk_file httpd_tmp_t;
   type_transition httpd_t tmp_t : sock_file httpd_tmp_t;

Found 2 named file transition rules:
   type_transition httpd_t tmp_t : file krb5_host_rcache_t "HTTP_23";
   type_transition httpd_t tmp_t : file krb5_host_rcache_t "HTTP_48";
```

The policy tells us that if a file, directory, symbolic link, or socket is created in a directory labeled `tmp_t`, then this resource gets the `httpd_tmp_t` context assigned (and not the default, inherited `tmp_t` one). But it also contains two named file transitions, which is a more flexible type of transition rule. The example also shows the granularity of SELinux again, with type transition rules for various classes: regular files, directories, and symbolic links or socket files. Other file system-related resource classes that SELinux supports are block devices (`blk_file`), character devices (`chr_file`) and pipes (`fifo_file`).

With **named file transitions**, the policy can take into account the name of the file (or directory) created to differentiate the target context. In the preceding example, if a file named `HTTP_23` or `HTTP_48` is created in a directory labeled `tmp_t`, then it does not get the assigned `httpd_tmp_t` context (as would be implied by the regular type transition rules), but the `krb5_host_rcache_t` type (used for **Kerberos** implementations) instead.

Type transitions not only give us insight into what labels are going to be assigned, but also give us some clues as to which types are related to a particular domain. In the web server example, we found out by querying the policy that its log files are most likely labeled `httpd_log_t` and its temporary files `httpd_tmp_t`.

Copying and moving files

File contexts can also be transferred together with the file itself during copy or move operations. By default, Linux will:

- Retain the file context in case of a move (`mv`) operation on the same file system (as this operation does not touch extended attributes, but merely adjusts the metadata of the file).
- Ignore the current file context in case of a move (`mv`) operation across a file system boundary, as this creates a new file, including content and extended attributes. Instead, it uses the inheritance (or file transitions) to define the target context.
- Ignore the file context in case of a copy (`cp`) operation, instead using the inheritance (or file transitions) to define the target context.

Luckily, this is just default behavior (based on the extended attribute support of these utilities) that can be manipulated freely.

We can use the `-Z` option to tell `mv` that the context for the file should be set to the default type associated with the target location. For instance, in the next example, two files are moved from a user's `home` directory to the `/tmp` directory. The first one will retain its file type (`user_home_t`) while the second one will receive the type associated with user files placed in `/tmp` (`user_tmp_t`):

```
$ mv test1.txt /tmp
$ mv -Z test2.txt /tmp
$ ls -ldZ /tmp/test*
-rw-r--r--. david users user_u:object_r:user_home_t:s0   test1.txt
-rw-r--r--. david users user_u:object_r:user_tmp_t:s0    test2.txt
```

Similarly, we can tell the `cp` command through the `--preserve=context` option to preserve the SELinux context while copying files. Using the same example, we now get the following:

```
$ cp test1.txt /tmp
$ cp --preserve=context test2.txt /tmp
$ ls -ldZ /tmp/test*
-rw-r--r--. david users user_u:object_r:user_tmp_t:s0  test1.txt
-rw-r--r--. david users user_u:object_r:user_home_t:s0 test2.txt
```

Most of the utilities that are provided through the `coreutils` package support the `-Z` option: `mkdir` (to create a directory), `mknod` (to create a device file), `mkfifo` (to create a named pipe), and so on. Even more so, many of these utilities allow the user to explicitly provide a context through the `--context` option.

For instance, to create a directory `/tmp/foo` with context `user_home_t`, using `mkdir` by default would not work:

```
$ sesearch -s user_t -t tmp_t -T -c dir
type_transition user_t tmp_t : dir user_tmp_t
```

With the `--context` option, we can tell the utility to set a particular context:

```
$ mkdir --context=user_u:object_r:user_home_t:s0 /tmp/foo
$ ls -ldZ /tmp/foo
drwxr-xr-x. lisa lisa user_u:object_r:user_home_t:s0 foo/
```

For other utilities, it is best to consult the manual page and see how the utility deals with extended attributes. For instance, to have `rsync` preserve the extended attributes, use the `-X` or `--xattrs` option:

```
$ rsync -av -X <source> <destination>
```

Temporarily changing file contexts

We can use the `chcon` tool to update the context of the file (or files) directly. In our previous example, we noticed that the DokuWiki files were labeled with `var_t`. This is a generic type for variable data and is not the right context for web content. We can use `chcon` to put the `httpd_sys_content_t` label on these files, which would allow web servers to have read access on these resources:

```
$ chcon -R -t httpd_sys_content_t /srv/www
```

Another feature that `chcon` offers is to tell it to label a file with the same context as a different file. In the next example, we use `chcon` to label `/srv/www/index.html` similarly to the context used for the `/var/www/index.html` file:

```
$ chcon --reference /var/www/index.html /srv/www/index.html
```

If we change the context of a file through `chcon` and set it to a context different from the one in the context list, then there is a possibility that the context will be reverted later: package managers might reset the file contexts back to their intended value, or the system administrator might trigger a full file system relabeling operation.

Up until now, we've only focused on the type part of a context. Contexts, however, also include a role part and SELinux user part. If UBAC is not enabled, then the SELinux user has no influence on any decisions, and resetting it has little value. If UBAC is enabled, though, it might be necessary to reset the SELinux user values on files. Utilities such as `chcon` are able to set the SELinux user as well:

```
# chcon -u system_u -R /srv/www
```

The role for a file is usually `object_r` as roles currently only make sense for users (processes).

In order to be able to change contexts, we do need the proper SELinux privileges, which are named `relabelfrom` and `relabelto`. These rights are granted on domains to indicate whether the domain is allowed to change a label from (`relabelfrom`) a particular type (such as `user_home_t`) and to (`relabelto`) another type (such as `httpd_sys_content_t`). If we find denials in the audit log related to these permissions, then it means that the domain is prohibited from changing the contexts.

Placing categories on files and directories

We focused primarily on changing types and briefly touched SELinux users, but another important part is to support categories (and sensitivity levels). With `chcon`, we can add sensitivity levels and categories as follows:

```
$ chcon -l s0:c0,c2 index.html
```

Another tool that can be used to assign categories is the `chcat` tool. With `chcat`, we can assign additional categories rather than having to reiterate them, as is the case with `chcon`, and even enjoy the human-readable category levels provided by the `setrans.conf` file:

```
$ chcat -- +Customer2 index.html
```

To remove a category, just use the minus sign:

```
$ chcat -- -Customer2 index.html
```

To remove all categories, use the `-d` option:

```
$ chcat -d index.html
```

Users and administrators should keep in mind that applications generally do not set categories themselves, so they need to be added ad hoc.

Using multilevel security on files

When the system uses an MLS policy, the `chcon` tool needs to be used. The syntax is the same as with categories. For instance, to set the sensitivity `s1` and category set `c2` and `c4` to `c10` on all files of a particular user's home directory, you'd do the following:

```
$ chcon -R -l s1:c2,c4.c10 /home/lisa
```

Keep in mind that the context of the user executing `chcon` and the context of the user who is going to use the data must of course be able to deal with the mentioned sensitivity.

Backing up and restoring extended attributes

Like with the regular file operation tools (such as `mv` and `cp`), backup software too needs to consider SELinux contexts. In fact, there are two important requirements for a backup tool when working with SELinux-enabled systems:

- The backup tool must run in a SELinux context that is capable of reading all files that are in the scope of the backup and restoring those files as well. If there is no specific SELinux policy for the backup tool, then it might need to run in an unconfined or highly privileged domain to succeed.
- The backup tool must be able to back up and restore extended attributes.

A popular tool for taking backups (or archives) is the `tar` application. When creating a tar archive, add `--selinux` to include SELinux contexts (both during the creation of the archive as well as when extracting files from the archive):

```
# tar cvjf home-20160815.tar.bz2 /home --selinux
```

Using mount options to set SELinux contexts

Not all file systems support extended attributes. When a file system is used without extended attribute support, then the SELinux context of a file is either based on the file system type itself (each file system has its own associated context) or is passed on to the system through a `mount` option.

The most used mount option in these situations is the context= option. When set, it will use the mentioned context as the context for all the resources in the file system. For instance, to mount an external USB drive that hosts a FAT file system while ensuring that end users can write to it, we could mount it with the user_home_t context:

```
# mount -o context="user_u:object_r:user_home_t:s0" /dev/sdc1 /media/usb
```

If the file system supports extended attributes but doesn't have all files labeled yet, then we can use the defcontext= option to tell Linux that if no SELinux context is available, then the provided default context should be used:

```
# mount -o defcontext="system_u:object_r:var_t:s0" /dev/sdc1 /srv/backups
```

Another mount option is fscontext=. This assigns a context on the file system type rather than the context of the files on the file system. For instance, a CD/DVD file system can be ISO 9660, Joliet or UDF. SELinux-wise, a compatible file system type is iso9660_t. This type definition on a file system level is used by SELinux to map permissions such as mount operations and file creation. Administrators might not want to allow an iso9660_t file system to be mounted anywhere else but inside /media. With the fscontext= option, this file system type can be set differently from what the default file system type would be.

The fscontext= option has little bearing on the contexts of the files inside this file system. For instance, a mounted ISO 9660 file system will probably use iso9660_t for the file system itself, while having its files accessible through the removable_t type:

```
# mount -o fscontext="system_u:object_r:iso9660_t:s0" /dev/sdc1 /mnt
```

The last option that can be used when mounting file systems is the rootcontext= option. This will force the root inode of the file system to have the given context even before the file system is visible to the user space. A file system root context can vary depending on where it is mounted, so forcing this through a mount option allows administrators to use consistent labeling regardless of the location:

```
# mount -o rootcontext="system_u:object_r:tmp_t:s0" -t tmpfs \
    none /var/cache/eix
```

That's it—these are all the context-related mount options. A final note though: the context= option is mutually exclusive to the defcontext= and fscontext= options. So while the defcontext= and fscontext= options can be used together, they cannot be used with the context= option.

SELinux file context expressions

When we think that the context of a file is wrong, we need to correct the context. SELinux offers several methods to do so, and some distributions even add in more. We can use tools such as `chcon`, `restorecon` (together with `semanage`), `setfiles`, `rlpkg` (Gentoo), and `fixfiles` (RHEL). Of course, we could also use the `setfattr` command, but that would be the least user-friendly approach for setting contexts.

Using context expressions

In the SELinux policy, there is a list of regular expressions that informs the SELinux utilities and libraries what the context of a file (or other file system resource) should be. Though this expression list is not enforced on the system, it is meant for administrators to see whether a context is correct, and for tools that need to reset contexts to what they are supposed to be. The list itself is stored on the file system in `/etc/selinux/targeted/contexts/files` in the `file_contexts.*` files.

As an administrator, we can query parts of this list through `semanage fcontext` as follows:

```
# semanage fcontext -l
SELinux fcontext         type         Context

/.*                      all files    system_u:object_r:default_t:s0
/[^/]+                   regular file system_u:object_r:etc_runtime_t:s0
/a?quota\.(user|group)   regular file system_u:object_r:quota_db_t:s0
...
```

An example of a tool that queries this information is `matchpathcon`, which we used earlier in this book:

```
# matchpathcon /etc/selinux/targeted
/etc/selinux/targeted   system_u:object_r:selinux_config_t:s0
```

Not all the entries are visible through the `semanage` application though. Entries related to specific user home directories (such as `/home/david/.ssh`) are not shown as these entries depend on the Linux user (and more importantly, its associated SELinux user).

But for all other entries, the output of the command contains:

- A regular expression that matches one or more paths
- The classes to which the rule is applicable, but translated in a more human-readable format
- The context to assign to the resources that match the expression and class list

The class list allows us to differentiate contexts based on the resource class. The `semanage fcontext` output uses human-readable identifiers, but for completeness' sake, we will cover the related options as well: resource classes can be a regular file (`--`), a directory (`-d`), a socket (`-s`), a named pipe (`-p`), a block device (`-b`), a character device (`-c`), or a symbolic link (`-l`). When it says *all files*, the line is valid regardless of the class.

Right now, we have not defined such rules yet, but after the next section, even defining custom SELinux context expressions will no longer hold any secrets. An important property of the context list is how it is prioritized—after all, we could easily have two expressions that both match. Within SELinux, the rule that is the most specific wins. The logic used is as follows (in order):

- If line A has a regular expression and line B doesn't, then line B is more specific
- If the number of characters before the first regular expression in line A is less than the number of characters before the first regular expression in line B, then line B is more specific
- If the number of characters in line A is less than in line B, then line B is more specific
- If line A does not map to a specific SELinux type (the policy editor has explicitly told SELinux not to assign a type) and line B does, then line B is more specific

Consider all the rules that match `/usr/lib/pgsql/test/regress/pg_regress` (shown through the `findcon` application, provided through the `setools-console` package in RHEL):

```
$ findcon /etc/selinux/strict/contexts/files/file_contexts -p \
/usr/lib/pgsql/test/regress/pg_regress
/.*                                 system_u:object_r:default_t
/usr/.*                             system_u:object_r:usr_t
/usr/(.*/)?lib(/.*)?                system_u:object_r:lib_t
/usr/lib/pgsql/test/regress(/.*)? system_u:object_r:postgresql_db_t
/usr/lib/pgsql/test/regress/pg_regress  --  \
                              system_u:object_r:postgresql_exec_t
```

Although the other rules match too, the last one is the most specific because it does not contain any expression. If that line didn't exist, then the line before is the most specific because the number of characters before the first regular expression is much more than the match before, and so on.

There is a caveat with the rule order, however. When additional rules are added through `semanage` (which is described in the next section), then the order of the added rules is used rather than its specificity. So the most recently added rule that matches the path is used.

Registering file context changes

Because changing a SELinux context using `chcon` is often just a temporary measure, it is seriously recommended to only use `chcon` when testing the impact of a context change. Once the change is accepted, we need to register it through `semanage`. For instance, to permanently mark `/srv/www` (and all its subdirectories) as `httpd_sys_content_t`, we need to execute the following:

```
# semanage fcontext -a -t httpd_sys_content_t "/srv/www(/.*)?"
# restorecon -Rv /srv/www
restorecon reset /srv/www context system_u:object_r:var_t:s0
  -> system_u:object_r:httpd_sys_content_t:s0
...
```

What we do here is register `/srv/www` and its subdirectories as `httpd_sys_content_t` through `semanage`. Then, we use `restorecon` to (recursively) reset the contexts of `/srv/www` to the value registered in the context list. This is the recommended approach for setting contexts on most resources.

These registrations are local (custom) context expressions and are stored in a separate configuration file (`file_contexts.local`). Considering the priority of (locally added) expressions, the following will not have the expected behavior since the most recent rule we add takes precedence:

```
# semanage fcontext -a -t httpd_sys_content_t "/srv/www(/.*)?"
# semanage fcontext -a -t var_t "/srv(/.*)?"
```

In this example, `/srv/www` would still be labeled as `var_t` instead of `httpd_sys_content_t` because the `var_t` rule was added later.

The `semanage fcontext` application can also be used to inform SELinux that a part of the file system tree should be labeled as if it were elsewhere. This allows us to use different paths for application installations or file destinations and tell `semanage` to apply the same contexts as if the destination were the default.

Let's make this more visible through an example and have everything under `/srv/www` be labeled as though it were located at `/var/www` (including subdirectories), so `/srv/www/icons` gets the same context as `/var/www/icons`. We use the `-e` option of `semanage fcontext` to create such an equivalency as follows:

```
# semanage fcontext -a -e /var/www /srv/www
```

This will create a substitution entry so that anything under `/srv/www` is labeled as if it were at the same location under `/var/www`.

Most distributions already configure a number of equivalence locations. The `semanage fcontext -l` command will show these equivalent locations at the end of its output, but you can also directly read that information from the `file_contexts.subs_dist` configuration file, available in `/etc/selinux/targeted/contexts/files`:

```
# cat /etc/selinux/targeted/contexts/files/file_contexts.subs_dist
/run /var/run
/run/lock /var/lock
/run/systemd/system /usr/lib/systemd/system
...
```

Using customizable types

Some SELinux types are meant for files whose paths cannot be accurately defined by administrators or where the administrator does not want the context to be reset when a relabeling operation is triggered. For these purposes, SELinux supports what it calls **customizable types**. When file context-managing tools such as `restorecon` encounter a file with a customizable type set, it will not revert its context to what is registered in the context's definition.

The customizable types are declared in the `customizable_types` file inside `/etc/selinux/strict/contexts`. To have `restorecon` relabel such files, administrators need to pass the force reset option (`-F`) before the tool resets the contexts.

Let's take a look at the contents of this `customizable_types` file:

```
$ cat /etc/selinux/strict/contexts/customizable_types
sandbox_file_t
svirt_image_t
home_bin_t
...
user_tty_device_t
```

As an example, we can mark a file in a home directory (in this example, the file is called `convert.sh`) as `home_bin_t`, which is a customizable type and as such will not be relabeled back to `user_home_t` when a file system relabeling operation is done:

```
$ chcon -t home_bin_t  ~/convert.sh
```

For now, marking types as customizable requires updating the `customizable_types` file. Because this file can be overwritten when a new policy package (by the distribution) is pushed to the system, it needs to be governed carefully.

That said, the use of customizable types has its advantages. As an administrator, we might want to create and support specific types usable by end users who can use `chcon` to set the contexts of individual files in their home directory. By having those types marked as customizable types, a relabeling operation against `/home` will not reset those contexts.

Most of the time, however, it is preferred you use `semanage fcontext` to add an expression and `restorecon` to fix the context of the files. Taking the `convert.sh` file as an example again, this would result in the following commands:

```
# semanage fcontext -a -t home_bin_t /home/myuser/convert\.sh
# restorecon -F /home/myuser/convert.sh
```

Most administrators will prefer to use directory-based labeling. User binaries and scripts are then located in the `~/bin` directory, with the context definition being as follows:

```
# semanage fcontext -a -t home_bin_t "/home/[^/]*/bin(/.*)?"
```

Compiling the different file_contexts files

Inside the `/etc/selinux/targeted/contexts/files` directory, five different `file_contexts` files can be found:

- The `file_contexts` file itself (without any suffix) is the basic expression file provided by the SELinux policy offered through the Linux distribution.
- The `file_contexts.local` file contains the locally added rules (through the `semanage fcontext` command, which we covered earlier in this chapter).
- The `file_contexts.homedirs` file contains the expressions for the user home directories. When new user mappings are created and managed through `semanage login` and `semanage user`, this file is adjusted to reflect the new situation.
- The `file_contexts.subs_dist` file contains equivalency rules provided by the SELinux policy offered through the Linux distribution, which tell SELinux to consider one part of the file system as requiring the same labeling rules as another location.
- The `file_contexts.subs` file contains equivalency rules, which are managed locally (through the `semanage fcontext` command, which we covered earlier in this chapter).

Alongside those files, you will find the associated `*.bin` files (so `file_contexts.bin` for the `file_contexts` file, `file_contexts.local.bin` for the `file_contexts.local` file, and so on). These files contain the same information as the main file, but are precompiled to make lookups faster. These `*.bin` files are automatically created, but in case of a discrepancy, administrators can rebuild the files themselves as well using the `sefcontext_compile` command:

```
# cd /etc/selinux/targeted/contexts/files
# sefcontext_compile file_contexts.local
```

Exchanging local modifications

When local modifications are registered through `semanage fcontext`, they only apply to a single system. If local definitions need to be reapplied on various systems, administrators can extract the local modifications and import them on another system.

To export the local modifications, use `semanage export`:

```
# semanage export -f local-mods.conf
```

The file where the local modifications are now stored (`local-mods.conf` in the example) can be adjusted at will. For instance, administrators can remove all lines except those they want to apply on other systems.

With the local modifications stored in the file, transport the file to the other system(s) and import them:

```
# semanage import -f ./local-mods.conf
```

The imported settings are immediately registered. Of course, in case of file system changes (`semanage fcontext`), don't forget to run `restorecon` against the target directories.

Modifying file contexts

We now know how to set SELinux contexts, both directly through tools such as `chcon` as well as through the `restorecon` application, which queries the SELinux context list to know what context a file should have. But `restorecon` is not the only application that considers this context list.

Using setfiles, rlpkg, and fixfiles

Using `semanage fcontext` and `restorecon` is the preferred method for changing file contexts, but other tools exist that impact file contexts on a system.

The `setfiles` application is an older one, which requires the path to the context list file itself in order to reset contexts. Although it is often used under the hood of other applications, most administrators do not need to call `setfiles` directly anymore:

```
# setfiles /etc/selinux/targeted/contexts/files/file_contexts /srv/www
```

Another set of tools are the `rlpkg` (Gentoo) and `fixfiles` (RHEL) applications. Both these applications have a nice feature: they can be used to reset the contexts of the files of a particular application rather than having to iterate over the files manually and run `restorecon` against them. In the next example, we're using these tools to restore the contexts of the files provided by the `openssh` package:

```
# rlpkg openssh
# fixfiles -R openssh restore
```

Another feature of both applications is that they can be used to relabel the entire file system without the need to perform a system reboot, like so:

```
# rlpkg -a -r
# fixfiles -f -F relabel
```

Relabeling the entire file system

The `rlpkg` and `fixfiles` commands are not the only available approaches for relabeling the entire file system when working with a RHEL (or derived) distribution. There are two other methods of asking the system to perform a full file system relabeling operation during (re)boot: a `touch` file or a kernel parameter.

The `touch` file is called `.autorelabel` and should be placed in the `root` file system. Once set, the system needs to be rebooted:

```
# touch /.autorelabel
# reboot
```

The same behavior is triggered if the `autorelabel` parameter is added to the kernel boot parameter list (similar to how the `selinux=` and `enforcing=` parameters can be set as discussed in `Chapter 2`, *Understanding SELinux Decisions and Logging*).

Asking the system to perform a full file system relabeling operation will take a while. When finished, the system will reboot again. If a `touch` file was used to trigger the relabeling operation, it will be removed automatically.

Automatically setting contexts with restorecond

Contexts can also be forced by the `restorecond` daemon. The purpose of this daemon is to enforce the expression list rules onto a configurable set of locations, defined in the `/etc/selinux/restorecond.conf` file.

The following set of files and directories is an example list of locations configured in the `restorecond.conf` file so that `restorecond` automatically enforces the SELinux contexts on these files and directories whenever it detects a context change:

```
/etc/resolv.conf
/etc/mtab
/var/run/utmp
/root/*
~/public_html
```

```
~/.mozilla/plugins/libflashplayer.so
```

In this case, if a file matches any of the previously created paths, `restorecond` will be notified of it (through the Linux **inotify** subsystem) and will relabel the file according to the expression list.

The use of `restorecond` is primarily for historical reasons, for back when SELinux didn't support named file transitions. Writing `resolv.conf` in `/etc` could not be differentiated from writing to the `passwd` file in `/etc`. The introduction of named file transitions has considerably reduced the need for `restorecond`.

The context of a process

As everything in SELinux works with labels, even processes are assigned a label, also known as the domain.

Getting a process context

We saw that the Apache web server runs in the `httpd_t` domain, which can be seen with the `ps -eZ` command, as follows:

```
# ps -eZ | grep httpd
system_u:system_r:httpd_t:s0 2270 ?        00:00:00 httpd
```

There are a number of other ways to obtain the process context as well. Although the method with `ps` is the most obvious, these other methods can prove useful in scripted approaches or through monitoring services.

A first approach is to read the `/proc/<pid>/attr/current` pseudo-file, which we've already encountered previously in the book. It displays a process' current security context:

```
# pidof httpd
1952 1951 1950 1949 1948 1947
# cat /proc/1952/attr/current
system_u:system_r:httpd_t:s0
```

To receive a somewhat more human-readable output, use the secon command for the given **process ID (PID)**:

```
# secon --pid 1952
user: system_u
role: system_r
type: httpd_t
sensitivity: s0
clearance: s0
mls-range: s0
```

Finally, the SELinux user space project has a helper utility called getpidcon, which is provided through the libselinux library. Although this utility is not available on RHEL, other distributions such as Gentoo have it. The utility requires a single PID and returns its context:

```
# getpidcon 1950
system_u:system_r:httpd_t:s0
```

Now, the Apache processes don't themselves inform SELinux that they need to run in the httpd_t domain. For that, transition rules exist in the SELinux policy that govern when and how processes are executed in a particular domain.

Transitioning towards a domain

Just as we have seen with files, if a process forks and creates a new process, this process by default inherits the context of the parent process. In the case of the web server, the main process is running in the httpd_t domain, so all the worker processes that are launched inherit the httpd_t domain from it.

In order to differentiate one process from another, domain transitions can be defined. A **domain transition** (also known as a **process transition**) is a rule in SELinux that tells SELinux another domain is to be used for a forked process (actually, it is when the parent process calls the execve() function, most likely after a fork() operation).

Similar to the files, domain transitions can be queried using `sesearch`. Let's look into the domains that are allowed to transition to the `httpd_t` domain:

```
$ sesearch -T | grep "process httpd_t"
type_transition piranha_pulse_t httpd_exec_t : process httpd_t;
type_transition kdumpctl_t httpd_exec_t : process httpd_t;
type_transition initrc_t httpd_exec_t : process httpd_t;
...
type_transition init_t httpd_exec_t : process httpd_t;
```

In this case, SELinux will switch the context of a launched web server to `httpd_t` if the parent process is running in one of the mentioned domains (such as the `initrc_t` domain) and is executing a file labeled as `httpd_exec_t` (which is the label assigned to the `httpd` binary).

But in order for this to truly happen, a number of other permissions (next to the type transition) need to be in place. The following list describes these various permissions:

- The source process (such as `initrc_t`) needs to be allowed to transition to the `httpd_t` domain, which is governed by the `transition` privilege on the `process` class:

  ```
  $ sesearch -s initrc_t -t httpd_t -c process -p transition -A
  ```

- The source process (such as `initrc_t`) needs to have the `execute` right on the file it is launching (`httpd_exec_t`):

  ```
  $ sesearch -s initrc_t -t httpd_exec_t -c file -p execute -A
  ```

- The `httpd_exec_t` type must be identified as an entry point for the `httpd_t` domain. An `entrypoint` is used by SELinux to ensure that a domain transition only occurs when that particular file context is used on the executing binary or script:

  ```
  $ sesearch -s httpd_t -t httpd_exec_t -c file -p entrypoint -A
  ```

- The target domain must be allowed for the role that the parent process is in. In case of system daemons, the role is `system_r`:

  ```
  $ seinfo -rsystem_r -x | grep httpd_t
  ```

A graphical representation of these rights is as follows:

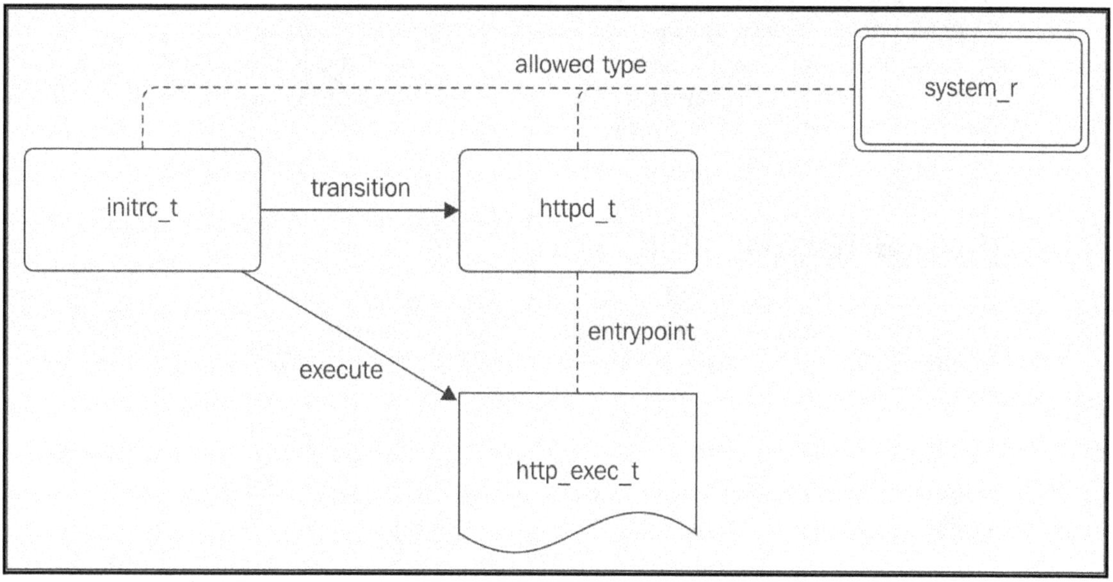

Graphical overview of the permissions involved in successfully transitioning from one domain to another

Only when all these privileges are allowed will a domain transition occur. If not, then either the execution of the application fails (if the domain has no `execute` or `execute_no_trans` rights on the file), or it executes but remains running in the same domain as the parent process.

Domain transitions are an important concept as they inform the administrator how an application gets into its privileged context. To analyze this, many security administrators look at how one context can transition to the next. This is documented further in `Chapter 9`, *Analyzing Policy Behavior*.

For policy writers, deciding when to create a domain transition and when to keep the processes running in the same (source) context is a matter of design. Generally, policy developers will try to keep the parent context confined so that every additional privilege is a source of consideration for switching to another domain (which has that particular privilege). In other words, a transition is prepared when the target application requires more or different permissions than the source domain.

That is also why the `unconfined_t` domain has few transitions when executing user applications compared to the confined user domains `user_t` or `guest_t`: the `unconfined_t` domain already holds many privileges, so there is little value in transitioning to a different domain. Note that this is a decision made by the policy writers or Linux distribution, not by the SELinux technology itself. All SELinux does is enforce the policy rules.

Verifying a target context

When executing applications, the SELinux policy might force the command to run in a different domain. Although we could start querying all rules with `sesearch`, there is a simpler command that tells us what the target context is when we execute a command or script.

The utility is called `selinuxexeccon` and is provided by the `libselinux-utils` package in RHEL or `sys-libs/libselinux` in Gentoo. It requires at least one argument (the path of the binary or script that would be executed) and an optional second (the source context).

For instance, to find out in which domain the `passwd` command would run when executed from the current context, we'd use this command:

```
# selinuxexeccon /usr/bin/passwd
unconfined_u:unconfined_r:passwd_t:s0
```

The following command would be used to find out in which domain the web server will run when executed from the `init_t` domain:

```
# selinuxexeccon /usr/sbin/httpd system_u:system_r:init_t:s0
system_u:system_r:httpd_t:s0
```

Other supported transitions

Regular domain transitions are the most common transitions in SELinux, but there are other transitions as well.

For instance, some applications (such as `cron` or `login`) are SELinux aware and will specify which domain to transition to. These applications call the `setexeccon()` method to specify the target domain and do not use a type transition rule. The other privilege requirements, however, still hold.

Some SELinux-aware applications are even able to change their current context (and not just the context of the application they execute). In order to do so, the application domain needs the `dyntransition` privilege (one of the privileges supported for process-level activities). One example of such an application is OpenSSH, which by default runs in the `sshd_t` domain but can transition to the `sftpd_t` type.

Querying initial contexts

If a label is absent (or invalid), SELinux will show the process as `unlabeled_t`. This is because for files, `unlabeled_t` is defined as the initial security context for a **security ID (SID)**.

The initial contexts for various security IDs can be queried using `seinfo`:

```
# seinfo --initialsid -x
Initial SID: 27
  devnull: system_u:object_r:null_device_t:s0
  scmp_packet: system_u:object_r:unlabeled_t:s0
  ...
  file: system_u:object_r:unlabeled_t:s0
  kernel: system_u:system_r:kernel_t:s0
```

Limiting the scope of transitions

For security reasons, Linux systems can reduce the ability for processes to gain elevated privileges under certain situations or provide additional constraints to reduce the likelihood of vulnerabilities to be exploitable. The SELinux developers too honor these situations.

Sanitizing environments on transition

When a higher-privileged command is executed (be it a `setuid` application or one where capabilities are added to the session), the **GNU C Library** (**glibc**) will sanitize the environment. This means that a set of sensitive environment variables is discarded to make sure that attackers or malicious persons or applications cannot influence the session.

This secure execution is controlled through an **Executable and Linkable Format** (**ELF**) auxiliary vector called `AT_SECURE`. When set, environment variables such as `LD_PRELOAD`, `LD_AUDIT`, `LD_DEBUG`, `TMPDIR`, and `NLSPATH` are removed from the session.

SELinux will force this sanitation on domain transitions as well, ensuring that the newly executed domain does not have access to these sensitive environment variables. Of course, sometimes the transitioned domain requires these variables (not all domains are security sensitive, so dropping the environment variables at all times might result in unusable application domains).

To allow transitions without sanitizing the environment, the `noatsecure` permission can be granted to domain transitions. For instance, when a Firefox plugin is executed (which results in a domain transition to `mozilla_plugin_t`) the environment variables need to be kept. As such, these transitions have `noatsecure` set:

```
# sesearch -t mozilla_plugin_t -p noatsecure -A
Found 4 semantic av rules:
  allow xguest_t mozilla_plugin_t : process { ... noatsecure };
  allow staff_t mozilla_plugin_t : process { ... noatsecure };
  allow user_t mozilla_plugin_t : process { ... noatsecure };
  allow unconfined_t mozilla_plugin_t : process { ... noatsecure };
```

Disabling unconstrained transitions

A second security constraint that Linux supports is to mount a file system with the `nosuid` option. When set, no `setuid` and `setgid` binaries on that file system will have any effect on the effective user or group ID of the executing session. In other words, a `setuid` application on a file system mounted with `nosuid` will act as if there were no `setuid` bit set.

For SELinux, any executable with a file context that would result in a domain transition will only result in a domain transition if the target domain is bounded by the parent domain. If it is not bounded, then the domain transition will not occur and the session will remain in the current context (or the command will fail to execute if the application is not allowed to run in the current context).

A bounded domain is not just calculated live based on the permissions though. SELinux has an explicit rule that enforces a target domain to be bounded by a parent domain. Even when permissions are later added to the bounded domain, they will be denied by the SELinux security subsystem as long as they aren't part of the parent domain either.

To view the current bounded domains, the `seinfo` application can be used. However, this functionality was only recently introduced (with the `setools` v4 release) and most distributions do not provide it yet. On Gentoo, the application is available:

```
# seinfo --typebounds
Typebounds: 1
  typebounds mozilla_t mozilla_plugin_t;
```

Using Linux's NO_NEW_PRIVS

The use of file systems mounted with `nosuid` is a specific case of Linux's **No New Privilege** (**NNP**) support. NNP is a process-specific attribute that tells the Linux kernel that the process is not to be granted additional privileges any more. From that point onwards, the constraints as mentioned before hold, and SELinux will only allow domain transitions if it is towards a bounded domain.

The parameter can be set by applications themselves using the process control function `prctl()`, but users can also influence this. The `setpriv` command can be used to launch applications with `PR_SET_NO_NEW_PRIVS` set (which is the parameter that applications can pass through the `prctl()` function).

As an example, create the following simple Python-based CGI script in a regular user's home directory:

```
$ mkdir ~/cgi-bin
$ cat > ~/cgi-bin/test.py << EOF
#!/usr/bin/env python
import sys, time
import subprocess
import cgi, cgitb
cgitb.enable()
print 'Content-Type: text/html;charset=utf-8\n'
PIPE = subprocess.PIPE
STDOUT = subprocess.STDOUT
pd = subprocess.Popen(['ping','-c','1','localhost'], stdout=PIPE,
stderr=STDOUT)
while True:
  output = pd.stdout.read(1)
  if output == '' and pd.poll() != None:
    break
  if output != '':
    sys.stdout.write(output)
    sys.stdout.flush()
EOF
```

With this CGI script now available, first launch a simple CGI-capable web server (we will pick port `6020` as unprivileged users should be able to have processes bind to this port) and connect to it:

```
$ python -m CGIHTTPServer 6020
```

In a different session, connect to the web server and call the `test.py` CGI script:

```
$ curl http://localhost:6020/cgi-bin/test.py
PING localhost (127.0.0.1) 56(84) bytes of data
64 bytes from localhost (127.0.0.1): icmp_seq=1 ttl=64 time=0.002 ms

-- localhost ping statistics --
1 packets transmitted, 1 received, 0% packet loss, time 0ms
rtt min/avg/max/mdev = 0.002/0.002/0.002/0.000 ms
```

Now, launch the same CGI-capable web server, but with NNP enabled:

```
$ setpriv --no-new-privs python -m CGIHTTPServer 6020
```

Again, connect to the web server and call the `test.py` CGI script:

```
$ curl http://localhost:6020/cgi-bin/test.py
ping: icmp open socket: Permission denied
```

Because Linux's NNP is enabled, the `ping` command is not able to obtain the higher privileges needed to open the socket.

Sometimes, the SELinux policy doesn't even allow an application to be executed without transitioning. In that case, an `execute_no_trans` denial will show up:

```
type=AVC msg=audit(1150125191.592:740): avc:  denied
  { execute_no_trans } for pid=2793 comm="pipe"
  name="PostFix.mail.SpamAssassin.spamfilter.sh" dev=md9 ino=56842
  scontext=system_u:system_r:postfix_pipe_t:s0
  tcontext=system_u:object_r:ql_spamassassin_client_exec_t:s0
  tclass=file permissive=0
```

Types, permissions, and constraints

Now that we know more about types (both for processes as well as files and other resources), let's look into how these are used in the SELinux policy in more detail.

Understanding type attributes

We have discussed the sesearch application already and how it can be used to query the current SELinux policy. Let's look again at the process transitions:

```
$ sesearch -s initrc_t -t httpd_t -c process -p transition -A
Found 1 semantic av rules:
   allow initrc_domain daemon : process transition ;
```

Even though we asked for the rules related to the initrc_t source domain and the httpd_t target, we get a rule back for the initrc_domain source domain and the daemon target. What sesearch did here was show us how the requested permission is allowed by SELinux, but through attributes assigned to the initrc_t and httpd_t types.

Type attributes in SELinux are used to group multiple types and assign privileges to those groups rather than having to assign the privileges to each type individually. In the case of initrc_domain, the following types are all *tagged* with the initrc_domain attribute, as can be seen through the seinfo application:

```
$ seinfo -ainitrc_domain -x
   initrc_domain
      piranha_pulse_t
      initrc_t
      openshift_initrc_t
      kdumpctl_t
      init_t
      glusterd_t
      cluster_t
      condor_startd_t
```

As we can see, the initrc_t type is indeed one of the types tagged with initrc_domain. Similarly, the daemon attribute is assigned to several types (several hundred, even). So the single allow rule mentioned earlier consolidates more than a thousand rules into one (hundreds of allow rules, each for the preceding eight initrc domains).

Attributes are being used increasingly in the policy as a way of consolidating and simplifying policy development. With seinfo -a, you can get an overview of all attributes supported in the current policy.

Querying domain permissions

The most common rules in SELinux are the allow rules, informing the SELinux subsystem what permissions a domain has. Allow rules use the following syntax:

```
allow <source> <destination> : <class> <permissions>;
```

The `<source>` field is almost always a domain, whereas the `<destination>` field can be of any kind of type.

The `<class>` field allows us to differentiate privileges based on the resource, whether it is for a regular file, a directory, a TCP socket, a capability, and so on. A full overview of all supported classes can be obtained from `seinfo -c`. Each class has a set of permissions assigned to it that SELinux can control. For instance, the `sem` class (used for semaphore access) has the following permissions associated with it:

```
$ seinfo -csem -x
   sem
      associate
      create
      write
      unix_read
      destroy
      getattr
      setattr
      read
      unix_write
```

In the `<permissions>` field, most rules will bundle a set of permissions through the use of curly brackets (`{ }`):

```
allow user_t etc_t : file { ioctl read getattr lock execute
                            execute_no_trans open };
```

This syntax allows policy developers to make very fine-grained permission controls. We can use the `sesearch` command to query these rules. The more options that are given to the `sesearch` command, the finer-grained our search parameters become. For instance, `sesearch -A` would give us all allow rules currently in place. Adding a source (`-s`) filters the output to only show the allow rules for this domain. Adding a destination or target (`-t`) filters the output even more. Other options that can be used to filter through allow rules with `sesearch` are the class (`-c`) and permission (`-p`) options.

The syntax also perfectly matches the information provided by the AVC denials:

```
type=AVC msg=audit(1371993742.009:15990): avc:  denied
  { getattr } for pid=31069 comm="aide"
  path="/usr/lib64/postgresql-9.2/bin/postgres"
  dev="dm-3" ino=803161 scontext=root:sysadm_r:aide_t
  tcontext=system_u:object_r:postgresql_exec_t tclass=file
```

If we wanted to *fix* this denial by granting it through a SELinux policy rule, then that rule would be as follows:

```
allow aide_t postgresql_exec_t : file { getattr };
```

Learning about constraints

The allow statements in SELinux, however, only focus on the type-related permissions. Sometimes, though, we need to restrict certain actions based on the user or role information. In SELinux, this is supported through constraints.

Constraints in SELinux are rules that are applied against a class and a set of its permissions that have to be true in order for SELinux to further allow the request. Consider the following constraint on process transitions:

```
constrain process
  { transition dyntransition noatsecure siginh rlimitinh }
  (
    u1 == u2 or
    (
       t1 == can_change_process_identity and
       t2 == process_user_target
    ) or (
       t1 == cron_source_domain and
       (
         t2 == cron_job_domain or
         u2 == system_u
       )
    ) or (
      t1 == can_system_change and
      u2 == system_u
       ) or (
         t1 == process_uncond_exempt
       )
);
```

This constraint says that at least one of the following rules has to be true if a `transition`, `dyntransition`, or any of the other three mentioned process permissions is invoked:

- The SELinux user of the source (`u1`) and that of the target (`u2`) have to be the same
- The SELinux type of the source (`t1`) has to have the `can_change_process_identity` attribute set, and the SELinux type of the target (`t2`) has to have the `process_user_target` attribute set
- The SELinux type of the source (`t1`) has to have the `cron_source_domain` attribute set, and either the target type (`t2`) should have `cron_job_domain` as an attribute or the target SELinux user (`u2`) should be `system_u`
- The SELinux type of the source (`t1`) has to have the `can_system_change` attribute set, and the SELinux user of the target (`u2`) has to be `system_u`
- The SELinux type of the source (`t1`) has to have the `process_uncond_exempt` attribute set

It is through constraints that UBAC is implemented, as follows:

```
u1 == u2
or u1 == system_u
or u2 == system_u
or t1 != ubac_constrained_type
or t2 != ubac_constrained_type
```

You can list the currently enabled constraints using `seinfo --constrain`, but the output expands the attributes immediately and uses a postfix notation, making it not that obvious to read.

Summary

In this chapter, we learned how file contexts are stored as extended attributes on the file system and how we can manipulate the contexts of files and other file system resources. Next, we found out where SELinux keeps its definitions on what contexts are to be assigned to which files.

We also learned to work with the `semanage` tool to manipulate this information and worked with a few tools that use this information to enforce contexts on resources.

On the process level, we got our first taste of SELinux policies, identifying when a process is launched inside a certain SELinux domain. With it, we covered the `sesearch` and `seinfo` applications to query the SELinux policy. Finally, we looked at some of Linux's security implementations that limit the transition scope of applications, which also influences SELinux domain transitions.

In the next chapter, we will expand our knowledge of protecting the operating system through the networking-related features of SELinux.

5
Controlling Network Communications

The SELinux mandatory access controls go much beyond its file and process access controls. One of the features provided by SELinux is the ability to control network communications. By default, the socket-based access control mechanism is used for general network access controls, but more detailed approaches are also possible.

In this chapter, we will:

- Learn how network access controls are governed by SELinux
- Cover what administrators can do to further strengthen network communications using `iptables`
- Describe how SELinux policies can be used for cross-system security through labeled IPsec

We'll finish the chapter with an introduction to CIPSO labeling and its integration with SELinux.

From IPC to TCP and UDP sockets

Linux applications communicate with each other either directly or over a network. But the difference between direct communication and networked communication, from an application programmer's point of view, is not always that big. Let's look at the various communication methods that Linux supports and how SELinux aligns with them.

Using shared memory

The method that is the least network-like is the use of shared memory. Applications can share certain parts of the memory with each other and use those shared segments to communicate between two (or more) processes. To govern access to the shared memory, application programmers can use **mutual exclusions** (**mutexes**) or **semaphores**. A semaphore is an integer that is atomically incremented or decremented (ensuring that two applications do not overwrite each other's values without knowing about the value change), whereas a mutex can be interpreted as a special kind of semaphore that only takes the values `0` or `1`.

On Linux, two implementations exist for shared memory access and control: SysV-style and POSIX-style. We will not dwell on the advantages and disadvantages of each, but rather look at how SELinux governs access to these implementations.

SELinux controls the SysV-style primitives through specific classes: `sem` for semaphores and `shm` for shared memory. The semaphores, mutexes, and shared memory segments inherit the context of the first process that creates them.

An example `AVC` denial for a SysV semaphore-related communication failure is as follows:

```
type=AVC msg=audit(1443147735.370:444): avc: denied
  { unix_read unix_write } for pid=1454 comm="gnome-shell"
  key=17908779 scontext=system_u:system_r:xdm_t:s0-s0:c0.c1023
  tcontext=system_u:system_r:xserver_t:s0-s0:c0.c1023
  tclass=sem permissive=0
```

Administrators who want to control the SysV-style primitives can use the various `ipc*` commands:

- With `ipcs`, the current SysV-style primitives (such as shared memory segments and semaphores) can be listed
- With `ipcrm`, these shared memory segments and semaphores can be removed/destroyed
- With `ipcmk`, new shared memory segments and semaphores can be created

For instance, let's first list the resources and then remove one of the semaphores:

```
# ipcs
------ Message Queues --------
key        msqid    owner    perms    used-bytes messages

------ Shared Memory Segments --------
key        shmid    owner    perms    bytes        nattch    status
0x01124612 0        root     600      1000         6         dest

------ Semaphore Arrays --------
key        semid        owner       perms       nsems
0x00000000 65536        apache      600         1
0x00000000 98305        apache      600         1
0x00000000 131074       apache      600         1
0x00000000 163843       apache      600         1
0x00000000 196612       apache      600         1
# ipcrm -s 98305
```

When POSIX-style semaphores, mutexes, and shared memory segments are used, SELinux controls those operations through the file-based access controls. The POSIX-style approach uses files in `/dev/shm`, which is simple for administrators to control and manage.

Communicating locally through pipes

A second large family of communication methods in operating systems is the use of pipes. As the name implies, pipes are generally one-way communication tunnels, with information flowing from one (or more) senders to one receiver (there are exceptions to this, such as Solaris pipes, which act as bidirectional channels, but those are not supported on Linux). Another name that is often used for a pipe is **first-in, first-out** (**FIFO**).

We have two types of pipes in Linux: **anonymous pipes** (also known as **unnamed pipes**) and **named pipes**. The difference is that a named pipe uses a special type of file in the regular file system as its identification, whereas anonymous pipes are constructed through the applications with no representation in the regular file system.

In both cases, SELinux will see the pipes as files of the `fifo_file` class. Named pipes will have their path associated with the regular file system and are created using the `mknod` or `mkfifo` commands (or through the `mkfifo()` function when handled within applications). Anonymous pipes, however, will be shown as being part of the `pipefs` file system. This is a pseudo-file system, not accessible to users but still represented as a file system through Linux's **virtual file system** (**VFS**) abstraction.

The following are two denials associated with FIFOs: the first one is a named pipe with the `/run/systemd/initctl/fifo` path while the second one is an anonymous one. Notice how the second is shown to be part of the `pipefs` device:

```
avc: denied { getattr } for pid=16755 comm="su"
  path="/run/systemd/initctl/fifo" dev="tmpfs" ino=822
  scontext=staff_u:sysadm_:sysadm_su_t:s0-s15:c0.c1023
  tcontext=system_u:object_r:initctl_t:s0
  tclass=fifo_file permissive=0
avc: denied { write } for pid=4445 comm="entrypoint.sh"
  path="pipe:[596879]" dev="pipefs" ino=596879
  scontext=system_u:system_r:svirt_lxc_net_t:s0:c845,c982
  tcontext=system_u:system_r:kernel_t:s0
  tclass=fifo_file permissive=0
```

From a SELinux policy point of view, access control is handled on the FIFO file level. Two domains that both have the correct set of privileges toward the context of the FIFO file will be able to communicate with each other.

Administrators can find out which process is communicating over FIFOs with other processes through tools such as `lsof` or by querying the `/proc` file system (as part of the `/proc/<pid>/fd` listings). For instance, the following snippet from `lsof` shows the pipe-based communication setup between two Postfix-related processes (the `NODE` column shows the FIFO identifier, which is the same for the two processes):

```
COMMAND PID USER     FD TYPE DEVICE SIZE/OFF  NODE  NAME
master 1320 root     5r FIFO 0,8    0t0       17553 pipe
qmgr   1345 postfix 92w FIFO 0,8    0t0       17553 pipe
```

Conversing over UNIX domain sockets

With pipes being for one-way communication only, any type of conversation between two processes would require two pipes. Also, true client/server-like communication with pipes is challenging to implement. To accomplish the more advanced communication flows between processes, sockets were introduced.

Most administrators are aware that TCP and UDP communication occurs over sockets. Applications can bind to a socket and listen for incoming communications or use the socket to connect to other, remote services. But even on a single Linux system, sockets can be used to facilitate the communication flows. These sockets are called **UNIX domain sockets**.

We can distinguish between two socket definitions, similar to pipes: unnamed sockets and named sockets. And like pipes, the distinction is in the path that is used to identify a socket. Named sockets are created on the regular file system, while unnamed sockets are part of the `sockfs` pseudo-file system. Similarly, sockets can be queried through utilities such as `lsof` or through the `/proc/<pid>/fd` listings.

There is another distinction regarding UNIX domain sockets though, and that is the type of communication that the UNIX domain socket allows. UNIX domain sockets can be created as **datagram sockets** (data sent to the socket is read in same-sized chunks and format) or **streaming sockets** (data sent to the socket can be read in different-sized chunks). This has some repercussions on the SELinux policy rules.

For SELinux, communicating over UNIX domain sockets requires both domains to have the proper communication privileges toward the socket file type (`open`, `read`, and `write`), depending on the direction of the communication.

Additionally, the sending (client) domain requires the following privileges as well toward the receiving (server) domain, which depends on the type of communication across the socket:

- The `connectto` privilege toward the `unix_stream_socket` class of the receiving (server) domain (in the case of stream sockets)
- The `sendto` privilege toward the `unix_dgram_socket` class of the receiving (server) domain (in the case of datagram sockets)

Like with pipes, SELinux denials will also reveal the type of UNIX domain socket used:

```
avc:  denied  { connectto } for  pid=2597 comm="nginx"
  path="/home/git/gitlab/tmp/sockets/gitlab.socket"
  scontext=system_u:system_r:httpd_t:s0
  tcontext=system_u:system_r:initrc_t:s0
  tclass=unix_stream_socket permissive=0
avc: denied { read write } for pid=31230 comm="iptables"
  path="socket:[224507]" dev=sockfs ino=224507
  scontext=unconfined_u:system_r:iptables_t:s0
  tcontext=unconfined_u:system_r:fail2ban_t:s0
  tclass=unix_stream_socket permissive=0
```

Understanding netlink sockets

A special case of UNIX domain sockets are netlink sockets. These are sockets that allow user space applications to communicate and interact with kernel processes. Unlike the regular UNIX domain sockets, whose target context is associated with the owner of that socket, netlink sockets are always *local* to the SELinux context.

In other words, when a domain such as `sysadm_t` wants to manipulate the kernel's routing information, it will open and communicate with the kernel through a netlink route socket, identified through the `netlink_route_socket` class:

```
# sesearch -s sysadm_t -t sysadm_t -c netlink_route_socket -A
allow sysadm_t sysadm_t : netlink_route_socket { ioctl... nlmsg_read };
```

As applications gain more features, it might be that some of these features are no longer allowed by the current SELinux policy. Administrators will then need to update the SELinux policy to allow the netlink communication.

An overview of supported netlink sockets can be devised from the netlink information in its manual page:

```
# man netlink
```

For instance, the `NETLINK_XFRM` socket is supported through the SELinux `netlink_xfrm_socket` class.

Dealing with TCP and UDP sockets

When we go further up the chain, we look at socket communication over TCP and UDP sockets. In this case, rather than the communication being directly between processes (and thus in Linux terminology between SELinux domains), the flows are from and to TCP and UDP sockets.

SELinux will assign types to TCP and UDP ports as well, and these types are then the types to use for the socket communication. For SELinux, a client application connecting to the DNS port (TCP port `53`, which is assigned the `dns_port_t` type in most SELinux policies) uses the `name_connect` permission over the `tcp_socket` class toward the typed port. For UDP services (and the `udp_socket` class), `name_connect` is not used. Daemon applications, on the other hand, use the `name_bind` privilege to bind themselves to the port.

Administrators can fine-tune which label is assigned to which TCP or UDP port. For this, the semanage port command can be used. For instance, to list the current port definitions, you'd use this command:

```
# semanage port -l
SELinux Port Type      Proto   Port Number
adb_port_t             tcp     5037
afs3_callback_port_t   tcp     7001
...
http_cache_port_t      tcp     3128, 8080, 8118, 10001-10010
http_port_t            tcp     80,443,488,8008,8009,8443
```

In this example, we see that the http_port_t label is assigned to a set of TCP ports. Web server domains that are allowed to bind to http_port_t are as such allowed to bind to any of the mentioned ports.

To allow a daemon, such as an SSH server, to bind to other (or additional) ports, we need to tell SELinux to map this port to the appropriate label. For instance, to allow the SSH server to bind to port 10122, we first check whether this port already holds a dedicated label or not. This can be accomplished using the sepolicy command (part of policycoreutils-devel in RHEL or sys-apps/policycoreutils in Gentoo):

```
# sepolicy network -p 10122
10122: tcp unreserved_port_t 1024-32767
10122: udp unreserved_port_t 1024-32767
```

The unreserved_port_t label is not a dedicated one, so we can assign the ssh_port_t label to it:

```
# semanage port -a -t ssh_port_t -p tcp 10122
```

Removing a port definition works similarly:

```
# semanage port -d -t ssh_port_t -p tcp 10122
```

When a specific port type is already assigned, then the utility will give the following error:

```
# semanage port -a -t ssh_port_t -p tcp 80
ValueError: Port tcp/80 already defined
```

If this is the case and another port cannot be used, then there is no other option than to modify the SELinux policy.

Listing connection contexts

Many of the tools in an administrator's arsenal are able to display security context information. Like with the core utilities, most of these tools use the `-Z` option for this. For instance, to list the running network-bound services, `netstat` can be used:

```
# netstat -naptZ | grep ':80'
tcp    0      0 0.0.0.0:80       0.0.0.0:*    LISTEN    2267/httpd \
  system_u:system_r:httpd_t:s0
```

Even `lsof` displays the context when asked to:

```
# lsof -i :80 -Z | grep httpd
httpd  2267 system_u:system_r:httpd_t:s0 root   3u IPv4  15962 \
  0t0       TCP   *:http (LISTEN)
```

Another advanced command for querying connections is the `ss` command. Just calling `ss` will display all the connections of the current system. When adding `-Z`, it adds the context information as well.

For instance, the following command queries for listening TCP services:

```
# ss -ltnZ
State    Recv-Q Send-Q  Local Address:Port   Peer Address:Port
LISTEN  0       128      *:22                  *:*   \
users:(("sshd",pid=747, \
proc_ctx=system_u:system_r:sshd_t:s0-s0:c0.c1023,fd=3))
```

More advanced queries can be called as well–consult the `ss` manual page for more information.

Linux netfilter and SECMARK support

The approach with TCP and UDP ports has a few downsides. One of them is that there is no knowledge of the target host, so you cannot govern where an application can connect to. There is also no way of limiting daemons from binding on any interface: in a multi-homed situation, we might want to make sure that a daemon only binds on the interface facing the internal network and not the Internet-facing one, or vice versa.

In the past, SELinux allowed support for this binding issue through the **interface** and **node** labels: a domain could only be allowed to bind to one interface and not on any other, or even on a particular address (referred to as the node). This support had its flaws though, and has been largely deprecated in favor of `SECMARK` filtering.

Introducing netfilter

Before explaining `SECMARK` and how administrators can control it, let's first take a quick look at Linux's netfilter subsystem, which is the de facto standard for local firewall capabilities on Linux systems.

Similar to LSM, the Linux netfilter subsystem provides hooks in various stages of its networking stack processing framework, which can then be implemented by one or more modules. For instance, `ip_tables` (which uses the `iptables` command as its control application) is one of those modules, while `ip6_tables` and `ebtables` are other examples of netfilter modules. When implementing processing logic on a hook, each module also tells the netfilter framework which priority the hook should be processed at. This enables controllable ordering in the execution of modules (as multiple calls for the same hook can and will be used together).

The `ip_tables` framework is the one we will be looking at in more detail, because it supports the `SECMARK` approach. As it is commonly best known through its control application, `iptables`, we will use `iptables` as the overarching name of this framework from now on.

`iptables` offers several tables, which are functionally oriented classifications for network processing. The common ones are as follows:

- The `filter` table enables the standard network-filtering capabilities
- The `nat` table is meant for modifying routing-related information from packets, such as the source and/or destination address
- The `mangle` table is used for modifying most of a packet's fields
- The `raw` table is enabled when administrators want to opt out certain packets/flows from the connection tracking capabilities of netfilter
- The `security table` is offered to allow administrators to label packets after regular processing is done

Within each table, `iptables` offers a default set of chains. These default chains specify where in the processing flow (and thus which hook in the netfilter framework) rules are to be processed. Each chain has a default policy, which is the default return value if none of the rules in a chain match. Within the chain, administrators can add several rules, which are processed sequentially. When a rule matches, a particular action is executed. This action can be to allow the packet to flow through this particular hook in the netfilter framework, be denied, or perform additional processing.

Commonly provided chains (not all chains are offered for all tables) are:

- The `PREROUTING` chain, which is the first packet-processing step once a packet is received
- The `INPUT` chain, which is for processing packets meant for the local system
- The `FORWARD` chain, which is for processing packets meant to be forwarded to another remote system
- The `OUTPUT` chain, which is for processing packets originating from the local system
- The `POSTROUTING` chain, which is the last packet-processing step before a packet is sent

Overly simplified, the implementation of these tables and their chains roughly associates with the priority of the calls within the netfilter framework. The chains are easily associated with the hooks provided by the netfilter framework, whereas the table tells netfilter which chain implementations are to be executed first.

Implementing security markings

With packet labeling, we can use the filtering capabilities of `iptables` (and `ip6tables`) to assign labels to packets and connections. The idea is that the local firewall is used to *tag* packets and connections and then use SELinux to grant (or deny) application domains the right to use those tagged packets and connections.

This packet labeling is known as **SECurity MARKings** (**SECMARK**). Although we use the term `SECMARK`, there are actually two markings: one for packets (`SECMARK`) and one for connections (`CONNSECMARK`). The `SECMARK` capabilities are offered through two tables: `mangle` and `security`. Only these tables currently have the action of tagging packets and connections available in their rule set.

The mangle table has a higher execution priority than most other tables. Implementing SECMARK rules on this level is generally done when all packets need to be labeled, even when many of these packets will eventually be dropped.

The security table is next in execution priority after the filter table. This allows the regular firewall rules to be executed first and only tag those packets that are allowed by the regular firewall to continue. Using the security table allows the filter table to implement the discretionary access control rules first and have SELinux execute its mandatory access control logic only if the DAC rules are executed successfully.

Once a SECMARK action is triggered, it will assign a packet type to the packet or communication. SELinux policy rules will then validate whether a domain is allowed to receive (recv) or send packets of a particular type. For instance, the Firefox application (running in the mozilla_t domain) will be allowed to send and receive HTTP client packets:

```
allow mozilla_t http_client_packet_t : packet { send recv };
```

Another supported permission set for SECMARK related packets is forward_in and forward_out. These permissions are checked when using forwarding in netfilter.

Important to know is that once a SECMARK action is defined, then all the packets that eventually reach the operating system's applications will have a label associated with them–even if no SECMARK rule was executed for that particular packet or connection. If that occurs, then the default unlabeled_t label is set. The default SELinux policy implemented in RHEL allows all domains to send and receive unlabeled_t packets, but this is not true for all Linux distributions.

Assigning labels to packets

When no SECMARK related rules are loaded in the netfilter subsystem, then SECMARK is not enabled and none of the SELinux rules related to SECMARK permissions are checked. The network packets are not labeled, so no enforcement can be applied to them. Of course, the regular socket-related access controls still apply–SECMARK is just an additional control measure.

Once a `SECMARK` rule is enabled, `SECMARK` becomes active and SELinux starts enforcing the packet-label mechanism. This means that all of the network packets now need a label on them (as SELinux can only deal with labeled resources). The default label (the initial security context) for packets is `unlabeled_t`, which means that no marking rule matches this particular network packet.

Because `SECMARK` rules are now being enforced, all domains that interact with network packets are checked to see whether they are allowed to send or receive these packets. In order to simplify management, some distributions enable send and receive rights against the `unlabeled_t` packets for all domains. Without these rules, all network services would stop functioning properly the moment a single `SECMARK` rule were enabled.

To assign a label to a packet, we need to define a set of rules that match a particular network flow and then call the `SECMARK` logic (to tag the packet or communication with a label), and perhaps immediately the `ACCEPT` target as well in order to allow this particular communication to reach the system.

Let's implement two rules: one is to allow communication toward websites (port 80) and tag the related network packets with the `http_client_packet_t` type (so that web browsers are allowed to send and receive these packets), while the other one is to allow communication toward the locally running web server (port 80) and tag its related network packets with the `http_server_packet_t` type (so that web servers are allowed to send and receive these packets). For each rule set, we also enable connection tracking so that related packets are automatically labeled correctly and passed.

Use these commands for the web server traffic:

```
# iptables -t filter -A INPUT -m conntrack \
  --ctstate ESTABLISHED,RELATED -j ACCEPT
# iptables -t filter -A INPUT -p tcp -d 192.168.100.15 \
  --dport 80 -j ACCEPT
# iptables -t security -A INPUT -p tcp --dport 80 -j SECMARK \
  --selctx "system_u:object_r:http_server_packet_t:s0"
# iptables -t security -A INPUT -p tcp --dport 80 \
  -j CONNSECMARK --save
```

Use these for the browser traffic:

```
# iptables -t filter -A OUTPUT -m conntrack \
  --ctstate ESTABLISHED -j ACCEPT
# iptables -t filter -A OUTPUT -p tcp --dport 80 -j ACCEPT
# iptables -t security -A OUTPUT -p tcp --dport 80 -j SECMARK \
  --selctx "system_u:object_r:http_client_packet_t:s0"
# iptables -t security -A OUTPUT -p tcp --dport 80 \
  -j CONNSECMARK --save
```

Finally, to copy connection labels to the established and related packets, use these:

```
# iptables -t security -A INPUT -m state \
  --state ESTABLISHED,RELATED -j CONNSECMARK --restore
# iptables -t security -A OUTPUT -m state \
  --state ESTABLISHED,RELATED -j CONNSECMARK --restore
```

Even this simple example shows that firewall rule definitions are an art by themselves, and that the `SECMARK` labeling is just a small part of it. However, using the `SECMARK` rules makes it possible to allow certain traffic while still ensuring that only well-defined domains are allowed to interact with that traffic. For instance, it can be implemented on kiosk systems to only allow one browser to communicate with the Internet while all other browsers and commands aren't: tag all browsing-related traffic with a particular label, and only allow that browser domain the `send` and `recv` permissions on that label.

Labeled networking

Another approach to further fine-tune the access controls on the network level is to introduce labeled networking. With labeled networking, security information is passed on between hosts (unlike `SECMARK`, which only starts when the packet is received by the netfilter subsystem). This is also known as **peer labeling**, as the security information is passed on between hosts (peers).

The advantage of labeled networking is that security information is retained across the network, allowing an end-to-end enforcement on mandatory access-control settings between systems as well as retaining the sensitivity level of communication flows between systems. The major downside however is that this requires an additional network technology (protocol) that is able to manage labels on network packets or flows.

SELinux currently supports two implementations as part of the labeled networking approach: NetLabel and labeled IPsec. With NetLabel, two implementations exist: fallback labeling and CIPSO. In both cases, only the sensitivity of the source domain is retained across the communication. Labeled IPsec supports transporting the entire security context with it.

There is actually an exception to this: NetLabel supports loopback-enabled full-label support. In that case, the full label (and not only the sensitivity and categories) is passed on. However, this only works for communications that go through the loopback interface.

Quite some time ago, support for NetLabel/CIPSO and labeled IPsec was merged into a common framework, which introduces three additional privilege checks in SELinux: interface checking, node checking, and peer checking.

These privilege checks are *only* active when labeled traffic is being used; without labeled traffic, these checks are simply ignored.

Fallback labeling with NetLabel

The NetLabel project supports fallback labeling, where administrators can assign labels to traffic from or to network locations that don't actually use labeled networking. By using fallback labeling, the peer controls that are mentioned in the next few sections can be applied even without labeled IPsec or NetLabel/CIPSO being in place.

Install the `netlabel_tools` package to obtain the `netlabelctl` command, which is used to control the NetLabel configurations. Once that is accomplished, we can start adding rules. Let's create a fallback label assignment for all traffic originating from the `192.168.100.1` address:

```
# netlabelctl unlbl add interface:eth0 address:192.168.100.1 \
    label:system_u:object_r:netlabel_peer_t:s0
```

To list the current definitions, use the following command:

```
# netlabelctl -p unlbl list
Accept unlabeled packets : on
Configured NetLabel address mappings (1)
 interface: eth0
   address: 192.168.100.1/32
     label: "system_u:object_r:netlabel_peer_t:s0"
```

With this rule in place, labeled networking is active. Any traffic originating from the 192.168.100.1 address will be labeled with the netlabel_peer_t:s0 label, while all other traffic will be labeled with the (default) unlabeled_t:s0 label.

Of course, the SELinux policy must allow all domains to have the recv permission from either the unlabeled_t peers or the netlabel_peer_t peers. If not, the following AVC denial will prevent that domain from receiving the network traffic:

```
avc:  denied  { recv } for  saddr=1.2.3.4 src=500 daddr=4.3.2.1
  dest=500 netif=eth0
  context=system_u:system_r:racoon_t:s0-s15:c0.c1023
  tcontext=system_u:object_r:unlabeled_t:s15:c0.c1023
  tclass=peer permissive=0
```

Fallback labeling is useful for supporting a mix of labeled networking environments and non-labeled networks.

Limiting flows based on the network interface

The idea behind interface checking is that each packet that comes into a system passes an ingress check on an interface, whereas a packet that goes out of a system passes an egress check. ingress and egress are the SELinux permissions involved, whereas interfaces are given a security context.

Interface labels can be granted using the semanage tool and are especially useful for assigning sensitivity levels and categories to interfaces, as we will do in the following example where the categories for the tap0 interface are set:

```
# semanage interface -a -t netif_t -r s0-s0:c0.c128 tap0
```

Similar to the other semanage commands, we can also view the current mappings as follows:

```
# semanage interface -l
SELinux Interface       Context
tap0                    system_u:object_r:netif_t:s0-s0:c0.c128
```

Keep in mind that for inbound communications, the acting domain is the peer. In the case of labeled IPsec, this would be the client domain initiating the connection, whereas in NetLabel/CIPSO, this is the associated peer label (such as netlabel_peer_t).

This is shown in the following denial:

```
avc:  denied  { ingress } for saddr=147.32.127.222 src=21
  daddr=10.0.2.15 dest=53060 netif=eth0
  scontext=system_u:object_r:netlabel_peer_t:s0
  tcontext=system_u:object_r:netif_t:s0-s15:c0.c1023
  tclass=netif permissive=0
```

By default, the interface is labeled with `netif_t` and without category constraints. This will, however, not be shown in the `semanage interface -l` output as its default output is empty.

Accepting peer communication from selected hosts

Nodes represent specific hosts (or a network of hosts) that data is sent toward (`sendto`) or received from (`recvfrom`) and are handled through the SELinux node class. Just like interfaces, these can be listed and defined by the `semanage` tool. In the following example, we mark the `10.0.0.0/8` network with the `node_t` type and associate a set of categories to it:

```
# semanage node -a -t node_t -p ipv4 -M 255.255.255.255 \
  -r s0-s0:c0.c128 192.168.100.1
```

Again, we can list the current definitions too:

```
# semanage node -l
IP Address     Netmask          Protocol Context
192.168.100.1  255.255.255.255  ipv4     \
          system_u:object_r:node_t:s0-s0:c0.c128
```

Similarly to the network interface flow control, the acting domain for incoming communications is the `peer` label. This can be seen from the following `AVC` denial:

```
avc:  denied  { recvfrom } for  pid=7204 comm="client.pl"
  saddr=10.4.2.1 src=56403 daddr=10.4.2.112 dest=7081
  netif=eth0 scontext=system_u:object_r:netlabel_peer_t:s0
  tcontext=system_u:object_r:node_t:s0 tclass=node permissive=0
```

By default, nodes are labeled with `node_t` and without category constraints. This will, however, not be shown in the `semanage node -l` output as its default output is empty.

Verifying peer-to-peer flow

The final check is a peer class check. In the case of labeled IPsec, this is the label of the socket that is sending out the data (such as mozilla_t). For NetLabel/CIPSO, however, the peer will be static, based on the source, as NetLabel (actually CIPSO) is only able to pass on sensitivity levels. A common label seen for NetLabel is netlabel_peer_t.

The following is an example of an AVC denial on the peer class, found in the audit logs of a web server that takes part in a labeled IPsec setup:

```
avc:  denied  { recv } for  pid=9 comm="rcu_preempt"
  saddr=192.168.100.1 src=40870 daddr=192.168.100.152 dest=80
  netif=eth0 scontext=system_u:system_r:httpd_t:s0
  tcontext=staff_u:staff_r:mozilla_t:s0 tclass=peer permissive=0
```

As we can see, unlike the interface and node checks, peer checks have the peer domain as the target rather than the source. In this example, we saw that the httpd_t domain (local) does not have the right to receive traffic from the mozilla_t peer.

In all of the previous examples, the process listed in the denial has nothing to do with the actual denial. This is because the denial is triggered from within a kernel subsystem rather than through a call made by a user process. As a result, an unrelated process that was interrupted while the denial was being prepared is listed.

To finish up, take a look at the following diagram, which gives an overview of these various controls and the level to which they apply:

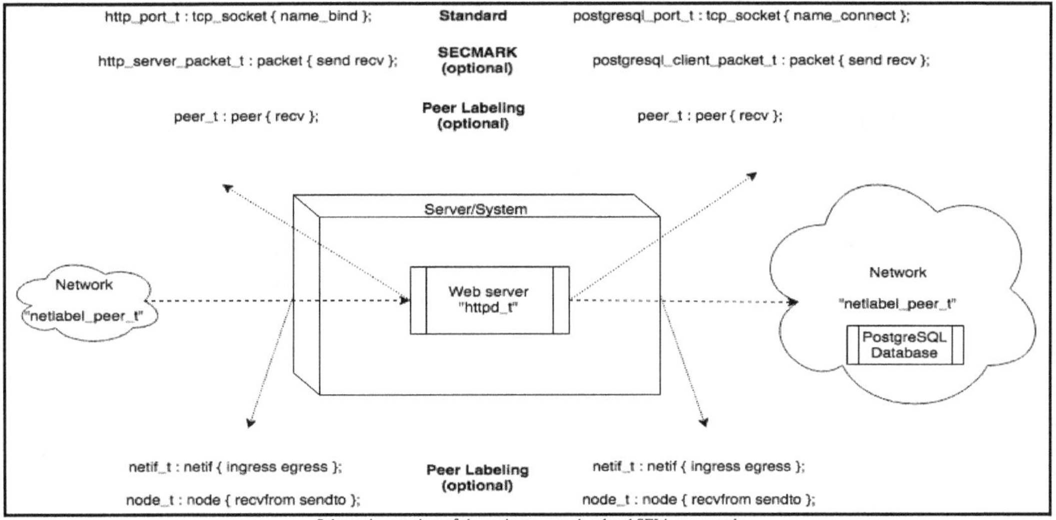

Schematic overview of the various network-related SELinux controls

The top-level controls are handled on the domain level (such as httpd_t) whereas the bottom-level controls are on the peer level (such as netlabel_peer_t).

Using old-style controls

Most Linux distributions enable what is called the network_peer_control capability. This is an enhancement within the SELinux subsystem that uses the previously mentioned peer class for verifying peer-to-peer flow.

However, SELinux policies can opt to return to the previous approach, where peer-to-peer flow is no longer controlled over the peer class, but uses the tcp_socket class for communication. In that case, the tcp_socket class will be used against the peer domain, and it will also use the recvfrom permission (on top of the existing tcp_socket permissions).

The current value of the network_peer_control capability can be queried through the SELinux file system:

```
# cat /sys/fs/selinux/policy_capabilities/network_peer_controls
1
```

If the value is 0, then the previously mentioned peer controls will be handled through the tcp_socket class instead of the peer class.

Policy capabilities cannot be controlled by the administrator: they are hardcoded by the SELinux policy itself.

Labeled IPsec

Although setting up and maintaining an IPsec setup is far beyond the scope of this book, let's look at a simple IPsec example to show how labeled IPsec is enabled on such a system. Remember that the labeled network controls on the interface, node, and peer levels, as mentioned earlier, are automatically enabled the moment labeled IPsec is used.

In an IPsec setup, there are two important concepts to be aware of:

- The **security policy database** (**SPD**) contains the rules and information for the kernel to know when communication has to be handled by a particular IP policy (and as a result, handled through a security association).
- The **security association database** (**SAD**) contains the individual security associations. A **security association** (**SA**) is a one-way channel between two hosts and contains all the security information about the channel. In the case of labeled IPsec, it also contains the context information of the client that caused the security association to materialize.

Security associations with a labeled IPsec setup are no longer purely indexed by the source and target address, but also the source context. As such, a Linux system that participates in a labeled IPsec setup will easily have several dozen SAs for a single communication flow, as each SA now also represents a particular client domain.

Labeled IPsec introduces a number of additional access controls through SELinux:

- Individual entries in the SPD are given a context. Domains that want to obtain an SA need to have the `polmatch` privilege (part of the `association` class) against this context. Also, they need to have the `setcontext` privilege (also part of the `association` class) against their own domain to allow them to initiate an SA.
- Only authorized domains are allowed to make modifications to the SPD, which is also governed through the `setcontext` privilege, but now also against the SPD context entries. This privilege is generally granted to IPsec tools such as `setkey` (`setkey_t`) and Racoon (`racoon_t`).
- Domains that participate in IPsec communication must have the `sendto` privilege to their own association and the `recvfrom` privilege to the association of the `peer` domain. The receiving domain also requires the `recv` privilege from the `peer` class associated with the `peer` domain.

So while labeled IPsec cannot govern whether `mozilla_t` can communicate to `httpd_t` (as `mozilla_t` needs to be able to send to its own association), it can control whether `httpd_t` allows or denies incoming communication from `mozilla_t` (as it requires the `recvfrom` privilege). This perhaps complex game of privileges is displayed in the following diagram:

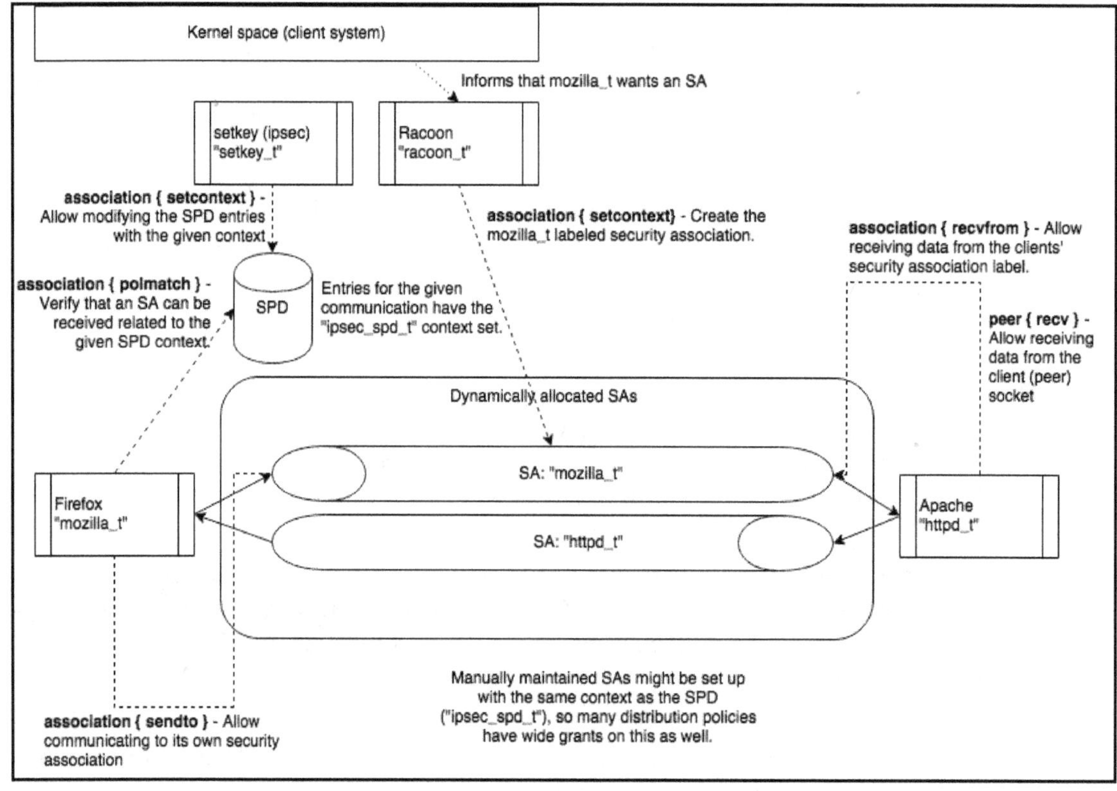

SELinux controls for labeled IPsec, mainly seen from the Firefox-to-Apache communication flow

In the next example, a simple IPsec tunnel is set up between two hosts using the `ipsec-tools` applications. Instructions for Libreswan are given after these sections.

Setting up regular IPsec

First, the racoon daemon is configured with information about the pre-shared key (to use during the handshake with the remote side), handshake details for the remote side, and association information for the *joined* networks. The following code is an excerpt from the racoon configuration file:

```
# File contains remote address with a shared key, like:
# 192.178.100.153 ThisIsABigSecret
path pre_shared_key "/etc/racoon/psk.txt";
remote 192.168.100.153 { ... };
sainfo address 10.1.2.0/24 any address 10.1.3.0/24 any { ... };
```

Most distributions offer sane defaults for the racoon configuration. In the preceding example, the 192.168.100.153 IP address is the address of the remote side, whereas the sainfo address ranges are used for the VPN (10.1.2.0/24 is local, 10.1.3.0/24 is remote).

The setkey information (to manipulate the IPsec SA/SP databases) looks like this:

```
#!/usr/sbin/setkey -f
flush; spdflush;
spdadd 10.1.2.0/24 10.1.3.0/24 any
  -P out ipsec esp/tunnel/192.168.1.5-192.168.100.153/require;
spdadd 10.1.3.0/24 10.1.2.0/24 any
  -P in ipsec esp/tunnel/192.168.100.153-192.168.1.5/require;
```

Finally, we adjust the system routing information so that any communication toward the 10.1.3.0/24 network is done over the 10.1.2.1 VPN gateway:

```
# ip addr add 10.1.2.1/24 dev eth0
# ip route add to 10.1.3.0/24 via 10.1.2.1 src 10.1.2.1
```

Enabling labeled IPsec

To enable labeled IPsec, we need to inform IPsec to add a context on the security policy database entries. Once enabled, racoon will automatically negotiate labeled IPsec support. Adding a context to the SPD is a matter of adding a -ctx option to the spdadd commands in the setkey configuration. For instance, we can add the ipsec_spd_t context to an IPsec security policy as follows:

```
spdadd ... -ctx 1 1 "system_u:object_r:ipsec_spd_t:s0" -P out ipsec ...
```

With this change in place, we can see the context in the output of `setkey -DP`, which displays the current SPD:

```
# setkey -DP
...
10.1.2.0/24[any] 10.1.3.0/24[any] 255
        out prio def ipsec
        esp/tunnel/192.168.100.152-192.168.100.153/require
        created: Jul  4 21:45:44 2013  lastused:
        lifetime: 0(s) validtime: 0(s)
        security context doi: 1
        security context algorithm: 1
        security context length: 33
        security context: system_u:object_r:ipsec_spd_t:s0
        spid=1 seq=0 pid=3237
        refcnt=1
```

When an application tries to communicate over IPsec with remote domains, Racoon (or any other IKEv2 client that supports labeled IPsec, such as Libreswan's pluto) will exchange the necessary information (including context) with the other side. Both sides will then update the SPD with the necessary SAs and associate the same **security policy information** (**SPI**) with it. From that point onward, the sending side will add the agreed-upon SPI information to the IPsec packets so that the remote side can immediately associate the right context to it again.

The huge advantage here is that the client and server contexts, including sensitivity and categories, are synchronized (they are not actually sent over the wire with each packet, but exchanged initially when the security associations are set up).

Using Libreswan

The previous instructions were related to the `ipsec-tools` applications. However, many other IPsec supporting utilities exist. RHEL uses Libreswan as its IPsec provider.

Configuring Libreswan is a matter of configuring Libreswan's main configuration file (`ipsec.conf`). Most distributions will use an `include` directory (such as `/etc/ipsec.d`) in which connection-specific settings can be placed. Generally, this `include` directory is used for the actual IPsec configurations, whereas the general `ipsec.conf` file is for Libreswan behavior.

To use labeled IPsec with Libreswan, use the `labeled_ipsec` and `policy_label` directives in the IPsec definition. For instance, to set up an IPsec definition between two hosts (`10.1.2.1` and `10.1.3.1`), the following configuration setting can be used:

```
# cat /etc/ipsec.d/selinuxtest.conf
conn selinuxtest
  auto=start
  rekey=no
  authby=secret
  type=transport
  left=10.1.2.1
  right=10.1.3.1
  ike=3des-sha1
  phase2=esp
  phase2alg=aes-sha1
    labeled-ipsec=yes
    policy-label=system_u:object_r:ipsec_spd_t:s0
  leftprotoport=tcp
  rightprotoport=tcp
```

The shared secrets used to authenticate the two sides of a connection are stored in `/etc/ipsec.secrets`. In RHEL, this file includes the secrets from `/etc/ipsec.d/*.secrets` so that IPsec definitions can be easily tuned through separate files.

For instance, for the preceding configuration, the secret could look like so:

```
# cat /etc/ipsec.d/selinuxtest.secrets
10.1.2.1 10.1.3.1: PSK "some preshared key"
```

When using Libreswan and `ipsec-tools` together in a single IPsec setup, it might be necessary to configure Libreswan to use the same attribute value for the security contexts as `ipsec-tools` does. `ipsec-tools` hardcodes this value to `10`, so we must adapt Libreswan to use this value as well. This is done in the `config setup` section, defined in the `ipsec.conf` file, where `secctx-attr-value = 10` has to be set.

NetLabel/CIPSO

With NetLabel/CIPSO support, traffic is labeled with sensitivity information that can be used across the network. Unlike labeled IPsec, no other context information is sent or synchronized. So when we see communication flows, they will originate from a single base context but will have sensitivity labels based on the sensitivity label of the remote side.

With NetLabel, mappings are defined that inform the system which communication flows (from particular interfaces, or even from particular IP addresses) are for a certain **Domain of Interpretation** (**DOI**). The CIPSO standard defines the DOI as a collection of systems that interpret the CIPSO label similarly or, in our case, use the same SELinux policy and configuration of sensitivity labels.

With the mappings in place, NetLabel/CIPSO will pass on the sensitivity information (and categories) between hosts. The context we will see on the communication flows will be `netlabel_peer_t`, a default context assigned to NetLabel/CIPSO originated traffic.

Consider the following `AVC` denial:

```
type=AVC msg=audit(1368735963.286:1998): avc: denied { recv }
  for pid=4773 comm="python-thinlinc" saddr=192.168.100.15
  src=46092 daddr=192.168.100.11 dest=9000 netif=eth0
  scontext=system_u:system_r:httpd_t:s0-s2:c0.c32
  tcontext=system_u:object_r:netlabel_peer_t:s0:c102
  tclass=peer permissive=0
```

The denial shows that traffic was received from a peer system with category `c102`, which is not allowed for the current `httpd_t` context (`s0-s2:c0.c32`).

Through this approach, we can start daemons with a particular sensitivity range and thus only accept connections from users or clients that have the right security clearance, even on remote, NetLabel/CIPSO-enabled systems.

Configuring CIPSO mappings

A preliminary requirement for having a good CIPSO-enabled network is to have a common understanding of which DOI will be used and what its consequences are. Labeled networks can use different Domains of Interpretation for specific purposes.

Along with the DOI, we also need to take care of how the categories and sensitivities are passed on over the CIPSO-enabled network. This is controlled by the CIPSO *tag*. There are three supported values for the tag:

- With `tag:1`, the categories are provided in the CIPSO package in a bitmap approach. This is the most common approach, but limits the amount of supported categories to `240` (from `0` to `239`).

- With `tag:2`, the categories are enumerated separately. This allows a wider range of categories (up to `65,534`), but only supports at most 15 enumerated categories. Try to use `tag:2` when you have many categories but for each *scope*, only a few categories need to be supported.
- With `tag:5`, the categories can be mentioned in a ranged approach (lowest and highest), with at most seven such low/high pairs.

Note that the CIPSO tag results are handled under the hood: system administrators only need to configure the NetLabel mapping to use a particular tag value.

Let's assume that we have two CIPSO-enabled networks, which have `10.1.0.0/16` associated with `doi:1` and `10.2.0.0/16` associated with `doi:2`. Both use the tag value `1`. First, we enable CIPSO and allow it to pass CIPSO-labeled packages with the DOI set to either `1` or `2`. We don't perform any translations (so the category and sensitivity set on the CIPSO package is the one used by SELinux):

```
# netlabelctl cipsov4 add pass doi:1 tags:1
# netlabelctl cipsov4 add pass doi:2 tags:1
```

If we need to translate (say that we use sensitivity `s0 - s3` while the CIPSO network uses sensitivity `100 - 103`), a command could look like so:

```
# netlabelctl cipsov4 add std doi:1 tags:1 levels:0=100,1=101,2=102
```

Next, we implement mapping rules, telling the NetLabel configuration which network traffic is to be associated with `doi:1` or `doi:2`:

```
# netlabelctl map del default
# netlabelctl map add default address:10.1.0.0/16 protocol:cipsov4,1
# netlabelctl map add default address:10.2.0.0/16 protocol:cipsov4,2
```

That's it. We removed the initial default mapping (as that would prevent adding new default mappings) and then configured NetLabel to tag traffic for the given networks with the right CIPSO configuration.

Adding domain-specific mappings

NetLabel can also be configured to ensure that particular SELinux domains use a well-defined DOI rather than the default one configured earlier on. For instance, to have the SSH daemon (running in the `sshd_t` domain) have its network traffic labeled with CIPSO `doi:3`, we'd use this:

```
# netlabelctl cipsov4 add pass doi:3 tags:1
# netlabelctl map add domain:sshd_t protocol:cipsov4,3
```

The mapping rules can even be more selective than that. We can tell NetLabel to use `doi:2` for SSH traffic originating from one network, use `doi:3` for SSH traffic originating from another network, and even use unlabeled network traffic when it comes from any other network.

```
# netlabelctl map del domain:sshd_t protocol:cipsov4,3
# netlabelctl map add domain:sshd_t address:10.1.0.0/16 protocol:cipsov4,1
# netlabelctl map add domain:sshd_t address:10.4.0.0/16 protocol:cipsov4,3
# netlabelctl map add domain:sshd_t address:0.0.0.0/0 protocol:unlbl
```

The NetLabel framework will try to match the most specific rule first, so `0.0.0.0/0` is only matched when no other rule matches.

Using local CIPSO definitions

As mentioned before, NetLabel by default only passes the sensitivity and categories. However, when using local CIPSO (that is, over the loopback interface), it is possible to use full label controls. When enabled, peer controls will not be toward the default `netlabel_peer_t` type, but immediately toward the client or server domain.

To use local CIPSO definitions, first declare the DOI for local use:

```
# netlabelctl cipsov4 add local doi:5
```

Next, have the local communication use the defined DOI (`5` in our example):

```
# netlabelctl map add default address:127.0.0.1 protocol:cipsov4,5
```

With this enabled, local communication will be associated with `doi:5` and use the local mapping, passing the full label toward the mandatory access-control system (SELinux).

Supporting IPv6 CALIPSO

Work is ongoing to implement the **Common Architecture Label IPv6 Security Option** (**CALIPSO**) by the NetLabel project. When CALIPSO support is needed, the protocol target is `calipso` rather than `cipsov4`.

There are a few small differences when using CALIPSO versus CIPSO in NetLabel, though:

- There is only one tag type supported (unlike CIPSO's three tag types). As such, there is no need to specify `tag:#` anywhere.
- CALIPSO only uses pass-through mode. Translations are not supported.
- The NetLabel CALIPSO implementation currently does not support local mode, in which the full label is passed on.

Beyond these differences, the use of CALIPSO is similar:

```
# netlabelctl calipso add pass doi:5
# netlabelctl map add domain:httpd_t protocol:calipso,5
```

Summary

SELinux by default uses access controls based on the file representation of communication primitives or the sockets that are used. In the case of TCP and UDP ports, administrators have some leeway in handling the controls through the `semanage` command without resorting to SELinux policy updates. Once we go into the realms of network-based communication, more advanced communication control can be accomplished through Linux netfilter support, using the `SECMARK` labeling, and through peer labeling.

In the case of `SECMARK` labeling, local firewall rules are used to map contexts to packets, which are then governed through SELinux policy. In the case of peer labeling, either the application context itself (in the case of labeled IPsec) or its sensitivity level (in the case of netfilter/CIPSO support) is used. This allows an almost application-to-application network flow control through SELinux policies.

In the next chapter, we will take a look at two platforms that use SELinux for their additional security controls: Linux virtualization and containerization with sVirt and Docker.

6

sVirt and Docker Support

More and more system tools have built-in support for SELinux or use SELinux's features to further harden their own service offerings. When we look at virtualization, two open source projects will definitely come to mind: **libvirt** and **Docker**. While the former supports full virtualization, the latter focuses on container management. In this chapter, administrators will:

- Learn how SELinux can help reduce the risks of virtualization
- Understand how SELinux's policy is tuned to support these services
- Deal with the secure virtualization option supported through the libvirt API

We'll end the chapter with a section on *Securing Docker containers* with SELinux.

SELinux-secured virtualization

Virtualization is part of many infrastructural services. Ever since its inception in the early 70s as a means of isolating workloads and abstracting hardware dependencies, virtualization implementations have grown. When we look at service offerings today, we realize that many cloud providers would be out of service if it weren't for virtualization.

One of the services that virtualization offers is isolation, which SELinux can support and augment quite nicely.

Introducing virtualization

When we look at virtualization, we look at the abstraction layers it provides in order to hide certain resource views (such as hardware or processing power). Virtualization contributes to the development of more efficient hardware usage (which results in better cost control), centralized views on resources and systems, more flexibility in the number of operating systems that the company can deal with, standardization of resource allocation, and even improved security services.

There are a number of virtualization types around:

- **Full system emulation**, where hardware is completely emulated through software. QEMU is an emulation software that is capable of handling full system emulation.
- **Native virtualization**, where main parts of the hardware are shared across instances, and guests can run unmodified on them. Linux's **Kernel-based Virtual Machine** (**KVM**), which is also supported through QEMU, is an example of this kind of virtualization.
- **Paravirtualization**, where the guest operating system uses specific APIs offered by the virtualization layer (on which unmodified operating systems cannot be hosted). Initial releases of Xen only supported paravirtualization. Using KVM with VirtIO drivers is another example.
- **OS-level virtualization or containerization**, where the guest uses the host operating system (kernel) but does not see the processes and other resources running on the host. Docker containers or LXC containers are examples of OS-level virtualization.
- **Application virtualization**, where the application runs under a specialized software runtime. A popular example here is the support for Java applications, running on the **Java Virtual Machine** (**JVM**).

Many virtualization platforms support a number of virtualizations. QEMU can range from full emulation to paravirtualization, depending on its configuration.

When we work with virtualization layers, a number of terms come up frequently:

- The **host** is the (native) operating system or server on which the virtualization software is running
- The **guest** is the virtualized service (generally an operating system or container) that runs on the host
- The **hypervisor** is the specialized virtualization software that manages the hardware abstraction and resource-sharing capabilities of the virtualization platform
- An **image** is a file or set of files that represent the file system of a guest
- A **virtual machine** is the abstracted hardware or resource set in which the guest runs

Reviewing the risks of virtualization

Virtualization comes with a number of risks though. If we ask architects or other risk-conscious people about virtualization, they will talk about VM sprawl, challenges related to the secure or insecure APIs, the higher complexity of virtualized services, and what not.

Going over the challenges of virtualization itself is beyond the scope of this chapter, but there are a few risks that play directly into SELinux's field. If we can integrate SELinux with a virtualization layer, then we can mitigate these risks more easily.

The first risk is **data sensitivity** within a virtual machine. Whenever multiple virtual machines are hosted together, you could have the risk that one guest is able (be it through a flaw in the virtualization software or its networking capabilities or through side-channel attacks) to access sensitive data on another virtual machine.

With SELinux, data sensitivity can be controlled through the use of MLS. Guests can run with different MLS labels so that the data sensitivity is guaranteed even on the virtualization layer.

Another risk is the **security of offline guest images**. Here, either administrators or misconfigured virtual machines might gain access to another guest image. SELinux can prevent this through properly labeled guest images and ensuring that images of offline virtual machines are typed differently from online virtual machines.

Virtual machines can also **exhaust the resources** on a system. On Linux systems, resources can be controlled through the **control groups** (**cgroups**) subsystem. As this subsystem is governed through regular file APIs, SELinux can be used to further control access to this facility, ensuring that the control groups maintained by Docker, for instance, remain solely under the control of Docker.

Break-out attacks, where vulnerabilities within the hypervisor are exploited to try and reach the host operating system, can be mitigated through SELinux's type enforcement as even a hypervisor does not require full administrative access to everything on the host.

SELinux can also be used to **authorize access to the hypervisor**, ensuring that only the right teams (through the role-based access controls) are able to control the hypervisor and its definitions

Finally, SELinux also offers improved **guest isolation**, which goes beyond just the guest image accesses. Thanks to SELinux's MCS implementation, guests can be separated from each other in a mandatory approach. And with type enforcement, the allowed behavior of guests can be defined and controlled. This is a key capability used by hosting providers as they allow running (for them) untrusted guest virtual machines.

Using nondynamic security models

SELinux, however, is not a full security solution for virtualization providers. One main disadvantage of SELinux is that it is not dynamic. When we assign a type to a virtual machine, this type is rigid and set in stone. Virtual machines, however, will have different behavior characteristics depending on the software that is running on them.

A virtual machine running a web server has a different behavior than one running a database or an e-mail gateway. Although SELinux policy administrators would be capable of creating new domains for each virtual machine, this is not efficient. As a result, most SELinux policies will only offer a few domains usable by the virtual machine with broad characteristics.

On RHEL, these domains are part of its sVirt implementation.

Reusing existing virtualization domains

With sVirt, Red Hat offers a reusable approach for supporting virtualization and containerization through SELinux. It does so through a number of domains and types that can be used regardless of the underlying virtualization platform.

These domains and types are as follows:

- The `virtd_t` domain is used by the hypervisor software.
- The `svirt_t` domain is used by guests (virtual machines) that do not require general use of host resources.
- The `svirt_qemu_net_t`, `svirt_kvm_net_t`, and `svirt_lxc_net_t` domains are used by guests that require more interaction with the host (be it due to paravirtualization or due to a semi-virtualization approach such as containerization).
- The `svirt_tcg_t` domain is used by guests that require more flexible memory accesses (executing writable memory segments). This is used for guests whose emulation/virtualization requires the use of a **Tiny Code Generator** (**TCG**).
- The `svirt_image_t` type is assigned to the image file that contains a guest's data.
- The `virt_image_t` type is assigned to image files that are not in use at the moment.
- The `virt_content_t` type is assigned to image files when they are used in a read-only fashion.

To enable some flexibility in what the domains are allowed to do, additional SELinux booleans are put in effect. To query these booleans and their current value, use the `semanage boolean` command, like so:

```
# semanage boolean -l | grep virt_
virt_rw_qemu_ga_data           (off  ,  off)
  Allow qemu-ga to manage qemu-ga date.
virt_use_nfs                   (on   ,   on)
  Allow confined virtual guests to manage nfs files
virt_use_comm                  (off  ,  off)
  Allow confined virtual guests to use serial/parallel communication ports
virt_sandbox_use_fusefs        (off  ,  off)
  Allow virt to sandbox use fusefs
...
virt_use_samba                 (off  ,  off)
  Allow confined virtual guests to manage cifs files
```

For instance, to allow virtual machines to manage NFS files, we'd use this command:

```
# setsebool -P virt_use_nfs on
```

Using SELinux booleans to control the confinement of virtualization domains should be carefully handled. Booleans influence the SELinux policy on the host level and cannot be used to change the access controls of individual guests. As such, the previous example allowing virtual machines to manage NFS files is applicable to all virtual machines running on the host.

If security-sensitive operations have to be allowed for a guest, it is advisable to run those guests on an isolated host where these operations are allowed, while running the other guests on hosts where the policy does not allow this particular action.

Administrators can also use different SELinux domains for specific guests, fine-tuning the access controls for an individual virtual machine. How this is accomplished depends on the underlying technology, of course. Later in this chapter, we will introduce this for libvirt-based virtualization and Docker-based containerization.

Understanding MCS

The SELinux domains and the mentioned types, however, are not sufficient to implement proper confinement and isolation between guests. sVirt adds another layer of security by using **Multi-Category Security** (**MCS**).

Within SELinux, some domains are marked as an MCS-constrained type. When this is the case, the domain will not be able to access resources that do not have the same set of categories (or more) assigned as the current context.

The sVirt implementation ensures that the virtualization domains mentioned earlier are all marked as such MCS-constrained types. This can be confirmed by asking the system which types are associated with the `mcs_constrained_type` attribute:

```
# seinfo -amcs_constrained_type -x | grep virt_
  svirt_kvm_net_t
  svirt_lxc_net_t
  svirt_tcg_t
  svirt_t
  svirt_qemu_net_t
```

If SELinux policy writers want to create a custom domain for use with the virtualization software, they will either need to mark it as an MCS-constrained type as well (using the `mcs_constrained()` macro) or mark it as a virtualization domain (using the `virt_domain_template()` macro). Building custom policies is briefly touched upon in `Chapter 8`, *Working with SELinux Policies*. A more extensive policy development-oriented resource is Packt's *SELinux Cookbook* (`https://www.packtpub.com/networking-and-servers/selinux-cookbook`).

Through the MCS constraints, sVirt enables proper isolation between guests. Every running virtual machine (generally running as `svirt_t`) will be assigned two (random) SELinux categories. The images that that virtual machine needs to use are assigned the same two SELinux categories.

Whenever a virtual machine wants to access a wrong image, the difference in MCS categories will result in SELinux denying the access. Similarly, if one virtual machine is trying to connect to/attack another virtual machine, the MCS protections will once again prevent these actions from happening.

sVirt selects two categories to allow a large amount of guests to run even when there are only a few categories available. Assume for instance that the hypervisor is running with the `c10.c99` category range. That means that the hypervisor can only select 90 categories. If each guest only receives a single category, then the hypervisor can support 90 guests before allowing multiple guests to interact with each other (assuming a vulnerability is found that allows that, of course–the hypervisor software will generally disallow such accesses as well). With two categories, however, the number of supported simultaneously running guests becomes `4005` (the number of unique pairs in a set of `90`, obtained through the formula $n*(n-1)/2$).

libvirt SELinux support

The libvirt project offers a virtualization abstraction layer, through which administrators can manage virtual machines without direct knowledge of or expertise in the underlying virtualization platform. As such, administrators can use the libvirt-offered tools to manage virtual machines running on QEMU, QEMU/KVM, Xen, and so forth.

To use the sVirt approach, libvirt can be built with SELinux support. When this is the case and the guests are marked as being governed (security-wise) through SELinux, then the sVirt domains and types are used/enforced by libvirt. The libvirt code will also perform the category selection to enforce guest isolation and will ensure that the image files are assigned the right label (image files that are in use should get a different label than inactive image files).

Thanks to the sVirt implementation, Red Hat was able to obtain a **Common Criteria at Evaluation Assurance Level 4+** (**CC EAL 4+**) certification (a measure of security trustworthiness of a platform) for the virtualization based on RHEL and KVM. This is of course not solely due to the sVirt technology, but it has contributed to this certification.

Differentiating between shared and dedicated resources

The different labels for images allow different use cases. The image that is used to host the main operating system (of the guest) is generally labeled with `svirt_image_t` and is assigned the same pair of categories as the guest runtime itself (running as `svirt_t`). This image is writable by the guest.

When an image is selected that needs to be writable for multiple guests, then libvirt can opt not to assign any categories to the file. Without categories, MCS constraints don't apply (well, they still apply, but any set of categories dominates an empty set, and as such, actions against those properly labeled files are allowed).

Images that need to be mounted read-only for a guest (such as bootable media) are assigned the `virt_content_t` type. If they are dedicated, then categories can be assigned as well. For shared read access, no categories need to be assigned.

Note that these label differences apply mainly to virtualization technologies and not container technologies.

Assessing the libvirt architecture

The libvirt project has a number of clients that interact with the `libvirtd` daemon. This daemon is responsible for managing the local hypervisor software (be it QEMU/KVM, Xen, or any other virtualization software) and is even able to manage remote hypervisors. This latter functionality is often used for proprietary hypervisors that offer the necessary APIs to manage the virtual resources on the host.

This high-level architecture is displayed in the next diagram:

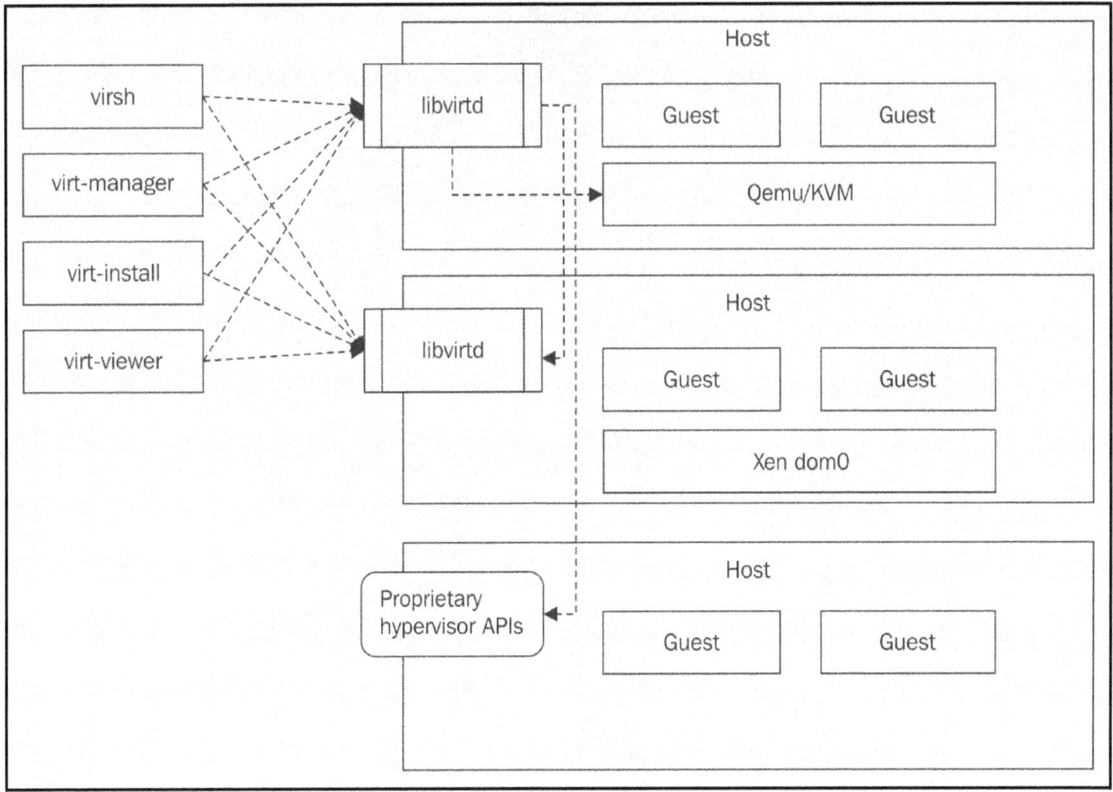

High-level architecture for the libvirt software

Due to the cross-platform and cross-hypervisor nature of the libvirt project, sVirt is a good match. Instead of hypervisor-specific domains, generic (yet confined) domains are used to ensure the security of the environment.

Configuring libvirt for sVirt

Most systems that support libvirt on SELinux systems (such as on RHEL) will have SELinux support automatically enabled. If this is not the case but SELinux support is possible, then all that it takes is to configure libvirt to allow the SELinux security model. For instance, for the QEMU-based virtualization driver, you'd do this:

```
# vim /etc/libvirt/qemu.conf
security_driver = "selinux"
```

When a guest is running on the platform, we can see proof of the use of sVirt through the assigned labels:

```
# ps -wwC qemu-kvm -o label,command
LABEL                                  COMMAND
system_u:system_r:svirt_t:s0:c23,c89  /usr/bin/qemu-kvm ...
system_u:system_r:svirt_t:s0:c48,c52  /usr/bin/qemu-kvm ...
```

To list the currently defined guests (called domains in libvirt), use this command:

```
# virsh list
Id   Name                    State
-------------------------------------
10   wastomcat1              running
12   wastomcat2              running
```

The current domain configuration can be queried using the `dumpxml` command with `virsh`:

```
# virsh dumpxml wastomcat1
<domain type='kvm' id='10'>
  <name>wastomcat1</name>
  ...
  <seclabel type='dynamic' model='selinux' relabel='yes'>
    <label>system_u:system_r:svirt_t:s0:c23,c89</label>
    <imagelabel>
      system_u:object_r:svirt_image_t:s0:c23,c89
    </imagelabel>
  </seclabel>
</domain>
```

The security label settings, part of the domain definition, tell libvirt how to apply security policies to this domain. In the previous example, the security model is based on SELinux (look at `model='selinux'`) and libvirt is allowed to dynamically allocate the labels and category sets (`type='dynamic'` and `relabel='yes'`).

Creating domains can be done using the `virt-install` command. As a result, an XML definition is created, which can be further edited. It is also possible to define a new domain through an XML file and then use that:

```
# virsh define SomeDomainDefinition.xml
```

To configure the domain definition with sVirt, use the `virsh edit` command:

```
# virsh edit wastomcat1
```

The next few subsections will show you how to update domains with specific SELinux-related tunings.

Using static labels

When managing domain definitions within libvirt, administrators can enforce the use of static labels. This will ensure that libvirt will not dynamically allocate labels and categories. Instead, the label defined by the administrator will be used.

In the case of static labels, the administrator can opt to enable or disable relabeling. If enabled, then libvirt will try to ensure that the resource (image file) label is applied/enforced on the images even though the domain label itself is fixed. If the administrator disables the relabeling, then libvirt will assume that the label on the resource (image file) is correct.

To set static labels, edit the domain and use the `type='static'` attribute in the `seclabel` entity:

```
# virsh edit wastomcat1
<domain>
  <name>wastomcat1</name>
  ...
  <seclabel type='static' model='selinux' relabel='no'>
    <label>system_u:system_r:svirt_t:c1,c2</label>
  </seclabel>
  ...
</domain>
```

Customizing labels

Administrators can choose to have different labels while retaining the dynamic nature of libvirt. For instance, administrators can request libvirt to use a particular domain but still govern the MCS categories, by selecting a base label:

```
# virsh edit wastomcat1
...
<seclabel type='dynamic' model='selinux'>
  <baselabel>system_u:system_r:custom_svirt_t:s0</baselabel>
</seclabel>
```

The dynamic model automatically implies relabeling on the resources.

Using different storage pool locations

When the storage location of the libvirt images differs from `/var/lib/libvirt/images/`, administrators will need to make sure that the new location is using the `virt_image_t` type. This is mandatory as the libvirt daemon can only relabel files with a virtualization label associated with it (except in RHEL, where `libvirtd` is running in a more unconfined domain and as such has more privileges).

For instance, if `/srv/virt/images` is used, we'd have this:

```
# semanage fcontext -a -t virt_var_lib_t "/srv/virt(/.*)?"
# semanage fcontext -a -t virt_image_t "/srv/virt/images(/.*)?"
# restorecon -R /srv/virt
```

If the storage pool is hosted on an NFS-mounted location, then enable the `virt_use_nfs` SELinux boolean:

```
# setsebool -P virt_use_nfs on
```

Interpreting output-only label information

When reading libvirt XML output, some security label information is added that cannot be altered. This is output-only information, specifically pertaining to the image (file) label.

Let's look at an example:

```
<seclabel type='dynamic' model='selinux' relabel='yes'>
  <label>system_u:system_r:svirt_t:s0:c192,c392</label>
  <imagelabel>
    system_u:object_r:svirt_image_t:s0:c192,c392
  </imagelabel>
</seclabel>
```

In this example, the security labeling is done dynamically. As a result, both the `<label>` and `<imagelabel>` fields are generated and are output-only. They show the administrator what the current labels are.

If an administrator edits a domain XML and includes the `<imagelabel>` information, it will be ignored (as this label is always output-only). The `<label>` field information might be interpreted depending on the type attribute defined in the `<seclabel>` entity.

Controlling available categories

When libvirt selects random categories, it does so based on its own category range. By default, MCS systems will have this range set to `c0.c1023`. To change the category range, the libvirt daemon (`libvirtd`) will need to be launched in the proper context.

On RHEL systems, this can be accomplished by updating the `systemd` unit file for `libvirtd` (by copying its original unit file from `/usr/lib/systemd/system` and placing it in `/etc/systemd/system`) and adding the `SELinuxContext=` attribute:

```
# vim /etc/systemd/system/libvirtd.service
...
[Service]
...
SELinuxContext=system_u:system_r:virtd_t:s0:c10.c99
```

On systems with a SysV-like init system, it is generally necessary to update the init script and include a `runcon` statement:

```
# vim /etc/rc.d/init.d/virtd
...
runcon -l s0:c10.c99 /usr/sbin/libvirtd --config \
  /etc/libvirt/libvirtd.conf --listen
```

Every time a new guest is launched, the libvirt code will randomly select two categories and check whether these categories are part of its own range as well as whether these two categories are already assigned to a guest. If they are, a new pair of categories is selected until a free pair is found.

Limiting supported hosts in a cluster

The libvirt project supports managing an environment spanning multiple hosts (cluster) and migrating guests from one host to another. When libvirt uses SELinux, one could imagine that each host must be running the same SELinux policy (or at least a policy that uses the same interpretation) as otherwise the security model definition used on the domain level cannot be guaranteed.

Although this approach is possible, it is not mandatory. With libvirt, administrators can tag the hosts that use the same SELinux policy and, while doing so, ensure that domains are only migrated between hosts with the same SELinux policy (or policy interpretation).

To accomplish this, libvirt uses the concept of a **domain of interpretation** (**DOI**). We have already seen a DOI, when talking about NetLabel/CIPSO. The DOI for libvirt has nothing to do with NetLabel/CIPSO, but serves a similar purpose. And just like the DOI with CIPSO, libvirt uses integers to differentiate systems with different policy implementations.

For instance, we could envision hosts where an MLS policy is enabled versus hosts where a default MCS policy is enabled. The hosts with an MLS policy could be assigned the DOI value `1` (one) whereas the others use a DOI value of `0` (zero).

The DOI setting can be configured by editing the proper virtualization configuration file (which depends on the virtualization technology being used) in `/etc/libvirt` and reviewed on the host using the `virsh capabilities` command:

```
# virsh capabilities
Connecting to uri: qemu:///system
<capabilities>
  <host>
    ...
    <secmodel>
      <model>selinux</model>
      <doi>0</doi>
    </secmodel>
  </host>
  ...
</capabilities>
```

Modifying default contexts

When libvirt decides on a domain label, it uses `svirt_t` or `svirt_tcg_t` as a default label. This is not hardcoded in libvirt but managed through a default context file. Two files, inside `/etc/selinux/targeted/contexts`, are used by libvirt to find default contexts:

- The `virtual_domain_context` file contains the default domain contexts for running guests (virtual machines)
- The `virtual_image_context` file contains the default types for images

Administrators can update these files to use different defaults but must keep in mind that these files are generally overwritten when a new policy package is deployed.

Therefore, it is advised to stick to the labeling options of libvirt itself.

Securing Docker containers

Until now, we've looked at libvirt and full virtualization. But a new type of virtualization has been gaining traction, called containerization–more specifically, Docker containers.

When working with containers, administrators have to be well aware that containers do not virtualize everything: the Linux kernel itself is shared, and all software running inside the container is interacting with the Linux kernel, just like software running outside the container. That does not mean that containers don't isolate, though. They are built based on Linux features such as namespaces and control groups.

Understanding container security

As the Linux kernel is shared, exploits on the kernel level impact the entire host and can compromise not only the container through which an exploit is executed, but also all other containers and software running on the host.

Generally, one could imagine using SELinux to prevent vulnerabilities to be exploited. Policies could be used to ensure that software running in the container cannot perform any action that is not acceptable behavior for that software.

However, as the Linux kernel is shared, containers have a different approach to SELinux support. While full virtualization allows the guest operating system to use SELinux as well, containers do not have this luxury. Right now, if in-container software checks whether SELinux is enabled, it receives a disabled status, even when this is not the case.

The reason behind this is that SELinux itself is not namespace-aware, while namespace isolation is the key part of containers on Linux. SELinux is part of the Linux kernel, and the policy is applicable to the entire host. As long as SELinux does not support policy layers (host-level policy and container-level policies) and namespace-aware access controls (ensuring that container-level policies cannot extend beyond the namespace scope), we will need to deal with SELinux on the host level only.

Controlling non-sVirt Docker SELinux integration

When the Docker installation is one that doesn't use sVirt technology, then most of the subsections following this one do not apply. But that does not mean that SELinux does not play a role. Containers will run through the `docker_t` or `container_runtime_t` type (which is an almost unconfined type), which has but a few handles that administrators can tune, using SELinux booleans.

There is no distinction between `docker_t` and `container_runtime_t`. The type name was changed to reflect the support of generic container runtimes (and not only Docker). In the remainder of this chapter, we stick to `docker_t`.

The important SELinux booleans that influence `docker_t` access controls are:

- The `docker_connect_any` boolean, which allows the `docker_t` type to connect to any TCP port (rather than just those specific to Docker management)
- The `selinuxuser_execheap` and `selinuxuser_execstack` booleans (on RHEL) or `allow_execheap` and `allow_execmem` booleans (on Gentoo), which generally (so more than just for the `docker_t` type) allow to execute writable memory segments

Of the security controls that are mentioned in the following subsections, the *using different SELinux contexts* subsection can be used even when the local Docker instance does not support sVirt. However, it requires Docker to be compiled with SELinux support and requires a SELinux policy that supports the necessary domain transitions.

Aligning Docker security with sVirt

Docker has a similar approach to virtualization as most other hypervisor-like solutions. It has a management component (the Docker daemon) and runs *guests* in which the container software runs. The guests here are processes that enable new namespaces–hiding the host-level view of files, processes, users, and so on–and run the container software as subprocesses.

By default, Docker does not have the sVirt technology (or the principles behind it) built in. This means that when running Docker on a SELinux-enabled host, the processes that act as the containers will run with the `docker_t` type, the type used for the Docker management daemon. And often, this works just like expected–but it does not isolate the guests much.

Red Hat is adapting Docker to support the sVirt principles. When running with Red Hat's Docker, new guests run within isolated domains (`svirt_lxc_net_t`) and receive a set of MCS categories to provide isolation between containers. We can expect Docker to further grow and embrace more SELinux access controls, and Red Hat's approach might become the standard in the near future.

For instance, an Nginx process running inside a Docker container is shown to be labeled with the `svirt_lxc_net_t` type and an MCS category pair:

```
~# ps -wwC nginx -o label,command
LABEL                                      COMMAND
system_u:system_r:svirt_lxc_net_t:s0:c232,c590 nginx: master ...
system_u:system_r:svirt_lxc_net_t:s0:c232,c590 nginx: worker ...
```

As Docker does not use the same concept of images as higher virtualization technologies (those supported through libvirt), the image-related types (such as `svirt_image_t` and `virt_content_t`) do not apply to the `svirt_lxc_net_t` type enforcement. Instead, host-level file types are used (such as `usr_t` for read-only access) with only the `svirt_sandbox_file_t` type being explicitly used for resources that can be fully managed by a container.

Unlike libvirt, Docker containers are not defined through XML files. Changing SELinux controls on containers is handled through the command line.

Limiting container capabilities

A strong feature of Docker is the ability to modify the capabilities of a container. Capabilities define coarse-grained authorizations on Linux and are used by Docker to limit what software running inside a container can do. For instance, shutting down the host (which is a kernel-level instruction) is not allowed by default from within a Docker container.

By default, Docker already limits the capabilities that are active for a container. Administrators can further fine-tune the capabilities, or even decide to only enable a given set of capabilities directly. By limiting container capabilities, kernel exploits can be further thwarted and container breakouts can be contained.

To remove capabilities, use the `--cap-drop` option of the `docker run` command (`nimmis/alpine-nginx` is the name of a publicly available microcontainer that hosts Nginx and is used here for example purposes):

```
~# docker run --cap-drop mknod --name nginx -d nimmis/alpine-nginx
```

We can use `pstree` (part of the `psmisc` package) to see the resulting processes that are started. With the `-S` option, it will even show which processes have switched namespaces (making it a bit more obvious which processes are the *containers*):

```
~# docker ps
CONTAINER ID   IMAGE          COMMAND      CREATED          ...
bb59d5e2ef4f   260f538c3be0   "/boot.sh"   46 minutes ago   ...
~# ps -ef | grep "boot.sh"
root    2955  2554  0 05:20 ?   00:00:00:00 /bin/sh /boot.sh
~# pstree -apS 2554
docker-current,2554,mnt daemon --exec-opt \
  native.cgroupdriver=systemd --selinux-enabled \
  --log-driver=journald
    |-boot.sh,2955,ipc,mnt,net,pid,uts /boot.sh
    |    `-runsvdir,3001 -P /etc/service...
    |        |-runsv,3003 crond
    |        |   `-crond,3006 -f
    |        |-runsv,3004 rsyslogd
    |        |   `-rsyslogd,3008 -n
    |        |       |-{rsyslogd},3010
    |        |       |-{rsyslogd},3011
    |        |       `-{rsyslogd},3012
    |        `-runsv,3005 nginx
    |            `-run,3007 ./run
    |                `-nginx,3009
    |                    `-nginx,3013
    |-{docker-current},2555
```

```
        |-{docker-current},2556
        |-{docker-current},2557
        |-{docker-current},2558
        |-{docker-current},2559
        |-{docker-current},2560
        |-{docker-current},2613
        |-{docker-current},2692
        |-{docker-current},2696
        |-{docker-current},2697
        `-{docker-current},2815
```

The capabilities of this running container can be checked through the status pseudo-file for the given PID (in the previous example, `2955`):

```
~# grep Cap /proc/2955/status
CapInh: 00000000a00425fb
CapPrm: 00000000a00425fb
CapEff: 00000000a00425fb
CapBnd: 00000000a00425fb
```

As this is a bitmap of the capabilities (`CapEff` showing the effectively active capabilities), it might be hard to deduce that the `mknod` capability is not active. We can use the `pscap` command (part of the `libcap-ng-utils` package on RHEL or `sys-libs/libcap-ng` on Gentoo) to show the current capabilities in a more human-readable format:

```
~# pscap | grep 2955
2554 2955 root boot.sh  chown, dac_override, fowner, fsetid,
  kill, setgid, setuid, setpcap, net_bind_service, net_raw,
  sys_chroot, audit_write, setfcap
```

Administrators can also drop all capabilities for a container and only add those that are needed:

```
~# docker run -d --cap-drop all --cap-add chown \
      --cap-add dac_override ...
```

Of course, we might want to adapt SELinux to accommodate the new capability list as well. After all, the default domain under which containers run (with sVirt support) will have a number of capabilities enabled as well.

There are a few SELinux booleans (only on RHEL) that influence the supported capabilities, but these booleans apply to all containers running on the same host. These are:

- `virt_sandbox_use_sys_admin`, which enables the `CAP_SYS_ADMIN` capability for the containers. This allows many system-administrative privileges, so it is wise to keep this off.
- `virt_sandbox_use_mknod`, which enables the `CAP_MKNOD` capability for the containers.
- `virt_sandbox_use_audit`, which enables the `CAP_AUDIT_WRITE` capability for the containers.
- `virt_sandbox_use_all_caps`, which enables all possible capabilities for the containers. This makes the sandbox run with full `root` privileges (SELinux-wise) and should only be used when the containers on the host are fully trusted.

A more fine-grained approach is to use separate SELinux domains for individual containers that require additional capabilities to be set. The next subsection describes how to set different SELinux contexts for Docker containers.

Using different SELinux contexts

Docker containers can be started with a different SELinux label through the `--security-opt` option. The security options that can be passed use the following syntax:

```
label:<key>:<value>
```

The following possible keys can be used:

- The `user` key sets the SELinux user for the container
- The `role` key sets the SELinux role for the container
- The `type` key sets the SELinux type (domain) for the container
- The `level` key sets the SELinux sensitivity level (MLS/MCS information) for the container
- The `disable` key (which takes no value) disables confinement for the container

For instance, to have a container run with the `custom_lxc_net_t` type rather than the default `svirt_lxc_net_t`, you'd use this command:

```
~# docker run --security-opt label:type:custom_lxc_net_t ...
```

Similarly, you'd use this when a container needs to run with a specific category set:

```
~# docker run --security-opt label:level:s0:c3.c5,c128 ...
```

The domains that Docker is allowed to transition to (SELinux-wise) is of course enforced through the policy. By default, `docker_t` can transition to guest domains that have the `svirt_sandbox_domain` attribute set:

```
~# seinfo -asvirt_sandbox_domain -x
  svirt_sandbox_domain
    svirt_kvm_net_t
    svirt_lxc_net_t
    openshift_initrc_t
    svirt_qemu_net_t
```

If custom domains are used, the SELinux policy administrator will need to ensure that the `docker_t` type can transition to the custom domain.

Relabeling volume mounts

Docker has a nice feature called **volume mounts**. When used, parts of the host file system are mounted into the container's file system view, allowing the container software to read or even write resources to a remote location. This is particularly useful for containers that need to persist data across container reboots, as containers by default do not persist their changes in their own environment: every time a container is started, it is pristine again.

Here's an example that mounts a host's `/srv/web/tomcat1` location into a container's `/srv/web` view:

```
~# docker run -v /srv/web/tomcat1:/srv/web -d --name wastomcat1 ...
```

With SELinux enabled though, volume mounts might not be readily accessible by the container. After all, the container is running within a confined domain (`svirt_lxc_net_t`), which might not have write access to the `/srv/web/tomcat1` location (which might be labeled as `httpd_sys_content_t`).

Administrators can relabel the resources manually, but luckily Docker has this covered.

When adding :z to the volume mount, Docker will relabel the content with the svirt_sandbox_file_t type, which is a type that sVirt containers have full manage rights on:

```
~# docker run -v /srv/web/tomcat1:/srv/web:z -d --name wastomcat1 ...
```

When adding :Z to the volume mount (notice the capitalized Z), Docker will not only relabel the content with the svirt_sandbox_file_t type, but will also assign the MCS category set of that particular container. As a result, the files will only be manageable by that particular container (and not be reusable by other containers):

```
~# docker run -v /srv/web/tomcat1:/srv/web:Z -d --name wastomcat1 ...
```

If you want to enable a location but with read-only access, administrators will need to relabel the files manually. Docker has no option (yet) for automatically relabeling content for read-only use.

Lowering SELinux controls for specific containers

Some Docker containers need to run with high privileges. Such containers are used to host management utilities (often to manage containers themselves) on hosts that are hardened and only contain the bare minimum for hosting Docker containers (such as CoreOS-based hosting).

When administrators run containers with SELinux confinement disabled (using the disable key with the security-opt option) Docker will run these containers in a much more privileged domain called spc_t. Think of the domain as being a **super-privileged container**, hence the spc_t name:

```
~# docker run --security-opt label:disable ...
```

This still has the container run confined from Docker's perspective, but no longer confined from the SELinux perspective. To even remove Docker's own confinement (such as the dropped capabilities), use the --privileged option:

```
~# docker run --privileged ...
```

Modifying default contexts

The sVirt technology supports modifying the default contexts. Docker does not hardcode the domain types and resource labels but obtains these values from a SELinux-provided configuration file, `lxc_contexts`, which is stored inside `/etc/selinux/targeted/contexts`.

The following snippet shows the default contents of this file and defines the labels used for various purposes:

```
process = "system_u:system_r:svirt_lxc_net_t:s0"
content = "system_u:object_r:virt_var_lib_t:s0"
file = "system_u:object_r:svirt_sandbox_file_t:s0"
sandbox_kvm_process = "system_u:system_r:svirt_qemu_net_t:s0"
sandbox_lxc_process = "system_u:system_r:svirt_lxc_net_t:s0"
```

Administrators can modify these defaults, but they must be aware that these files are part of the SELinux policy packages and might be overwritten when an updated policy is deployed.

Therefore, it is advised to stick to the labeling features of Docker itself.

Summary

In this chapter, we looked at virtualization and the risks associated with it. We discussed how some of these risks can be mitigated through the same set of controls that SELinux offers, such as type enforcement (limiting what guests can do) and MCS confinement (isolating guests from each other).

Next, we covered how libvirt supports several virtualization technologies on Linux platforms and how it includes a technology called sVirt that enables SELinux integration, offering guest isolation and access controls. We saw how administrators can manipulate the sVirt logic within libvirt, such as using different domain labels or category sets.

Finally, we looked at Docker, a popular container technology, and how here too sVirt can provide container confinement both from an access control approach (limiting exploits and break-outs) as well as isolation (protecting one container from the actions of another). Here too, we looked at how the various SELinux controls can be fine-tuned by administrators, ranging from defining the domain label of a container up to volume-mounted SELinux labeling.

In the next chapter, we'll look at another pair of SELinux-aware technologies: D-Bus and systemd.

7
D-Bus and systemd

System-controlling services such as D-Bus and systemd are core components of a Linux system, now more than ever. Where D-Bus offers system- and session-wide cross-service communication and process life cycle management, systemd is a core daemon offering multiple features. Both services use SELinux to further harden their operations, and allow administrators to fine-tune the access controls applicable.

In this chapter, we will learn about:

- SELinux's policy implementation for D-Bus and systemd
- Tuning service access controls on D-Bus
- Handling access permissions for services

We will end the chapter with an explanation of how D-Bus can use SELinux as its policy source for tightening the authorizations on its services.

The system daemon (systemd)

Systemd is a core component of many Linux distributions. Since its birth in 2010, systemd has gradually been adopted as the core init system, responsible for handling services and boot-up operations.

Throughout its development phase, several other components have been added to the systemd portfolio:

- D-Bus has been merged with systemd and offers a system and session bus service, allowing the use of D-Bus for inter-application communication
- Udev has been merged with systemd as well, offering a flexible device-node management application
- Login capabilities have been added to systemd, enabling fine-grained control over user sessions
- The `journald` daemon has been added to provide a new approach to system and service logging, replacing some of the functionality of standard system loggers
- The `timerd` daemon provides support for the time-based execution of tasks, replacing some of the functionality of standard cron daemons
- Network configurations can be managed by `systemd-networkd`

This ongoing approach of absorbing several system services into a single application suite has not gone unnoticed and isn't without controversy. Some distributions even refuse to have systemd as the default init system.

Gentoo Linux gives users the choice of which init system they want: OpenRC or systemd. With RHEL (from version 7 onward), systemd is the only available option.

The systemd project has included SELinux support for most of its services. The specific details of this SELinux support is detailed next.

Service support in systemd

The main capability of the system daemon that most people know is its support for system services. Unlike the traditional SysV-compatible init systems, systemd does not use scripts to manage services. Instead, it uses a declarative approach for the various services, documenting the wanted state and configuration parameters while using its own logic to ensure that the right set of services is started in due time.

Understanding unit files

Systemd uses unit files to declare how a service should behave. These unit files use the INI-style syntax, supporting sections and key/value pairs within each file. A service can have multiple unit files that influence the service at large. It is important to remember that different unit files for the same service are all related:

- The `*.service` unit files define how a system service should be launched, what its dependencies are, how systemd should treat sudden failures, and so on.
- The `*.socket` unit files define which socket(s) should be created and which permissions should be assigned to it. This is used for services that can be launched on request rather than directly at boot.
- The `*.timer` unit files define what time or frequency the service should be launched at. This is used for services that do not necessarily run daemonized but need to execute a certain logic at defined intervals.

Other unit files exist as well, although those have more in common with generic system configurations (such as slice definitions, paths, and automount settings) and less with particular services.

When an application is installed on a system, it places its default unit files inside `/usr/lib/systemd/system`, from where they are picked up by systemd. At runtime, updates can be placed inside `/run/systemd/system`, which will override the unit files in the default location. System administrators can override the configurations by placing unit files in `/etc/systemd/system`. These unit files override settings in `/run/systemd/system` and `/usr/lib/systemd/system`.

As an example, check out the default `dnsmasq` service unit file:

```
# cat /usr/lib/systemd/system/dnsmasq.service
[Unit]
Description=DNS caching server
After=network.target

[Service]
ExecStart=/usr/sbin/dnsmasq -k

[Install]
WantedBy=multi-user.target
```

This unit file declares the command to use to launch `dnsmasq` and informs systemd that the service should be launched after the `network` target has been reached (which is a kind of milestone in the boot process, allowing proper dependency handling) and is needed for the `multi-user` target (which is the equivalent of the default run level when using SysV-style init services).

Setting the SELinux context for a service

When systemd launches a service, it executes the command defined through the `ExecStart=` configuration entry in the service unit file. By default, a standard domain transition will occur as defined through the SELinux policy.

When a SysV-style init script is used, the service is launched from within the `initrc_t` context. With systemd, the context is the one from the daemon itself, generally `init_t`. Not all Linux distributions have a SELinux policy that is already modified to suit the systemd service approach and might be missing domain transitions from `init_t` to the various service daemons.

Package developers and system administrators can, however, update the service unit files to have the service launched in an explicitly mentioned domain. To accomplish this, the `[Service]` section of the unit file can be extended with the `SELinuxContext=` configuration entry.

For instance, to ensure that `dnsmasq` is launched with the `dnsmasq_t:s0:c0.c128` context, you'd use this:

```
[Unit]
Description=DNS caching server
After=network.target

[Service]
ExecStart=/usr/sbin/dnsmasq -k
SELinuxContext=system_u:system_r:dnsmasq_t:s0:c0.c128

[Install]
WantedBy=multi-user.target
```

Of course, it is also possible to use this to have a service running with a completely different context, which can be useful when developing custom policies for daemons.

Using transient services

Systemd can also be used to launch applications as if they are services and have them under systemd's control. Such applications are then called **transient services**, as they lack the unit files that generally declare how systemd should behave.

Transient services are launched through the `systemd-run` application:

```
# systemd-run bittorrent-sync
Running as unit run-2603.service
```

As transient services do not have unit files to manage, changing the SELinux context has to be accomplished through the command line as well. Of course, this is only needed if the standard domain transitions defined in the policy do not result in the wanted behavior.

The `systemd-run` application supports this (starting with systemd version v230) through the `--property` or `-p` option:

```
# systemd-run \
    -p SELinuxContext=system_u:system_r:bittorrent_sync_t:s0 \
    bittorrent-sync
Running as unit run-6523.service
```

Requiring SELinux for a service

Some services should only run when SELinux is enabled or disabled. With systemd, this can be defined through its conditional parameters.

A service unit file can contain a number of conditions that need to be valid before systemd will consider the service. These conditionals can point to the system type (virtualized or not), kernel command-line parameters, files that do or don't exist, and so on. The one we are interested in is `ConditionSecurity`, which is `true` if the given security system is enabled.

For instance, look at the `rhel-autorelabel.service` unit file:

```
# cat /usr/lib/systemd/system/rhel-autorelabel.service
[Unit]
Description=Relabel all filesystems, if necessary
DefaultDependencies=no
Requires=local-fs.target
```

```
Conflicts=shutdown.target
After=local-fs.target
Before=sysinit.target shutdown.target
ConditionSecurity=selinux
ConditionKernelCommandLine=|autorelabel
ConditionPathExists=|/.autorelabel

[Service]
ExecStart=/lib/systemd/rhel-autorelabel
Type=oneshot
TimeoutSec=0
RemainAfterExit=yes
StandardInput=tty
```

This unit file declares three conditionals:

- The `ConditionSecurity=selinux` condition ensures that the service is only launched if SELinux is active
- The `ConditionKernelCommandLine=|autorelabel` condition informs systemd that the kernel command line should be checked, and if it contains `autorelabel`, this service should be triggered (the `|` prefix makes this conditional a trigger)
- The `ConditionPathExists=|/.autorelabel` condition informs systemd that the `/.autorelabel` file should be searched, and if it exists, this service should be triggered

Similarly, the `rhel-autorelabel-mark.service` file is provided by RHEL. This service ensures that if the system is booted without SELinux being active and no `/.autorelabel` file exists yet, then this file needs to be created to ensure that when the system is rebooted with SELinux support, the relabeling operation occurs.

We can see this check by looking at the `rhel-autorelabel-mark.service` file:

```
# cat /usr/lib/systemd/rhel-autorelabel-mark.service
[Unit]
Description=Mark the need to relabel after reboot
DefaultDependencies=no
Requires=local-fs.target
Conflicts=shutdown.target
After=local-fs.target
Before=sysinit.target shutdown.target
ConditionSecurity=!selinux
ConditionPathIsDirectory=/etc/selinux
ConditionPathExists=!/.autorelabel
```

```
[Service]
ExecStart=-/bin/touch /.autorelabel
Type=oneshot
RemainAfterExit=yes
```

Relabeling files during service startup

Due to its more declarative approach to service management, a number of services are harder to control through systemd than they were when using SysV-style service scripts. This is of course due to the open and flexible use of scripts to perform any service-specific preparation, which is harder to accomplish with systemd.

One of the actions that many services require is the preparation of service-specific runtime directories, such as `/run/httpd` for the Apache service. Systemd has resolved this by supporting what it calls `tmpfiles.d`. These are files and locations that are requested to be provided or updated immediately (at boot time) but are not placed in the (persisted) file system.

For instance, the package that provides the Apache daemon installs the following definition by default on the system:

```
# cat /usr/lib/tmpfiles.d/httpd.conf
d /run/httpd   710 root apache
d /run/httpd/htcacheclean  700 apache apache
```

Similar to the systemd unit files, the files that contain these settings should be declared in one of the following three locations. Each of these locations overrides the settings of the previous one.

- The default, package-provided location is `/usr/lib/tmpfiles.d`
- Runtime declarations can be placed in `/run/tmpfiles.d`
- Local sysadmin-provided declarations are placed in `/etc/tmpfiles.d`

The definitions can go much further than just directory creation. Through the `tmpfiles.d` application, definitions can be set to create files, empty directories up front, create sub-volumes, manage special files such as symbolic links or block devices, set extended attributes, and more.

One of its features is to set the file mode and ownership and restore the SELinux context on a file (`z`) or recursively against a location (`Z`). This can be used to change contexts on files that have a proper context definition in the policy but whose context is not properly assigned.

For instance, Red Hat has the following definition active:

```
# cat /usr/lib/tmpfiles.d/selinux-policy.conf
z /sys/devices/system/cpu/online - - -
Z /sys/class/net - - -
z /sys/kernel/uevent_helper - - -
w /sys/fs/selinux/checkreqprot - - - - 0
```

The relabeling inside `/sys` is needed because this location will, by default, be labeled with `sysfs_t`, whereas some of its files are requested to have a different label. The `/sys/devices/system/cpu/online` file for instance needs to be labeled with `cpu_online_t`:

```
# matchpathcon /sys/devices/system/cpu/online
/sys/devices/system/cpu/one  system_u:object_r:cpu_online_t:s0
```

The definition ensures that this (pseudo-)file is relabeled at boot so that all other processes that rely on the file being labeled with `cpu_online_t` can happily continue working.

The other arguments to the definition are explicitly marked with a dash (-) in the previous example, meaning that there are no other parameters to be set. They can be used to set the mode, UID, GID, age, and argument related to the rule.

An example configuration that uses some of these other parameters with the `z` or `Z` state is the `systemd.conf` file:

```
# grep ^[zZ] /usr/lib/tmpfiles.d/systemd.conf
z /run/log/journal 2755 root systemd-journal - -
Z /run/log/journal/%m ~2750 root systemd-journal - -
z /var/log/journal 2755 root systemd-journal - -
z /var/log/journal/%m 2755 root systemd-journal - -
```

For more information about the definition format, see `man tmpfiles.d`.

Using socket-based activation

The system daemon also supports socket-based activation. When configured, systemd will create the socket on which the daemon usually listens and will have the daemon launched when the socket is used. This allows systems to be booted quickly (as many daemons do not need to be launched immediately).

When a client only places information in the socket (such as with the /dev/log socket), the client does not even need to wait for the daemon to be activated. The data is stored in a buffer until the daemon can read it–only when the buffer is full will the operation block until the daemon has flushed the buffer.

Take a look at the systemd-journald socket unit file:

```
# cat /usr/lib/systemd/system/systemd-journald.socket
[Unit]
Description=Journal Socket
DefaultDependencies=no
Before=sockets.target
IgnoreOnIsolate=yes

[Socket]
ListenStream=/run/systemd/journal/stdout
ListenDatagram=/run/systemd/journal/socket
ListenDatagram=/dev/log
SocketMode=0666
PassCredentials=yes
PassSecurity=yes
ReceiveBuffer=8M
```

If one of the mentioned sockets (/run/systemd/journal/stdout, /run/systemd/journal/socket, or /dev/log) is used, then the systemd-journald.service unit file is used to launch the service.

Inside the [Socket] section, a SELinux-specific entry can be defined: SELinuxContextFromNet=true. When this entry is set, the MLS/MCS information is obtained from the client context (the application connecting to the socket) and appended to the context of the service.

Governing unit operations access

Until now, we've looked at configuration settings related to systemd's SELinux support. But systemd also uses SELinux to control access to services defined through the unit files. When a user wants to perform a particular operation against a unit (such as starting a service or checking the state of a running service), systemd queries the SELinux policy to see whether this operation is allowed.

The system daemon uses the service class to validate whether an operation is allowed or not. For instance, to validate whether a user context `user_t` is allowed to view the status of the service associated with the `sshd.service` unit file, it checks the context of this file (such as `sshd_unit_file_t`) and then validates if the status permission is granted:

```
# sesearch -s user_t -t sshd_unit_file_t -c service -p status -A
```

In this case, no output is shown, so the user does not have the permissions to query this information. Other supported permissions are `disable`, `enable`, `kill`, `load`, `reload`, `start`, and `stop`.

Whenever the SELinux policy denies the operation, it will be shown as follows:

```
# systemctl status sshd
Failed to issue method call: SELinux policy denies access.
```

In the audit logs, this will be available through a `USER_AVC` denial message:

```
type=USER_AVC msg=audit(1348750450.105:135): pid=1 uid=0
  auid=4294967295 ses=4294967295 subj=system_u:system_r:init_t:s0
  msg='avc:  denied  { status } for auid=3267 uid=0 gid=0
    path="/usr/lib/systemd/system/sshd.service"
    cmdline="/bin/systemctl status sshd.service"
    scontext=user_u:user_r:user_t:s0-s0:c0.c1023
    tcontext=system_u:object_r:sshd_unit_file_t:s0
    tclass=service exe="/usr/lib/systemd/systemd" sauid=0
    hostname=? addr=? terminal=?'
```

What is important to know here is that the SELinux policy contains the access rules related to these service operations but is not responsible for enforcing the rules. It is systemd that acts based on the policy content (unlike file system operations, which are governed by the Linux kernel and are as such enforced through the kernel as well).

Logging with systemd

As mentioned before, systemd is not only responsible for service management: it takes up several other tasks as well. One of these tasks is log management, which is traditionally implemented through a system logger.

While systemd still supports running with a traditional system logger, it now suggests the use of `systemd-journald`. One of the advantages of the journal daemon is that it is not limited to textual, single-line log messages. Daemons can now use binaries as well as multiline messages as part of its logging capabilities.

The journal daemon also registers information about the sending process alongside the log messages itself. This additional information contains ownership data (process owner) including the SELinux context of the sending process.

Retrieving SELinux-related information

The traditional approach to receive SELinux-related information (excluding the audit events we tackled before) is to `grep` through the log information. With the journal daemon, this is accomplished like so:

```
# journalctl -b | grep -i selinux
```

The `-b` option passed on to the journal control application informs the journal daemon that we are only interested in the log messages that originated for a specific boot.

Querying logs given a SELinux context

A unique feature of the journal daemon is to use the information associated with the log messages as part of the query to be launched against the journal database. For instance, we can ask the journal daemon to only show those messages that originated from a daemon or application running in the `udev_t` context:

```
# journalctl _SELINUX_CONTEXT=system_u:system_r:udev_t:s0-s0:c0.c1023
-- Logs begin at Sat 2016-09-24 05:04:58 EDT,
   end at Sat 2016-09-24 10:35:04 EDT. --
Sep 24 05:04:59 selinuxtest systemd-udevd[429]: starting version 219
Sep 24 05:04:59 selinuxtest systemd-udevd[429]: Network interface
  NamePolicy= disabled on kernel command line, ignoring.
Sep 24 07:00:37 selinuxtest systemd-udevd[4507]: starting version 219
Sep 24 07:00:37 selinuxtest systemd-udevd[4507]: Network interface
  NamePolicy= disabled on kernel command line, ignoring.
```

```
Sep 24 07:00:38 selinuxtest systemd-udevd[4507]: Network interface
  NamePolicy= disabled on kernel command line, ignoring.
```

Using setroubleshoot integration with journal

On RHEL systems, the SELinux troubleshooting daemon is also integrated with `systemd-journald`. Any alert that comes up from `setroubleshootd` is also available through the journal daemon.

This helps administrators as they will quickly find out about SELinux denials when investigating problems. For instance, when the Apache web server is not working properly, a quick investigation of the status of the service will reveal that the SELinux policy is preventing some actions:

```
# systemctl status httpd
* httpd.service - The Apache HTTP Server
   Loaded: loaded (/usr/lib/systemd/system/httpd.service; disabled;
           vendor preset: disabled)
   Active: active (running) since Sat 2016-09-24 13:47:23 EDT;
           8min ago
     Docs: man:httpd(8)
           man:apachectl(8)
 Main PID: 3183 (httpd)
   Status: "Total requests: 9; Current requests/sec: 0;
            Current traffic:   0 B/sec"
   CGroup: /system.slice/httpd.service
           ├─3183 /usr/sbin/httpd -DFOREGROUND
           ├─3184 /usr/sbin/httpd -DFOREGROUND
           ├─3185 /usr/sbin/httpd -DFOREGROUND
           ├─3186 /usr/sbin/httpd -DFOREGROUND
           ├─3187 /usr/sbin/httpd -DFOREGROUND
           ├─3188 /usr/sbin/httpd -DFOREGROUND
           └─3336 /usr/sbin/httpd -DFOREGROUND

Sep 24 13:47:23 selinuxtest systemd[1]: Starting The Apache HTTP Server...
Sep 24 13:47:23 selinuxtest systemd[1]: Started The Apache HTTP Server.
Sep 24 13:48:12 selinuxtest python[10112]: SELinux is preventing
  /usr/sbin/httpd from read access on the file
  /srv/web/localhost/htdocs/dokuwiki/doku.php
```

To get more information about the message, use `journalctl`:

```
# journalctl -r -o verbose -u httpd.service
-- Logs begin at Sat 2016-09-24 12:04:39 EDT, end at
   Sat 2016-09-24 13:59:34 EDT. --
Sat 2016-09-24 13:48:12.382005 EDT
[s=0e131d2da8174be59dc9dd50b5aa7aa9;i=772;b=e0177f4aefb046ab807e22725b85086
d;m=16f715bc2;t=53d447cbcf970;x=72b681410ee05ceb]
    PRIORITY=6
    _UID=0
    _GID=0
    _BOOT_ID=e0177f4aefb046ab807e22725b85086d
    _MACHINE_ID=02f1ddb1415c4feba9880b2b8c4c5925
    _HOSTNAME=selinuxtest
    SYSLOG_FACILITY=3
    SYSLOG_IDENTIFIER=systemd
    _TRANSPORT=journal
    _PID=1
    _COMM=setroubleshootd
    _EXE=/usr/bin/python27
    _CMDLINE=/usr/bin/python27 -Es /usr/sbin/setroubleshootd -f
    _CAP_EFFECTIVE=1ffffffff
    _SYSTEMD_CGROUP=/
    _SELINUX_CONTEXT=system_u:system_r:setroubleshootd_t:s0-s0:c0.c1023
    MESSAGE_ID=39f53479d3a045ac8e11786248231fbf
    RESULT=done
    UNIT=httpd.service
    MESSAGE= SELinux is preventing /usr/sbin/httpd from read access on the
file /srv/web/localhost/htdocs/dokuwiki/doku.php

***** Plugin restorecon (92.2 confidence) suggests
****************

If you want to fix the label.
/srv/web/localhost/htdocs/dokuwiki/doku.php default label should be
httpd_sys_content_t.
Then you can run restoreon.
Do
# /sbin/restorecon -v /srv/web/localhost/htdocs/dokuwiki/doku.php

***** Plugin catchall_boolean (7.83 confidence) suggests
****************
...
```

Using systemd containers

Another feature that systemd supports is `systemd-nspawn`. This service provides container capabilities in systemd and allows systemd to manage these containers. It uses the same primitives as the LXC project and Docker. SELinux-wise, the software that is running inside the container will not have a correct view on the SELinux state (as is the case with Docker).

However, unlike Docker and libvirt, the `systemd-nspawn` approach does not support the sVirt technology that we covered in the previous chapter. In other words, it will not dynamically reset the SELinux contexts of the used files, nor will it search for a free category pair to associate with the files and the processes.

Initializing a systemd container

To create a systemd container, first create a root file system in which the software that the container should run is deployed. It is advised to use the `/var/lib/machines` location, with a subdirectory per container, as this location will be the default location for further automation within `systemd-nspawn`.

For instance, an `nginx` container would have its `root` file system at `/var/lib/machines/nginx`.

The `root` file system of the container must look like an operating system tree, as otherwise systemd will refuse to start it. Use tools such as `debootstrap` or `dnf` to build a minimal operating system environment inside this location.

Next, to start the container, use the `systemd-nspawn` command like so:

```
# systemd-nspawn -D /var/lib/machines/nginx
```

If the container hosts a relatively complete distribution, use the `-b` option:

```
# systemd-nspawn -bD /var/lib/machines/nginx
```

Support for systemd-managed containers is still nascent at the time of writing this. In the near future, the `machinectl` command will be used to manage containers.

Using a specific SELinux context

Like with Docker, systemd-nspawn also allows administrators to pass on the SELinux context in which the processes of the container should run as well as the context that should be used for the files of the container.

To accomplish this, systemd-nspawn supports the following two options:

- The --selinux-context= option allows the administrator to define the SELinux context for the runtime processes of the container
- The --selinux-apifs-context= option allows the administrator to define the SELinux context for the files and file system of the container

Here's an example that runs a container with the svirt_lxc_net_t type, the svirt_image_t type for the files, and the c32,c42 categories:

```
# systemd-nspawn \
  --selinux-context=system_u:system_r:svirt_lxc_net_t:s0:c32,c42 \
  --selinux-apifs-context=system_u:object_r:svirt_image_t:s0:c32,c42
  -D /var/lib/machines/nginx
```

Handling device files

Linux has had a long history of device managers. Initially, administrators needed to make sure that the device nodes were already present on the file system (/dev was part of the persisted file system). Gradually, more dynamic approaches were used for device management.

Nowadays, device files are managed through a combination of a pseudo file system (devtmpfs) and a user space device manager called **udev**. This device manager has been merged in systemd as well, becoming systemd-udevd.

There are projects, such as **eudev**, which provide udev functionality without requiring systemd to be installed and enabled on the system.

The device manager listens on a kernel socket for kernel events. These events inform the device manager about detected or plugged-in devices (or the removal of such devices) and allow the device manager to take appropriate action. For udev, these actions are defined in udev rules.

Using udev rules

The main configuration of udev is handled through udev rules. These rules are one-liners that contain a matching part and an action part.

The matching part is made up of validations that are executed against the event(s) that udev receives from the Linux kernel. This is based on key/value pairs that are obtained from the event and include the kernel-provided device name (`KERNEL`), device subsystem (`SUBSYSTEM`), kernel driver (`DRIVER`), specific attributes (`ATTR`), and environment variables that are active (`ENV`).

The Linux kernel will also inform the device manager about the device hierarchy. This allows rules to be defined based on, for instance, the USB controller through which a USB device is plugged in. Hierarchically related information is provided through key/value pairs whose key is defined in *plural* form: `SUBSYSTEMS` instead of `SUBSYSTEM`, `DRIVERS` instead of `DRIVER`, and so on.

For instance, to match a particular USB webcam, the match-related pairs could look like so:

```
KERNEL=="video[0-9]*", SUBSYSTEM=="video4linux", \
SUBSYSTEMS="usb", ATTR{idVendor}=="05a9", ATTR{idProduct}=="4519"
```

The second part of a udev rule is the action to take. The most common action is to create a symbolic link to the created device file, ensuring that applications can always reach the same device through the same symbolic link, even when the device from the kernel point of view is named differently. The preceding example could for instance become this:

```
KERNEL=="video[0-9]*", SUBSYSTEM=="video4linux", \
SUBSYSTEMS="usb", ATTR{idVendor}=="05a9", \
ATTR{idProduct}=="4519",  SYMLINK+="webcam1"
```

The udev application supports many more actions than just defining symbolic links, of course. It can associate ownership (OWNER) or group membership (GROUP) on the device, controlling who can access the devices. Udev can also set environment variables (ENV) and be configured to run a command (RUN). It is probably sensible to only run a command when the device is added, in which case a match such as ACTION=="add" should be added.

ENV can be seen as both a matching key as well as an action key. The difference is with the operation (single = sign or double) that is performed. ENV{envvar}=="value" is a match (is the envvar environment variable set to "value"?) whereas ENV{envvar}="value" is an action (the envvar environment variable is set to "value").

Udev rules are by default provided through the /usr/lib/udev/rules.d location. This is where distributions and applications/drivers will store their default rules. Additional rules or rule overrides can be placed in /etc/udev/rules.d.

Important to remember is that udev will continue processing rules even when a matching rule is found and executed. This can be changed on a per-rule basis through the OPTIONS action, like with OPTIONS+="last_rule", which informs udev that it can stop processing further rules for this event.

Setting a SELinux label on a device node

One of the actions that udev supports is to assign a particular SELinux context on the device node. This is done through the SECLABEL{selinux} action:

```
KERNEL=="fd0", ..., \
SECLABEL{selinux}="system_u:object_r:my_device_t"
```

Note that this action is only applicable to the device node that is created. If the rule also sets a symbolic link, then the symbolic link itself is left untouched (and will inherit the default device_t context).

D-Bus communication

The D-Bus daemon provides an inter-process communication channel between applications. Unlike the traditional IPC methods, D-Bus is a higher-level communication channel that offers more than simple signaling or memory sharing. Applications that want to chat over the D-Bus link with one of the many D-Bus compatible libraries, such as libdbus, sd-bus (part of systemd), GDBus, and QtDBus.

The D-Bus daemon is part of the systemd application suite.

Understanding D-Bus

Linux generally supports two D-Bus types: system-wide and session-specific D-Bus instances:

- The system-wide D-Bus is the main instance used for system communication. Many services or daemons will associate themselves with the system D-Bus to allow others to communicate with them through D-Bus.
- The session-specific D-Bus is an instance running for a particular, logged-in user. It is commonly used by graphical applications to communicate with each other within a user session.

Both D-Bus instances are provided through the `dbus-daemon` application. However, the system-wide D-Bus will run with the `--system` option whereas a session-specific instance will run with the `--session` option.

Applications register themselves against the D-Bus through a particular namespace. Conventionally, this namespace is based on the domain name of the project. For instance, systemd uses the `org.freedesktop.systemd1` namespace whereas D-Bus is at `org.freedesktop.DBus`.

The currently associated applications can be queried using D-Bus clients, such as `qdbus` (provided through the `qt` package):

```
# qdbus --system
:1.1
 org.freedesktop.login1
:1.186
:1.2
 org.fedoraproject.FirewallD1
:1.3
 com.redhat.ifcfgrh1
```

```
 org.freedesktop.NetworkManager
:1.4
:1.5
 fi.epitest.hostap.WPASupplicant
 fi.w1.wpa_supplicant1
:1.6
 org.freedesktop.PolicyKit1
:1.65
 org.freedesktop.systemd1
:1.66
 com.redhat.tuned
org.freedesktop.DBus
```

Each application then provides objects on the bus that can be reached by other objects (other applications)—of course, assuming they have the privileges to do so. These objects are represented through a path-like syntax and generally also use the domain of the project as a prefix.

For instance, to list the objects currently associated with `org.freedesktop.systemd1`, you'd use this command:

```
# qdbus --system org.freedesktop.systemd1
/
/org/freedesktop/systemd1/unit/firewalld_2eservice
/org/freedesktop/systemd1/unit/machines_2etarget
/org/freedesktop/systemd1/unit/sys_2ddevices_2dpnp0_2d00_3a05_2dtty_2dttyS0
_2edevice
/org/freedesktop/systemd1/unit/getty_2etarget
/org/freedesktop/systemd1/unit/lvm2_2dlvmpolld_2eservice
...
```

Applications can then trigger methods on these objects or through these methods send messages to the applications that are bound to these objects.

For instance, to read all properties exposed by the hostname service, we call the `org.freedesktop.DBus.Properties.GetAll` method of the object bound at `/org/freedesktop/hostname1` provided by `org.freedesktop.hostname1`. We pass on the `org.freedesktop.hostname1` string to this method:

```
# dbus-send --system --print-reply --type=method_call \
  --dest=org.freedesktop.hostname1 \
  /org/freedesktop/hostname1 \
  org.freedesktop.DBus.Properties.GetAll \
  string:"org.freedesktop.hostname1"
method return sender=:1.192 -> dest=:1.193 reply_serial=2
  array [
    dict entry(
```

```
        string "Hostname"
        variant   string "selinuxtest"
      )
  ...
      dict entry(
        string "KernelName"
        variant   string "Linux"
      )
      dict entry(
        string "KernelRelease"
        variant   string "3.10.0-327.13.1.el7.x86_64"
      )
      dict entry(
        string "KernelVersion"
        variant   string "#1 SMP Thu Mar 31 11:10:31 CDT 2016"
      )
      dict entry(
        string "OperatingSystemPrettyName"
        variant   string "Red Hat Enterprise Linux Server 7.2 (Maipo)"
      )
      dict entry(
        string "OperatingSystemCPEName"
        variant   string \
                  "cpe:/o:redhat:enterprise_linux:7.2:GA:server"
        )
   ]
```

Controlling service acquisition with SELinux

The D-Bus application, like systemd, will query the SELinux policy to identify whether a particular operation is allowed. Again, it is the D-Bus application itself that enforces the policy and not a Linux kernel subsystem.

The first control that administrators can enable within D-Bus is to ensure that only well-established domains can acquire a particular object within D-Bus. Without this control, malicious code could register itself as being `org.freedesktop.login1`, for instance, and act as a system daemon on the bus. Other applications might mistakenly send out sensitive information to the application.

Applications store this *policy* information in files hosted in `/etc/dbus-1/system.d/`. The login service for instance has the following policy snippet installed:

```
# cat /etc/dbus-1/system.d/org.freedesktop.login1.conf
<?xml version="1.0"?>
<!DOCTYPE busconfig PUBLIC
  "-//freedesktop//DTD D-BUS Bus Configurqtion 1.0//EN"
  "http://www.freedesktop.org/standards/dbus/1.0/busconfig.dtd">
<busconfig>
  <policy user="root">
    <allow own="org.freedesktop.login1" />
    <allow send_destination="org.freedesktop.login1" />
    <allow receive_sender="org.freedesktop.login1" />
  </policy>
  <policy context="default">
    ...
  </policy>
</busconfig>
```

As the login daemon runs in the `systemd_logind_t` domain, we could enhance this configuration as follows:

```
<?xml version="1.0"?>
<!DOCTYPE busconfig PUBLIC
  "-//freedesktop//DTD D-BUS Bus Configurqtion 1.0//EN"
  "http://www.freedesktop.org/standards/dbus/1.0/busconfig.dtd">
<busconfig>
  <selinux>
    <associate
      own="org.freedesktop.login1"
      context="system_u:system_r:systemd_logind_t:s0" />
  </selinux>
</busconfig>
```

D-Bus will then check whether the application (which we presume is running in the `systemd_logind_t` context) has the `acquire_svc` permission (of the `dbus` class) against the `systemd_logind_t` context. By default, the SELinux policy does not have this permission, and as such, the registration fails:

```
systemd-logind[538]: Failed to register name: Permission denied
systemd-logind[538]: Failed to fully start up daemon:
                     Permission denied
```

In the audit logs, we notice the following denial:

```
time->Sat Sep 24 11:53:23 2016
type=USER_AVC msg=audit(1474732403.120:404): pid=521 uid=81
  auid=4294967295 ses=4294967295
  subj=system_u:system_r:system_dbusd_t:s0-s0:c0.c1023
  msg='avc:  denied  { acquire_svc } for
    service=org.freedesktop.login1 spid=2313
    scontext=system_u:system_r:systemd_logind_t:s0
    tcontext= system_u:system_r:system_dbusd_t:s0
    tclass=dbus  exe="/usr/bin/dbus-daemon" sauid=81
    hostname=? addr=? terminal=?'
```

When we add the following SELinux policy rule (something we'll discuss in the next chapter), the registration of `systemd-logind` will succeed, as expected:

```
allow systemd_logind_t self:dbus acquire_svc;
```

By limiting which domains can obtain a given service, we ensure that only trusted applications are used. Non-trusted applications will generally not run within the domain of that application (end users for instance cannot trigger a transition to such a domain) even if they receive the `root` privileges (which is another check that D-Bus does for the login service, as shown in the first `busconfig` snippet).

Administrators can enhance this D-Bus configuration without having to alter the existing configuration files. For instance, the previously mentioned SELinux-governing `busconfig` snippet could very well be saved as a different file.

Governing message flows

A second control that D-Bus validates is which applications are allowed to communicate with each other. This is not configurable through the service configurations, but is a pure SELinux policy control.

Whenever a source application is calling a method of a target application, D-Bus validates the `send_msg` permission between the two domains associated with the source and target applications.

For instance, communication over D-Bus between a user domain (`sysadm_t`) and service domain (`systemd_logind_t`) will check the following permissions:

```
allow sysadm_t systemd_logind_t : dbus send_msg;
allow systemd_logind_t sysadm_t : dbus send_msg;
```

If these permissions are not in effect, then D-Bus will not allow the communication to happen.

If at any point the application context cannot be obtained (which is not possible with UNIX domain sockets, but might occur if D-Bus eventually supports other communication approaches), then the bus daemon context will be used.

Summary

In this chapter, we started out with an introduction to systemd and a strong focus on the service management capabilities that systemd offers. We learned how to start a service with a custom SELinux context as well as how additional files can be properly labeled upon boot. Alongside the service management, through systemd's unit files, this chapter also covered transient services and how to immediately associate the right SELinux context.

Other systemd capabilities and services were touched upon as well. We saw how SELinux contexts are registered as part of the systemd journal and how to query for events using this context. Journal daemon integration with the SELinux troubleshooting daemon was covered as well. We learned how systemd supports containers and what administrators can do to fine-tune the SELinux context associated with the container. Finally, we took a brief look at udev and how its rules can be used to support administrators in managing devices. One of its actions is to set the SELinux context of the device node.

We finished the chapter with an introduction to D-Bus, how SELinux can be used to control the association of applications with services, and how D-Bus uses the `send_msg` permission to validate communications across its channels.

In the next chapter, we will learn how the SELinux policy can be tuned and even how custom SELinux policies can be developed and loaded.

8

Working with SELinux Policies

Until now, we have been working with an existing SELinux policy by tuning our system to deal with the proper SELinux contexts and assigning the right labels to files, directories, and even network ports. In this chapter, we will:

- Manipulate conditional SELinux policy rules through booleans
- Learn to create new custom SELinux policy modules
- Develop user and application domains
- Replace existing policies with new, custom ones

We'll end the chapter with a few examples of custom policies that augment our SELinux experience and fine-tune the policy to match the security requirements that the administrator has in mind.

SELinux booleans

One of the methods of manipulating SELinux policies is by toggling SELinux booleans. Ever since `Chapter 2`, *Understanding SELinux Decisions and Logging,* in which we used the `secure_mode_policyload` boolean, these tunable settings have been popping up over the course of this book. With their simple on/off state, they enable or disable parts of the SELinux policy. Policy administrators use SELinux booleans to manage parts of the policy that are not always needed (or wanted) but still have a common use case.

Listing SELinux booleans

An overview of SELinux booleans can be obtained using the `semanage` command with the `boolean` option. On a regular system, we can easily find over a hundred SELinux booleans, so it is necessary to filter out the description of the boolean we need:

```
# semanage boolean -l | grep policyload
secure_mode_policyload    (off, off)
```

Boolean to determine whether the system permits loading policy, setting enforcing mode, and changing boolean values. Set this to `true` and you have to reboot to set it back.

The output not only gives us a brief description of the boolean, but also the current value (actually, it gives us the value that is pending a policy change and the current value, but this will almost always be the same).

Another method for getting the current value of a boolean is through the `getsebool` application, as follows:

```
# getsebool secure_mode_policyload
secure_mode_policyload --> off
```

If the name of the boolean is not exactly known, we can ask for an overview of all booleans (and their values) and filter out the one we need:

```
# getsebool -a | grep policy
secure_mode_policyload --> off
```

Another utility that can be used to view SELinux boolean descriptions is the `sepolicy booleans` command:

```
# sepolicy booleans -b secure_mode_policyload
secure_mode_policyload=_("Boolean to determine whether the system
    permits loading policy, setting enforcing mode, and changing
    boolean values.  Set this to true and you have to reboot to
    set it back.")
```

This command, however, does not show the current value of the boolean.

Finally, booleans are also represented through the `/sys/fs/selinux` file system:

```
# cat /sys/fs/selinux/booleans/secure_mode_policyload
0
```

Here, booleans can be read as if they were regular files, and they return the value 0 (zero) for off, and 1 (one) for on.

Changing boolean values

We can change the value of a boolean using the setsebool command. For instance, to toggle the SELinux boolean, we can use httpd_can_sendmail (which enables or disables the policy rules that allow web servers to send e-mails):

```
# setsebool httpd_can_sendmail on
```

On Gentoo Linux, another command called togglesebool exists, which just flips the current state of a boolean. This command is provided by libselinux, but is absent in RHEL.

SELinux booleans have a default state defined by the policy administrator. Changing the value using setsebool updates the current access controls, but this does not persist across reboots.

In order to keep the changes permanently, add the -P option to setsebool as follows:

```
# setsebool -P httpd_can_sendmail on
```

In the background, the updated SELinux boolean value is included in the policy store: the current policy file is rebuilt and loaded. As a result, the policy file (called policy.29, for instance, inside /etc/selinux/targeted/policy/) is regenerated.

Another way to change and persist the boolean settings is to use the semanage boolean command, as follows:

```
# semanage boolean -m --on httpd_can_sendmail
```

In this case, the boolean value is modified (-m) to on (--on).

Persisting the changes will take a while as the SELinux policy is being rebuilt (non-persistent changes are almost instantaneous). The larger the SELinux policy on a system, the more time it takes.

Inspecting the impact of a boolean

To find out what policy rules a boolean manipulates, the description usually suffices, but sometimes, we might want to know which SELinux rules change when a boolean is toggled. With the `sesearch` application, we can query the SELinux policy, displaying the rules that are affected by a boolean. To show this information in detail, we use the `-b` option (for the boolean), `-A` option (show allow rules), and `-C` option (to show conditional rules):

```
# sesearch -b httpd_can_sendmail -AC
Found 46 semantic av rules:
DT allow httpd_sys_script_t bin_t : dir { getattr search open } ;
  [ httpd_can_sendmail ]
DT allow httpd_sys_script_t bin_t : lnk_file { read getattr } ;
  [ httpd_can_sendmail ]
DT allow system_mail_t httpd_suexec_t : process sigchld ;
  [ httpd_can_sendmail ]
DT allow system_mail_t httpd_suexec_t : fd use ;
  [ httpd_can_sendmail ]
DT allow system_mail_t httpd_suexec_t : fifo_file { ioctl ... } ;
  [ httpd_can_sendmail ]
DT allow httpd_t bin_t : dir { getattr search open } ;
  [ httpd_can_sendmail ]
DT allow httpd_t bin_t : lnk_file { read getattr } ;
  [ httpd_can_sendmail ]
DT allow httpd_t smtp_client_packet_t : packet { send recv } ;
  [ httpd_can_sendmail ]
...
```

In the example, we can see that the rules are prefixed with two characters: `DT`. These inform us about the state of the boolean in the policy (first character) and when the SELinux rule is enabled (second character).

With `setools` version 4, the `-C` option is no longer available in the `sesearch` command. When a boolean is selected using the `-b` option, only those rules affected by the boolean are shown. The output is also slightly different, showing only the active state of the rule (**true** or **false**) rather than the two-character state that is displayed in the previous example.

The state reflects whether the SELinux policy rule is currently enabled (`E`) or disabled (`D`) and whether the rule becomes active when the boolean is on/true (`T`) or off/false (`F`). So `DT` means that the rule is currently not active but will become active if the boolean is toggled to the `on` state.

When we query the SELinux policy, it makes sense to always add the conditional option so that we can easily see whether the policy supports a certain access based on one or more booleans.

Consider the web server domain (`httpd_t`), which has many policy rules governed through SELinux booleans. We might want to see which rules are applicable between the web server domain (`httpd_t`) and user content type (`user_home_t`):

```
# sesearch -s httpd_t -t user_home_t -AC
Found 7 semantic av rules:
   allow daemon user_home_t : file { getattr append } ;
   allow httpd_t file_type : filesystem getattr ;
   allow httpd_t file_type : dir { getattr search open } ;
DT allow httpd_t user_home_type : file     { ioctl read getattr lock open }
; [ httpd_read_user_content ]
DT allow httpd_t user_home_type : dir { getattr search open } ;
   [ httpd_enable_homedirs ]
DT allow httpd_t user_home_type : dir
   { ioctl read getattr lock search open } ;
   [ httpd_read_user_content ]
DT allow httpd_t user_home_type : lnk_file { read getattr } ;
   [ httpd_enable_homedirs ]
```

Enhancing SELinux policies

Not all situations can be perfectly defined by policy writers. At times, we will need to make modifications to the SELinux policy. As long as the changes involve adding rules, we can create additional SELinux modules to enhance the policy. If the change is more intrusive, we might need to remove an existing SELinux module and replace it with an updated one.

Listing policy modules

SELinux policy modules are, as mentioned at the beginning of this book, sets of SELinux rules that can be loaded and unloaded. These modules, with `.pp` or `.cil` suffixes, can be loaded and unloaded as needed by the administrator. Once loaded, the policy module is part of the SELinux policy store and will be loaded even after a system reboot.

To list currently loaded SELinux policy modules, it is recommended to use the `semodule` command. Depending on the version of the SELinux user space tools (in this case, the version of the `policycoreutils` package), listing modules will show module versions as well (old version) or just the module name (new version). On RHEL 7.2, the old SELinux user space is still active:

```
# semodule -l
abrt        1.4.1
accountsd   1.1.0
acct        1.6.0
afs         1.9.0
...
```

The more recent SELinux user space no longer uses module versions but instead introduces priorities. Modules can be loaded with a higher priority, overriding previous modules, or with lower priority (in which case the module is loaded but not active). On Gentoo Linux, for instance, we get the following output, which shows the priority as well as **policy module** format:

```
# semodule --list-modules=full
400 also        pp
400 android     pp
400 application pp
400 archi       pp
...
```

The SELinux utilities will copy the active policy modules into a policy-specific location. As such, listing this directory also provides an overview of the currently loaded modules:

```
# ls /etc/selinux/targeted/modules/active/modules/
abrt.pp     cockpit.pp     gitosis.pp     lvm.pp     oracleasm.pp
...
```

On older SELinux user space versions, this location is at `/etc/selinux` whereas the more recent SELinux user space has it at `/var/lib/selinux`.

Loading and removing policy modules

In later sections in this chapter, we will learn how to write new policy modules. Once created, they need to be loaded and removed. This is done with `semodule` as well, regardless of the policy format (`.pp` or `.cil`):

```
# semodule -i screen.pp
```

On recent SELinux user space utilities, administrators can pass on a priority. This allows administrators to load an updated module with a higher priority while retaining the older one (just inactive). For instance, you'd use this command to load the `archi.cil` policy module with a priority `500`:

```
# semodule -i archi.cil -X 500
```

Removing modules is done with the `--remove` or `-r` option. In this case, we are not referring to the package format but to the loaded module, so no package suffix needs to be provided:

```
# semodule -r screen
```

Again, with the newer SELinux user space, it is possible to remove a module from a given priority. Here's an example to remove the `archi` module from priority `300`:

```
# semodule -r archi -X 300
```

Finally, it is possible to keep a module but disable it. This keeps the module in the policy store but disables all the SELinux policy rules inside of it. We use the `--disable` or `-d` option to accomplish this:

```
# semodule -d archi
```

Re-enabling the policy is done with the `--enable` or `-e` option:

```
# semodule -e archi
```

Creating policies using audit2allow

When SELinux prevents certain actions, we already know it will log the appropriate denial in the audit logs. This denial can be used as the source to generate a custom SELinux policy that allows the activity.

Consider the following denials, which occurred when a user called `setkey` after switching his active SELinux role to `sysadm_r` through the `newrole` command:

```
type=AVC msg=audit(1373121736.897:6882): avc:  denied  { use } for
  pid=15069 comm="setkey" path="/dev/pts/0" dev="devpts" ino=3
  scontext=root:sysadm_r:setkey_t:s0-s0:c0.c1023
  tcontext=root:staff_r:newrole_t:s0-s0:c0.c1023
  tclass=fd permissive=0
type=AVC msg=audit(1373121736.907:6883): avc:  denied  { search }
  for  pid=15069 comm="setkey" name="/" dev="dm-4" ino=2
  scontext=root:sysadm_r:setkey_t:s0-s0:c0.c1023
```

```
tcontext=system_u:object_r:var_t:s0
tclass=dir permissive=0
```

If there is no solution offered by `sealert` other than running `audit2allow`, and a quick investigation reveals that there are no SELinux booleans that we can toggle to allow this, then we only have a few options left. We can refuse to handle this solution, telling the user to trigger the `setkey` command through a different path (without switching the SELinux role), as a sort of work around. But if we are certain that the action is correct and there is no mismatch of contexts of any kind, then we might want to allow the currently denied actions.

The `audit2allow` application transforms a denial or a set of denials into SELinux `allow` rules. These rules can then be saved in a file, ready to build into a SELinux policy module based on these `allow` rules, which we can then load in memory.

To generate SELinux policy `allow` rules, pipe the denials through the `audit2allow` application:

```
# grep setkey /var/log/audit/audit.log | audit2allow
#============= setkey_t ==============
allow setkey_t newrole_t:fd use;
allow setkey_t var_t:dir search;
```

Based on the denials, two `allow` rules are prepared. We can also ask `audit2allow` to immediately create a SELinux module, as follows:

```
# grep setkey /var/log/audit/audit.log | audit2allow -M localpolicy
********** IMPORTANT **********
To make this policy package active, execute:
semodule -i localpolicy.pp
```

A file called `localpolicy.pp` will be available in the current directory, which we can load in memory using the given command.

If the denials that occurred are, however, cosmetic in nature (meaning that the system functions as expected), you can use `audit2allow` to generate `dontaudit` rules rather than `allow` rules. In that case, the denials will no longer occur even though the action is not allowed:

```
# grep setkey /var/log/audit/audit.log | audit2allow -D -M localpolicy
********** IMPORTANT **********
To make this policy package active, execute:
semodule -i localpolicy.pp
```

It is likely, after including the necessary rules (assuming the rules are `allow` rules), that the action that was taken still fails. It just fails in another phase, which it couldn't reach before. As long as the previous AVC denials are still available in the audit logs, it is sufficient to regenerate the policy and continue. After all, `audit2allow` will take into account all AVC denials that it encountered, even those that were present before the new policy was loaded.

Another approach would be to put the system (or the specific domain) in permissive mode to generate and fill up the audit logs with all the AVC denials related to the action. Although this generates more AVC denials to work with, it could also result in *wrong* decisions being taken by the `audit2allow` command. Always verify the denials before generating new policy constructs!

When the previous AVC denials are no longer available inside the audit log, a new policy module needs to be generated, as otherwise, the previously fixed accesses will be denied again: the newly generated policy will no longer contain the `allow` rules that were hit before, and when the new policy is loaded, the old one is no longer active.

Using sensible module names

In the previous example, the `audit2allow` command was instructed to generate a policy module named `localpolicy`. However, this is bad practice.

Once a (binary) policy is created (the `localpolicy.pp` file), it is very hard for administrators to find out which rules were part of this module. Although it is possible to unpack the `.pp` file (using `semodule_unpackage`) and then disassemble the resulting `.mod` file into a `.te` file, it requires software that is not readily available on most distributions (the `dismod` application, which is part of the `checkpolicy` software, is not often included). To just get insight into the rules that are part of a module, this is a very elaborate and time-intensive approach.

On systems with a recent SELinux user space, the content of a module can be somewhat deduced from the generated **Common Intermediate Language** (**CIL**) code. For instance, an active screen module will have its code available at `/var/lib/selinux/mcs/active/modules/400/screen` in a file called `cil`. Still, having to dive into the rules to know what `localpolicy` is actually about is not only bad practice, but also requires sufficient privileges to be able to read these files.

Instead, it is a best practice to name the generated modules for their intended purpose. A SELinux policy module that fixes a few AVC denials that come up when `setkey` is executed after a role-switch operation triggered by `newrole` is better called `custom_setkey_newrole`.

It is also recommended to prefix (or suffix) the custom policies with a string that identifies that the module has been added by the administrator (or organization) and not through the distribution's policy. In the previous example, having all custom policies start with `custom_` makes it easier to see which of the currently installed policies are custom ones:

```
# semodule -l | grep ^custom_
custom_setkey_newrole
custom_sysadmin_powertop
custom_debug_xorg
custom_alsa_qemu
```

Using refpolicy macros with audit2allow

The reference policy project provides distributions and policy writers with a set of functions that simplify the development of SELinux policies. As an example, let's see what the macros can do with the previous situation:

```
# grep setkey /var/log/audit/audit.log | audit2allow -R
require {
        type setkey_t;
        type newrole_t;
        class fd use;
}

#============= setkey_t ==============
allow setkey_t newrole_t:fd use;
files_search_var(setkey_t)
```

As `audit2allow -R` uses an automated approach for finding potential functions, we need to review the results carefully. Sometimes it selects a method that creates far more privileges for a domain than needed.

One of the rules in the example has been written as `files_search_var(setkey_t)`. This is a reference policy macro that explains a particular SELinux rule (or set of rules) in a more human-readable way. In this case, it allows the `setkey_t` domain to search through the `var_t` labeled directories.

All major distributions base their SELinux policies upon the macros and content provided by the reference policy. The list of methods we can call while building SELinux policies is available online (`http://oss.tresys.com/docs/refpolicy/api/`) but can also be installed on the local file system at `/usr/share/doc/selinux-base-*` (for Gentoo, with `USE="doc"` enabled while building the `sec-policy/selinux-base` package) or `/usr/share/doc/selinux-policy` (for RHEL, after installing the `selinux-policy-doc` package).

These named methods bundle a set of rules that are related to the functionality that SELinux policy administrators want to enable. For instance, the `storage_read_tape()` method allows us to enhance a SELinux policy module to allow the given domain read access to storage tape devices.

Using selocal

On Gentoo, a script called `selocal` is available that allows administrators to add simple, one-line rules to the policy. These are then made part of a policy module managed by `selocal` (by default called `selocal`).

For instance, to allow all domains to send and receive unlabeled packets, we could execute `selocal` as follows:

```
# selocal -a "allow domain unlabeled_t:packet { send recv };" -Lb
```

As a more advanced example, let's go back to the denials related to `setkey_t` we encountered previously. Here, `setkey_t` was trying to use a `newrole_t` file descriptor. If we investigate the `newrole_t` type a bit further, we can use `seinfo` to view its associated attributes. Here, we see that `newrole_t` has an attribute called `privfd`:

```
$ seinfo -tnewrole_t -x
  newrole_t
    privfd
    mlsprocsetsl
    can_change_object_identity
    kernel_system_state_reader
    ...
```

One of the reference policy methods available is `domain_use_interactive_fds()`, which allows the domains to use file descriptors of types with the `privfd` attribute set.

We can allow this for the `setkey_t` domain using `selocal`:

```
# selocal -a  "domain_use_interactive_fds(setkey_t)" \
    -c "Get output of setkey after newrole" -L -b
```

Understanding which method to call and when to call it is a matter of SELinux development principles. In this chapter, we touch upon basic SELinux policy-development aspects. However, in-depth development of SELinux policies is outside the scope of this book. For this, I recommend *SELinux Cookbook* at `https://www.packtpub.com/networking-and-servers/selinux-cookbook`, another Packt publication, which focuses on SELinux policy development intensively.

The `selocal` application by default maintains a single SELinux policy module, unlike `audit2allow`, where we need to continuously create new SELinux policy modules as time goes by. The application also builds this module on request (`-b`) and loads it in memory (`-L`).

To list the currently available SELinux rules in the `selocal` managed policy, use the `selocal -l` command:

```
# selocal -l
23: files_mountpoint(portage_tmp_t) # Mount tmpfs on /var/tmp/portage
24: domain_use_interactive_fds(setkey_t)
                                 # Get output of setkey after newrole
```

To remove a specific line, pass on the line number displayed in the listing output. For instance, to remove the previously added line, use this command:

```
# selocal -d 24
Removing line 24 from module selocal (/root/.selocal/selocal.te)
Removed following line: domain_use_interactive_fds(setkey_t) \
               # Get output of setkey after newrole
```

Creating custom modules

We can always maintain our own SELinux policy modules as well. To accomplish this, we either need to have at least a file with the `.te` suffix (which stands for type enforcement) and optionally a file context (`.fc`) file and interface (`.if`) file or, when using the new policy format, a `.cil` file. All these files need to have the same base name, which will be used as a module name later.

There are several formats in which SELinux policy modules can be written:

- The first format we call **SELinux native**. It does not understand reference policy macros, but it is the base policy development approach that is still in use. The reference project even relies on this format to build its own set of rules.
- The second format we call **reference policy style**. Here, macros are provided that facilitate SELinux policy development while still supporting most of the syntax that SELinux native uses. Transitioning from SELinux native to reference policy style is therefore quite simple.
- The third format is CIL. This is a completely new language for SELinux policy development, but of course still maps to the well-known SELinux language constructs. The recent SELinux user space will translate the first two formats into CIL format under the hood.

The use of custom modules (instead of relying on `audit2allow`) is preferred as it provides the administrator more control over the added policy rules. It also allows administrators to keep track of policy updates, including comments inside the policy rules explaining why the rules were added.

We will briefly look at the three approaches in the next few subsections.

Building SELinux native modules

A native SELinux policy language module starts with a line defining the name of the module, followed by a set of requirements (types or attributes, classes, and permissions) and then the rules themselves.

An example of this is given through the following policy file:

```
# cat localpolicy.te
module localpolicy 1.0;
require {
  type setkey_t;
  type newrole_t;
  class fd { use };
}
allow setkey_t newrole_t:fd use;
```

The `localpolicy.te` file can then be transformed into an intermediate module file, which will be called `localpolicy.mod`. This is accomplished using the `checkmodule` command, as follows:

```
$ checkmodule -M -m -o localpolicy.mod localpolicy.te
```

Finally, the SELinux policy module is built, generating a loadable `localpolicy.pp` module. For this, we use the `semodule_package` command:

```
$ semodule_package -o localpolicy.pp -m localpolicy.mod
```

The resulting `localpolicy.pp` file can now be loaded in memory using the `semodule` application.

Building reference policy modules

In the case of a reference policy module, a similar structure as with the native format is used, but now leveraging functions provided by the various SELinux policy module definitions. Again, it starts with a module declaration, followed by a declaration of required types (or other SELinux objects), and finally, the set of policy rules that the module holds.

What's important is that the first line calls a macro, namely, the `policy_module()` method:

```
# cat localpolicy.te
policy_module(localpolicy, 1.0)
gen_require('
  type setkey_t;
')
domain_use_interactive_fds(setkey_t)
```

The `localpolicy.te` file can then be built using a reference policy project provided `Makefile`, which transforms the functions to the raw SELinux policy rules and builds the policy packages afterwards.

On Gentoo systems, this `Makefile` resides in `/usr/share/selinux/targeted/include`, while RHEL has it in `/usr/share/selinux/devel`:

```
$ make -f /usr/share/selinux/devel/Makefile localpolicy.pp
Compiling targeted localpolicy module
/usr/bin/checkmodule:  loading policy configuration from
                       tmp/localpolicy.tmp
/usr/bin/checkmodule:  policy configuration loaded
/usr/bin/checkmodule:  writing binary representation (version 17) to
                       tmp/localpolicy.mod
Creating targeted localpolicy.pp policy package
rm tmp/localpolicy.mod.fc tmp/localpolicy.mod
```

Afterward, the `localpolicy.pp` file can be loaded using the `semodule` application.

Building CIL policy modules

The CIL format uses a different policy development style, which might make it easier for software to parse but sometimes more challenging for users to develop. Still, there are a number of advantages to CIL files that will make it a popular approach. Note, however, that CIL support is only available in the recent SELinux user space. RHEL 7.2 does not support CIL yet.

The following `localpolicy.cil` file has similar content as the SELinux native example given earlier on:

```
# cat localpolicy.cil
(allow setkey_t privfd (fd (use)))
```

One of the advantages of using CIL is that it does not require packaging commands. Hence, the generated file can be loaded immediately:

```
# semodule -i localpolicy.cil
```

Adding file context definitions

SELinux policy modules can also contain context definitions, which inform the user space what label to assign to file system resources. For instance, we might want to assign the `httpd_sys_content_t` label to `/opt/dokuwiki/htdocs` content.

Although we have seen that `semanage fcontext` can be used to assign contexts to the right location on the file system, the use of context definitions inside modules gives us the advantage that they become part of the main policy (and thus are validated using the specificity rules as described in `Chapter 4`, *Process Domains and File-Level Access Controls*).

For SELinux native development, this would be written as follows:

```
# cat localpolicy.fc
/opt/dokuwiki/htdocs(/.*)?                    \
    system_u:object_r:httpd_sys_content_t:s0
# checkmodule -M -m -o localpolicy.mod localpolicy.te
# semodule_package -o localpolicy.pp -m localpolicy.mod -f localpolicy.fc
```

For reference policy style, this would be written as follows:

```
# cat localpolicy.fc
/opt/dokuwiki/htdocs(/.*)?                    \
    gen_context(system_u:object_r:httpd_sys_content_t,s0)
# make -f /usr/share/selinux/devel/Makefile localpolicy.pp
```

For CIL style, this is added to the `.cil` file itself:

```
# cat localpolicy.cil
(filecon "/opt/dokuwiki/htdocs(/.*)?" any
  (system_u object_r httpd_sys_content_t ((s0) (s0)))
)
```

Creating roles and user domains

One of the best features of SELinux is its ability to confine end users and only grant them the rights they need to do their job. To accomplish this, we need to create a restricted user domain that these users should use (either immediately or after switching from their standard role to the more privileged role).

Such user domains and roles need to be created through SELinux policy enhancements. These enhancements, however, require a deep understanding of the available permission checks, reference policy macros, and more, which one can only obtain through experience (or assistance). Still, that shouldn't prevent us from providing a working example of how to create a special end user role and domain for the PostgreSQL administration.

Creating the pgsql_admin.te file

First, let's look at the SELinux policy file that includes our user related rules. Each line is commented to explain why the next policy line is used.

The `pgsql_admin.te` file looks as follows:

```
# cat pgsql_admin.te
policy_module(pgsql_admin, 1.0)

# Define the pgsql_admin_r role
role pgsql_admin_r;

# Create a pgsql_admin_t type that has minimal rights a regular
# user domain would need in order to work on a Linux system
userdom_base_user_template(pgsql_admin)

# Allow the pgsql_admin_t type to execute regular binaries
# such as id.
corecmd_exec_bin(pgsql_admin_t)

# Allow the user domain to read its own selinux context
selinux_getattr_fs(pgsql_admin_t)

# Allow the user to administer postgresql, but do not fail
# if no postgresql SELinux module is loaded yet
optional_policy(`
        postgresql_admin(pgsql_admin_t, pgsql_admin_r)
')

# Allow transitioning from staff_r to pgsql_admin_r
gen_require(`
        role staff_r;
')

allow staff_r pgsql_admin_r;
```

This policy file can be built (using the reference policy approach) and loaded.

Creating the user rights

With this policy loaded, the pgsql_admin_r role and pgsql_admin_t type are now available. Next, we create a SELinux user called pgsql_admin_u that is allowed access to the staff_r role (for non-privileged activities), system_r role (for handling the PostgreSQL service), and pgsql_admin_r role (for administering the PostgreSQL files and commands).

As seen in Chapter 3, *Managing User Logins*, we can accomplish this with the semanage user command:

```
# semanage user -a -R staff_r -R system_r -R pgsql_admin_r \
  pgsql_admin_u
```

In the same chapter, we saw how to map this to Linux users. Assuming the Linux user is called janedoe, we assign the pgsql_admin_u SELinux user to her as follows:

```
# semanage login -a -s pgsql_admin_u janedoe
```

Now, we need to reset the contexts of the user, as the contexts of all files now need to be changed. We use restorecon for this:

```
# restorecon -RvF /home/janedoe
```

Finally we need to edit the sudoers file so that every command the user launches through sudo will be with the pgsql_admin_r role (and in the pgsql_admin_t domain).

The following /etc/sudoers snippet should suffice:

```
janedoe ALL=(ALL) ROLE=pgsql_admin_r TYPE=pgsql_admin_t ALL
```

With these changes in place, the user can now log in and handle PostgreSQL. By default, janedoe will remain logged in through the staff_r role (and in the staff_t domain) so that most end user commands work. The moment a more privileged activity needs to be launched, janedoe has to use sudo. As the user is not in the wheel group, using su to get a root shell is not possible.

The pgsql_admin_t domain has enough rights to manage PostgreSQL. For instance, the janedoe user can restart the service and even edit its configuration file:

```
$ sudo rc-service postgresql-9.2 start
* Starting PostgreSQL...    [ ok ]
$ sudo vim /etc/postgresql-9.2/pg_hba.conf
```

As additional rights are most likely going to be needed, all the administrator has to do is update the pgsql_admin.te file accordingly, rebuild the policy, and load it. This allows the pgsql_admin_t domain to become a better match for the requirements that the users have while retaining the secure state of the system.

Granting interactive shell access

Eventually, users might want to ask for shell access, either indirectly (through sudo) or perhaps immediately after login (so that the user can log in to the pgsql_admin_r role directly). This is not a problem for SELinux, even if that user were granted a root shell: SELinux still prevents the user from making changes or performing activities that the user is not allowed to.

The most common approach to allowing interactive shell usage within a SELinux role is to use the userdom_login_user_template() call instead of the userdom_base_user_template() call. If the generated role is a more privileged administrative role, it might even be better to use userdom_admin_user_template(). By switching the template that is called in the policy file (pgsql_admin.te in our case), additional SELinux rules are added that are meant for more interactive use.

If we want a user to be logged in directly to the new type, a few more changes are needed.

First, we need to create a default context file for the SELinux user (in /etc/selinux/mcs/contexts). We can work from a copy (for instance, from staff_u) and substitute staff_r with pgsql_admin_r everywhere. This file will tell SELinux what the default type should be when a login is handled through one of the mentioned contexts.

Next, the /etc/selinux/mcs/default_type file has to be updated to tell SELinux that the pgsql_admin_t domain is the default type for the pgsql_admin_r role (as a fallback).

With these changes in place, we can update the role mappings for the user to only contain pgsql_admin_r system_r (don't forget to reset the contexts of the user files afterwards), as follows:

```
# semanage user -m -R "pgsql_admin_r system_r" pgsql_admin_u
```

Generating skeleton user policy files

The SELinux user space utilities offer a tool that generates skeleton files for custom policies. This tool is called `sepolgen` (or `sepolicy generate`) and is provided through the `policycoreutils-devel` package (in RHEL) or `sys-apps/policycoreutils` (in Gentoo).

To generate a skeleton file set for the `pgsql_admin` role, we can use the `--term_user` option to generate code for interactive users:

```
# sepolgen --term_user -n pgsql_admin
Created the following files:
pgsql_admin.te # Type Enforcement file
pgsql_admin.if # Interface file
pgsql_admin.fc # File Contexts file
pgsql_admin_selinux.spec # Spec file
pgsql_admin.sh # Setup Script
```

The first three files are the same files we created earlier on. The two additional files allow administrators to quickly introduce the generated policies on their systems:

- The `pgsql_admin_selinux.spec` file is used to build RPM (originally named Red Hat Package Manager) files, allowing administrators to deploy custom policies through their standard software life cycle management system
- The `pgsql_admin.sh` script, which builds the policy, loads it on the system, generates a standard manual page for the module, updates the context files on the system to accommodate the new user, and finally builds the RPM package (using the `.spec` file mentioned earlier)

The use of `sepolgen` (or `sepolicy generate`) allows administrators to easily start off with a common set of policy files.

Other supported user templates with `sepolgen` are as follows:

- `--admin_user` for administrative, privileged user domains
- `--confined_admin` for administrative, but otherwise limited user domains
- `--desktop_user` for standard end user domains
- `--x_user` for low-privilege end user domains that can use the X server

Creating new application domains

By default, Linux distributions come with many prepackaged application domains. However, we will most likely come across situations where we need to build our own application policy or include a custom policy that is offered through third-party means.

Unlike users and roles, application domains usually have file context-related information with them.

Creating the mojomojo.* files

The following SELinux policy is for `mojomojo`, an open source, catalyst-based wiki. The code is pretty lightweight as it is a relatively simple web application (infrastructure-wise). In it, we call the `apache_content_template()`, which provides most of the necessary rules out of the box:

```
# cat mojomojo.te
policy_module(mojomojo, 1.1.0)

# Create all types based on the apache content template
apache_content_template(mojomojo)

# Only call creation of alias on RHEL systems
ifdef(`distro_rhel',`
  apache_content_alias_template(mojomojo,mojomojo)
')

# Needed by the mojomojo application
allow httpd_mojomojo_script_t httpd_t:unix_stream_socket
rw_stream_socket_perms;

# Network connectivity
corenet_sendrecv_smtp_client_packets(httpd_mojomojo_script_t)
corenet_tcp_connect_smtp_port(httpd_mojomojo_script_t)
corenet_sendrecv_smtp_client_packets(httpd_mojomojo_script_t)

# Additional File system access
files_search_var_lib(httpd_mojomojo_script_t)

# Networking related activities (name resolving & mail sending)
sysnet_dns_name_resolve(httpd_mojomojo_script_t)
mta_send_mail(httpd_mojomojo_script_t)
```

This is not much different from the user domain module we created earlier. Obviously, there are lots of different calls, but the method is the same.

Let's look at the file context definition file (`mojomojo.fc`):

```
# cat mojomojo.fc
/usr/bin/mojomojo_fastcgi\.pl   --
    gen_context(system_u:object_r:httpd_mojomojo_script_exec_t,s0)
/usr/share/mojomojo/root(/.*)?
    gen_context(system_u:object_r:httpd_mojomojo_content_t,s0)
/var/lib/mojomojo(/.*)?
    gen_context(system_u:object_r:httpd_mojomojo_rw_content_t,s0)
```

The first column is the same as we used with the `semanage fcontext` command. The `--` in the first line tells the SELinux policy that the regular expression is only for a regular file–again, just like what we could do with `semanage fcontext`.

The last column is again a reference policy macro. The macro generates the right context based on the target policy. If the target policy is MLS enabled, then the sensitivity level is also used (`s0`); otherwise, it is dropped.

Creating policy interfaces

When we are building a policy for end user applications, we will eventually need to tell SELinux that existing (and new) roles and types are allowed to execute the new application. Although we can do this through standard SELinux rules, it is much more flexible to create an interface for this. Regular rules that refer to several types break the isolation provided by SELinux policy modules. Interfaces allow us to group rules coherently.

As an example, let's look at the interfaces of the `zosremote` module (in the `zosremote.if` file), which can be found in the `contrib/` subdirectory of `/usr/share/selinux/devel/include/` (for RHEL) or `/usr/share/selinux/targeted/include/` (for Gentoo Linux). If we ignore the comments, then its contents are as follows:

```
# cat zosremote.if
interface(`zosremote_domtrans',`
        gen_require(`
                type zos_remote_t, zos_remote_exec_t;
        ')
        corecmd_search_bin($1)
        domtrans_pattern($1, zos_remote_exec_t, zos_remote_t)
')
interface(`zosremote_run',`
```

```
        gen_require(`
                attribute_role zos_remote_roles;
        ')
        zosremote_domtrans($1)
        roleattribute $2 zos_remote_roles;
')
```

The interface file provides the following interfaces:

- `zosremote_domtrans` allows a given domain to transition to the `zosremote_t` domain upon executing a file labeled `zos_remote_exec_t`
- `zosremote_run` allows a given domain to transition to the `zosremote_t` domain, but also ensures that `zosremote_t` is allowed for the given role

The difference lies with the use: `zosremote_domtrans` will be used for transitions between applications, whereas `zosremote_run` will be used for users (and user roles). For instance, to allow our PostgreSQL user to run `zosremote` applications, we need to include the following SELinux policy rule code in the `pgsql_admin.te` file:

```
zosremote_run(pgsql_admin_t, pgsql_admin_r)
```

When building custom interface files, the interface file (such as `mojomojo.if`) needs to be available in either the current directory (where other custom policy modules are built) or in `/usr/share/selinux/devel/include`, in either the `contrib/` location or the `apps/` location. Otherwise, policies that would use the interfaces of the `mojomojo` module will not be able to locate the interface definitions.

Generating skeleton application policy files

Similar to the user policy files, we can use `sepolgen` to generate application-directed policies. In the case of `mojomojo`, we can use the `--cgi` template:

```
# sepolicy generate --cgi -n mojomojo /usr/bin/mojomojo_fastcgi.pl
Loaded plugins: fastestmirror
Created the following files:
mojomojo.te # Type Enforcement file
mojomojo.if # Interface file
mojomojo.fc # File Contexts file
mojomojo_selinux.spec # Spec file
mojomojo.sh # Setup Script
```

For applications, the `sepolicy generate` command requires the `main` command to be passed on as an argument. This will be used to generate a simple file context (`.fc`) file.

Other supported application-related templates for `sepolicy generate` are as follows:

- `--application` to generate standard, command-line application policies
- `--dbus` to generate D-Bus managed applications
- `--inetd` to generate inetd-operated system service domains (daemons)
- `--init` to generate system service domains (daemons)

Replacing existing policies

When adding custom SELinux policies, all that users can do is to add more `allow` rules. SELinux does not have a *deny* rule that can be used to remove currently allowed access rules from the active policy.

If the current policy is too permissive to the administrator's liking, then the administrator will need to update the policy rather than just enhance it. And that implies that the administrator has access to the current SELinux policy rules used.

Replacing existing policies depends on the SELinux user space utilities (the more recent one supports priority-based loading) and the source of the current policy. Let's look at two approaches: one for RHEL and another for Gentoo Linux.

Replacing RHEL policies

To replace an active Red Hat policy, we need to download the source RPM of the SELinux policy package and use the `rpmbuild` application to extract the files. Once extracted, we update the policy files, rebuild them, and then install them on the system.

First, find out what the current version of the SELinux policy is:

```
# rpm -qi selinux-policy
Name        : selinux-policy
Version     : 3.13.1
Release     : 60.el7_2.9
Architecture: noarch
Install Date: Sat 24 Sep 2016 07:00:07 AM EDT
Group       : System Environment/Base
Size        : 180
License     : GPLv2+
```

```
Signature   : DSA/SHA1, Thu 15 Sep 2016 11:05:48 AM EDT, Key ID
b0b4183f192a7d7d
Source RPM  : selinux-policy-3.13.1-60.el7_2.9.src.rpm
Build Date  : Wed 14 Sep 2016 01:19:26 PM EDT
Build Host  : sl7.fnal.gov
Relocations : (not relocatable)
Packager    : Scientific Linux
Vendor      : Scientific Linux
URL         : http://oss.tresys.com/repos/refpolicy/
Summary     : SELinux policy configuration
Description :
SELinux Reference Policy - modular.
Based off of reference policy: Checked out revision  2.20091117
```

Next, we try to obtain the source RPM shown in the output. If the system does not use an active subscription, then the source RPM can still be obtained through third-party repositories, such as those offered by CentOS. If the package is really difficult to find, you can try to find it through `https://rpmfind.net`.

Download the source RPM, and then install it on the system:

```
# rpm -i selinux-policy-3.13.1-60.el7_2.src.rpm
```

Next, use the `rpmbuild` utility (part of the `rpm-build` package) to extract the source RPM:

```
# rpmbuild -bp ~/rpmbuild/SPECS/selinux-policy.spec
```

When finished, the SELinux policy source code can be found inside `~/rpmbuild/BUILD/serefpolicy-3.13.1`. For instance, the `screen.te` file can be found in the `./policy/modules/contrib` subdirectory.

The policy files can now safely be copied over, manipulated at will, and built to replace the existing policy. It is not necessary to first remove the module from the policy; just inserting the new policy module (with the same name) will replace it.

Replacing Gentoo policies

To replace Gentoo Linux SELinux policies, we will first download the policies through Git and then check out the state of the repository for a given version. Then, we can copy over the files, update them, and insert them at a higher priority.

The repository for the Gentoo Linux SELinux policy is called `hardened-refpolicy.git`:

```
# git clone https://anongit.gentoo.org/git/proj/hardened-refpolicy.git
Cloning into 'hardened-refpolicy'...
remote: Counting objects: 23027, done.
remote: Compressing objects: 100% (7186/7186), done.
remote: Total 23027 (delta 18788), reused 19384 (delta 15768)
Receiving objects: 100% (23027/23027), 3.98 MiB | 3.38 MiB/s, done.
Resolving deltas: 100% (18788/18788), done.
```

Next, find the current version of the policy that is installed:

```
# qlist -ICv selinux-base-policy
sec-policy/selinux-base-policy-2.20151208-r4
```

Now check out the `2.20151208-r4` tag (or whatever the current version on the system is) in the `git` repository:

```
# git checkout tags/2.20151208-r4
```

The source code can now be copied over, manipulated, and built. Once a build is ready, load it at a higher priority than the default (for instance, use priority `500`):

```
# semodule -i screen.pp -X 500
```

Other uses of policy enhancements

Throughout the book, we've covered quite a few technological features of SELinux. By creating our own SELinux policies, we can augment this further.

Creating customized SECMARK types

A use case for building our own policy is to create a custom `SECMARK` type and make sure that a particular domain is the only domain that is allowed to handle this communication.

The following SELinux rules create an `invalid_packet_t` type (to match packets that should not be sent out: for example, the PostgreSQL communication that is directed to the Internet rather than the internal network) and an `intranet_packet_t` type (to match packets being sent to an intranet server):

```
# cat custom_packets.te
policy_module(custom_packets, 1.0)
```

```
type invalid_packet_t;
corenet_packet(invalid_packet_t)

type intranet_packet_t;
corenet_packet(intranet_packet_t)
```

With these rules loaded, we can now create `SECMARK` rules that label packets with `invalid_packet_t` and `intranet_packet_t`.

The next step is to allow certain domains to send and receive `intranet_packet_t`. For instance, for `nginx_t` (a reverse proxy application), you'd use this:

```
allow nginx_t intranet_packet_t:packet { send recv };
```

We could also create an interface to accomplish the same:

```
# cat custom_packets.if
    interface(`corenet_sendrecv_intranet_packets',`
      gen_require(`
        type intranet_packet_t;
      ')
      allow $1 intranet_packet_t : packet { send recv };
    ')
```

With that interface in place, the Nginx policy would be enhanced with the following:

```
corenet_sendrecv_intranet_packets(nginx_t)
```

Auditing access attempts

Some applications have privileges that we still want to be notified about when they are used. The Linux auditing subsystem has powerful features to be notified about various activities on the system, and SELinux enhances those capabilities by supporting the `auditallow` statement.

The `auditallow` SELinux statement has a similar syntax as the regular `allow` statement. But instead of telling SELinux that the access is allowed, it tells SELinux that the access, if it is allowed, should still be logged to the audit subsystem.

For instance, to audit write accesses to files labeled with the `etc_runtime_t` type, you'd use this:

```
auditallow domain etc_runtime_t : file { write };
```

When this occurs, we will see a `granted` statement (rather than a denial), as follows:

```
type=AVC msg=audit(1373135944.183:209339): avc:  granted  { write }
  for  pid=23128 comm="umount" path="/etc/mtab" dev="md3" ino=135500
  scontext=pgsql_admin_u:sysadm_r:mount_t
  tcontext=root:object_r:etc_runtime_t
  tclass=file permissive=0
```

From the (`granted`) message, we can deduce that the `pgsql_admin_u` SELinux user called `umount`, which resulted in the modification of `/etc/mtab`.

Creating customizable types

To create a customizable type, we need to create the type definition in SELinux (which is a regular file type), grant the correct users (and applications) access to the type, and then register the type as customizable (so that a relabel operation does not change the type back).

For instance, we want to have a separate type for an embedded database file used by end users through the `sqlite3` command (which does not run in its own domain, but in the caller domain, so `user_t` or `staff_t`). By using a separate type, other access to the file (by non-privileged applications that run in a different domain) is by default denied, even when those other applications have access to the (standard) `user_home_t` type:

```
# cat custom_mydb_embedded.te
policy_module(custom_mydb_embedded, 1.0)

type mydb_embedded_t;
files_type(mydb_embedded_t)

gen_require(`
  type user_t;
')

admin_pattern(user_t, mydb_embedded_t, mydb_embedded_t)
```

Next, we edit the `/etc/selinux/targeted/contexts/customizable_types` file and add the `mydb_embedded_t` type to it.

With those steps completed, all users (in the `user_t` domain) can now use the `chcon` command to label a file as `mydb_embedded_t` and (still) use this file through `sqlite` (or other application programs that run in the user domain).

Summary

We saw how to toggle SELinux policy booleans using tools such as `setsebool` and how to get more information about booleans, both from their description (using the `semanage boolean` command) and the rules they influence (using `sesearch`).

Next, we saw how custom SELinux policy modules can be loaded and removed and which different types of development formats can be used for building custom SELinux policies. We created our own policy modules to enhance the SELinux policy using various examples such as user domain definitions, web application types, and `SECMARK` types.

We also saw how existing policies can be replaced rather than just augmented with additional rules. Replacing policies is, after all, the only way that a policy can be reduced (less permissive).

In the next chapter, we will use various tools to analyze the existing SELinux policy. This is needed for administrators to verify that the policy supports the security rules that the administrator has in mind and that confined users cannot break out of the confined domains.

9
Analyzing Policy Behavior

Although SELinux policies enforce wanted behavior on a system, knowing how a policy will act up front is necessary for administrators. It assists in the execution of assessments as well as root-cause analysis activities. In this chapter, we will:

- Learn how to query the SELinux policy in depth
- Use a multitude of tools to query process transitions
- Be able to analyze information flows

We'll end the chapter with a few smaller analysis tools, including one that shows the differences between two policy files.

Single-step analysis

In the previous chapters, we covered a few methods of analyzing SELinux policies through command-line utilities such as `seinfo` and `sesearch`. These utilities are able to assist users in performing single-step analysis: they either provide immediate information about a SELinux object (which is mainly what `seinfo` is about) or are capable of querying direct SELinux rules (which is the scope of `sesearch`).

These utilities are provided through the `setools` package. This package has recently received an overhaul with the release of `setools` version 4, but at the time of writing this, it has not been included yet by RHEL. It offers new capabilities but also a slightly adjusted output. Throughout this chapter, the displayed outputs will not be accompanied with a warning that the output might be different from system to system.

Not all capabilities of the seinfo and sesearch utilities have been discussed yet though. The next few subsections will go a bit deeper into how these utilities can be used to query and analyze a SELinux policy.

Using different SELinux policy files

The seinfo and sesearch utilities can do their job for the currently loaded policy or for a selected policy file. The latter allows developers to query SELinux policies of systems they do not have direct access to or for which direct access is cumbersome (such as mobile devices, where Android has its SELinux policy available as the /sepolicy file).

For instance, to analyze an Android SELinux policy file named sepolicy, the following command applies:

```
$ seinfo sepolicy
```

When it is not passed on a policy file, the seinfo or sesearch applications will try to query the current active policy (and not necessarily the last installed one) through the /sys/fs/selinux/policy pseudo-file.

Displaying policy object information

The main purpose of the seinfo application is to display SELinux object information. This information is presented through the types of objects that SELinux (and the seinfo application) supports. Various SELinux object types are supported, ranging from the well-known types, attributes, roles, and users to the more specialized fs_use_* declarations or genfscon statements.

A complete list of supported object types (and their resulting seinfo options) can be found in the seinfo manual page, or through the direct help utility:

```
$ seinfo --help
usage: seinfo [-h] [--version] [-x] [--flat] [-v] [--debug] [-a [ATTR]]
              [-b [BOOL]] [-c [CLASS]] [-r [ROLE]] [-t [TYPE]] [-u [USER]]
              [--category [CAT]] [--common [COMMON]] [--constrain [CLASS]]
              [--default [CLASS]] [--fs_use [FS_TYPE]] [--genfscon
[FS_TYPE]]
              [--initialsid [NAME]] [--netifcon [DEVICE]] [--nodecon
[ADDR]]
              [--permissive [TYPE]] [--polcap [NAME]]
              [--portcon [PORTNUM[-PORTNUM]]] [--sensitivity [SENS]]
              [--typebounds [BOUND_TYPE]] [--validatetrans [CLASS]] [--all]
```

```
               [--ioportcon] [--iomemcon] [--pcidevicecon] [--pirqcon]
               [--devicetreecon]
               [policy]
...
```

Regardless of the object type that the user is interested in, `seinfo` has three main modus operandi.

In the **first mode**, it lists the objects of a given type. For this, only the option has to be passed on, without additional information. For instance, to list all object classes available in the policy, you'd use this command:

```
$ seinfo --class
Classes: 83
  appletalk_socket
  association
  blk_file
  capability
  capability2
  ...
```

In the **second mode**, it can confirm (or deny) the presence of an object instance. To accomplish this, add the instance name to the command. For instance, to validate whether the `memprotect` class is available in the policy, use this command:

```
$ seinfo --class memprotect
Classes: 1
  memprotect
```

Sadly, if the given instance is not available, it is only shown as part of the output. The return code of the application is the same, regardless of whether the instance has been found or not. This makes it less interesting to use in scripts, where the use of `grep` is recommended:

```
$ seinfo --class | grep -q -E "^[ ]*memprotect$"
```

The **third mode** displays expanded information about a selected instance. Although not all information objects support an expanded set, most of the common ones do. The expanded information generally shows a list of (different) instances that are related to the initial query.

For instance, for class information, the expanded information displays the supported permissions of this class:

```
$ seinfo --class memprotect -x
Classes: 1
  class memprotect
{
    mmap_zero
}
```

Finally, `seinfo` can display all information immediately through the `--all` option. This will not show the expanded information though:

```
$ seinfo --all
```

Understanding sesearch

Where the `seinfo` application displays information about SELinux objects, the `sesearch` application is used to query SELinux rules and behavior information between a source and a target resource.

We have been using the `sesearch` application to query standard `allow` rules (type enforcement related access controls) as well as the impact of SELinux booleans on these `allow` rules. The `sesearch` application allows us to not just query rules based on the rule type, but also filter out those rules that match a given source expression using `--source` (-s) and/or target expression using `--target` (`-t`).

The `sesearch` application can deal with indirect source or target information. For instance, when querying information related to the `java_domain` attribute, it will also display rules of all types that have this attribute. In the previous `setools` versions, this behavior can be disabled with the `-d` option. In the recent `setools` versions, this can be selectively used on either source (using `-ds`) or target (using `-dt`).

As this provides the bulk of SELinux's behavior, let's go through the various rules and the impact they have on a system.

Querying allow rules

The first set of rules are the allow rules, which provide type enforcement to allow a source domain to take a type of action against a target resource, assuming the `resource` class matches:

```
$ sesearch --allow -s guest_t -t cgroup_t -c dir
allow guest_usertype cgroup_t:dir { search read lock ... open };
allow guest_usertype filesystem_type:dir { getattr open search };
```

In the recent SELinux policy support (in the Linux kernel) and `setools` package, this includes support for the `allowxperm` rule, which is an extended `allow` rule that takes additional information into account (extended permission information-hence the name). This is used to fine-tune access controls related to IO operations currently, but might be extended further in the future.

Related to the `allow` rules are the `auditallow` rules (showing which `allow` rules, when used, result in audit events being logged) and `dontaudit` rules (showing which actions, when triggered by a domain but not allowed by the policy, will not result in audit events being logged).

Querying type transition rules

A second set of rules are type transition rules. These show how actions (such as creating new files, directories, or even processes) result in a change in security context. A very common analysis done here is to see which type transitions occur that result in a different domain:

```
$ sesearch -T -s guest_t -c process
type_transition guest_t abrt_helper_exec_t:process abrt_helper_t;
type_transition guest_t chfn_exec_t:process chfn_t;
...
```

In this output, we can see that even the guest domain (`guest_t`) has a number of rules that allow transitioning into different domains.

This kind of analysis will be used later too when we look at domain transition analysis.

Querying other type rules

After the type transition rules, there are two other translation-related rules that are part of the SELinux policy, but are not enforced through the operation itself but through a SELinux-aware application which queries these rules.

The first rule is the `type_change` rule, which tells the SELinux-aware application that when it is asked to relabel a certain resource (*target*) for a given domain (*source*), then the relabeling operation should result in the given type. This is used when a resource is created first by another (*parent*) domain, after which it is *handed over* to the source domain. In this case, the parent domain will invoke SELinux functions to ensure that the generated resource gets the right context.

To query it using `sesearch`, use the `--type_change` option:

```
$ sesearch --type_change -s guest_t
type_change guest_t ajaxterm_devpts_t:chr_file user_devpts_t;
type_change guest_t console_device_t:chr_file user_tty_device_t;
...
```

The second rule is the `type_member` rule, which is used for polyinstantiated resources. Here, again, the parent application that initiates the polyinstantiation is SELinux aware and will call the necessary SELinux functions to ensure that the instantiated resource gets the right context.

To query it using the `sesearch` application, use the `--type_member` option:

```
$ sesearch --type_member -s guest_t
type_member guest_t tmp_t:dir user_tmp_t;
type_member guest_t user_home_dir_t:dir user_home_dir_t;
```

Querying role related rules

The previous set of rules was strictly related to types. However, SELinux also has rules related to role activities. With the `sesearch` application, we can query which roles are allowed to be accessed from other roles and when a role transition (such as switching from a user role to the system role) is performed.

The `--role_allow` option shows the allowed roles:

```
$ sesearch --role_allow -s webadm_r
allow webadm_r system_r;
```

With `--role_trans`, we can see when an automatic transition takes place:

```
$ sesearch --role_trans -s webadm_r
role_transition webadm_r httpd_initrc_exec_t:process system_r;
```

Analyzing role transitions and role allow rules helps administrators deduce which roles are powerful or could result in potential security issues. For instance, having the `webadm_r` role be able to switch to the `system_r` role through the `httpd_initrc_exec_t` type might allow that role to invoke actions outside its scope if it has the rights to modify `httpd_initrc_exec_t` resources.

According to the following query, this does not seem to be the case:

```
$ sesearch -s webadm_t -t httpd_initrc_exec_t -A
allow webadm_t httpd_initrc_exec_t:file { read open ... execute };
```

However, it is not sufficient to just look at the main user type. A decent analysis would need to include all types that are reachable by the `webadm_r` role. This in-depth, multi-step analysis is the subject of the next few sections.

Browsing with apol

A decent tool to perform policy analysis is `apol`, offered through the `setools` package. The `apol` tool is graphical in nature and allows analysts and administrators to perform a wealth of analytical actions against the SELinux policy.

Once started, the first action to take with `apol` is to load a target policy (either the currently active policy or a file copied over from a different system). This can be accomplished through the **Open Policy** button or by navigating to **File** | **Open Policy**.

The tool will then display a generic overview of the loaded policy:

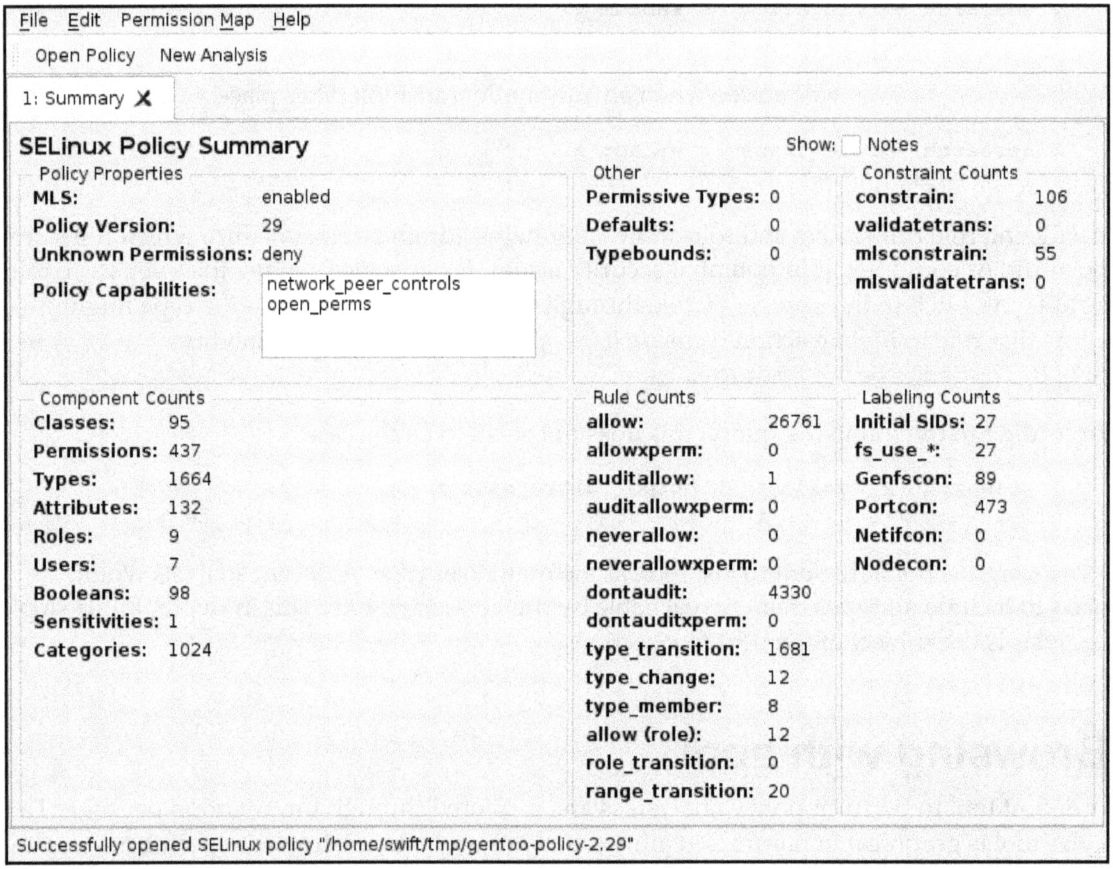

File Edit Permission Map Help

Open Policy New Analysis

1: Summary

SELinux Policy Summary

Show: Notes

Policy Properties

MLS:	enabled
Policy Version:	29
Unknown Permissions:	deny
Policy Capabilities:	network_peer_controls open_perms

Other

Permissive Types:	0
Defaults:	0
Typebounds:	0

Constraint Counts

constrain:	106
validatetrans:	0
mlsconstrain:	55
mlsvalidatetrans:	0

Component Counts

Classes:	95
Permissions:	437
Types:	1664
Attributes:	132
Roles:	9
Users:	7
Booleans:	98
Sensitivities:	1
Categories:	1024

Rule Counts

allow:	26761
allowxperm:	0
auditallow:	1
auditallowxperm:	0
neverallow:	0
neverallowxperm:	0
dontaudit:	4330
dontauditxperm:	0
type_transition:	1681
type_change:	12
type_member:	8
allow (role):	12
role_transition:	0
range_transition:	20

Labeling Counts

Initial SIDs:	27
fs_use_*:	27
Genfscon:	89
Portcon:	473
Netifcon:	0
Nodecon:	0

Successfully opened SELinux policy "/home/swift/tmp/gentoo-policy-2.29"

The apol application after loading a policy file

Most analytical functions in `apol` are supported in both `setools` version 3 and 4. The graphical interface has been revamped though. The screenshots used in this chapter are from `setools` version 4.

Once it has been loaded, select **New Analysis** to initiate the policy analysis functions:

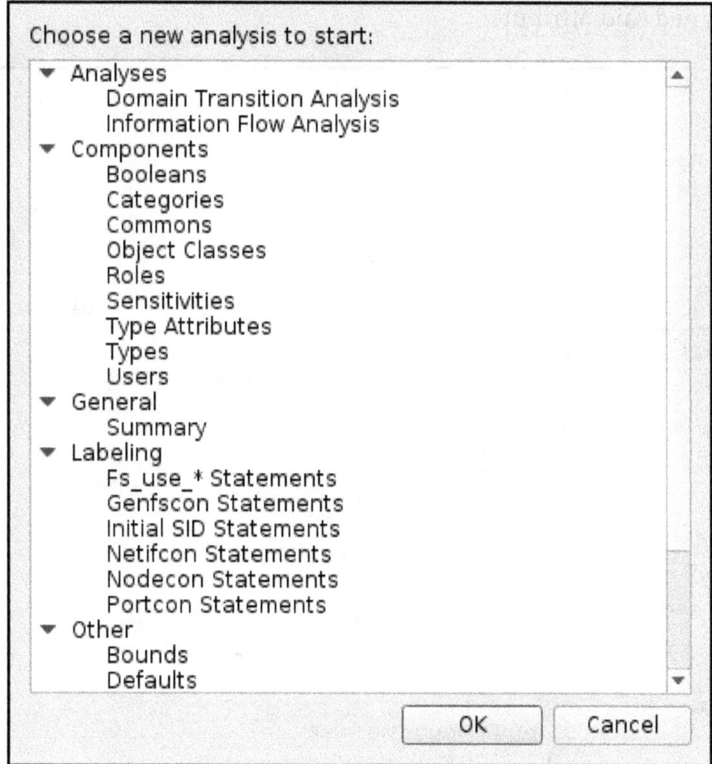

Apol's overview of supported analysis methods

A number of analysis methods are provided. Let's select **Types** to find the next screen, allowing us to browse through the available types, or select an attribute to find out which domains are assigned said attribute:

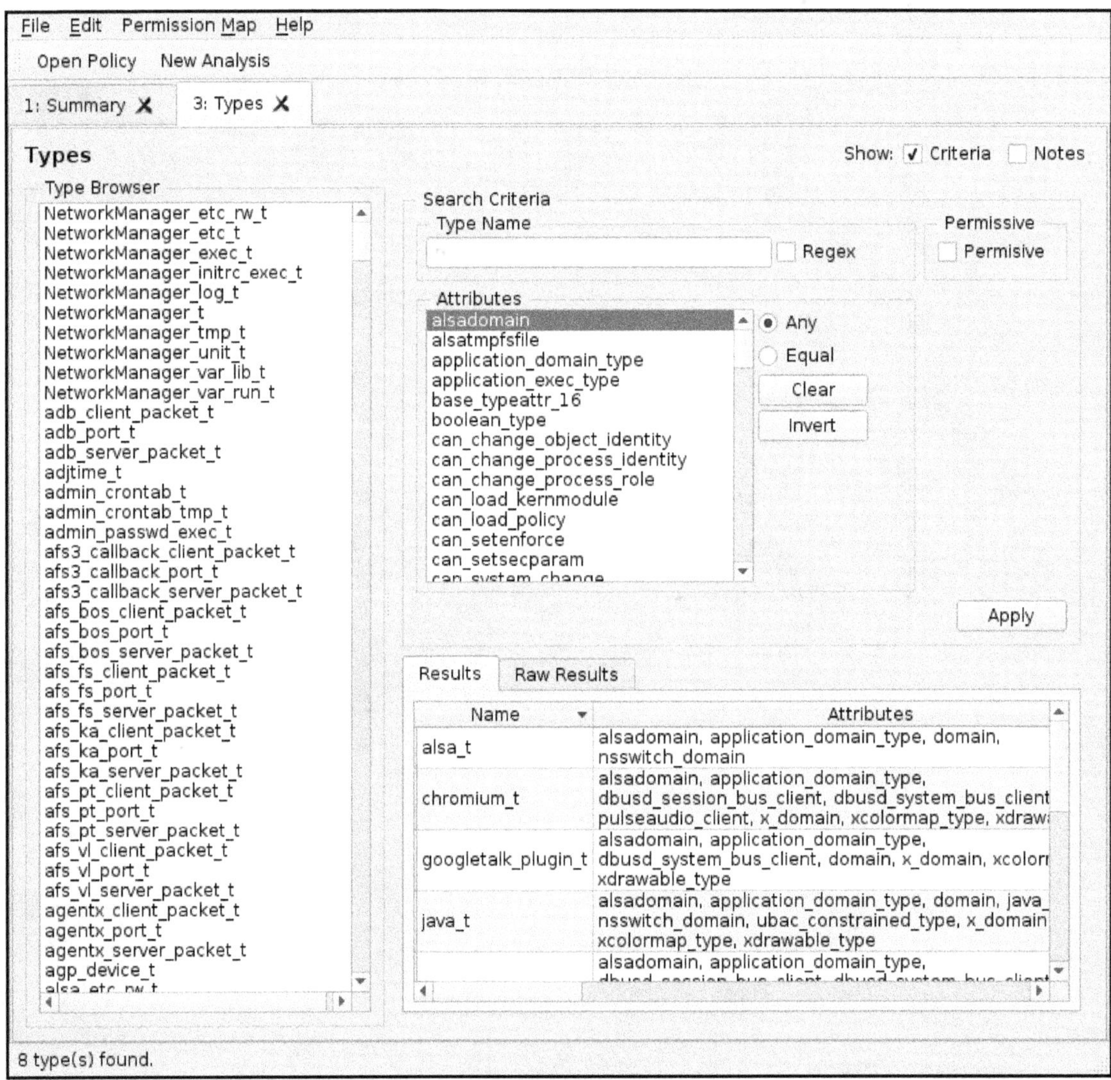

Type browsing within apol: the result pane shows which types are associated with the alsadomain attribute

Similarly, with the **TE Rules** analysis, we can perform the same analysis as with the `sesearch` application:

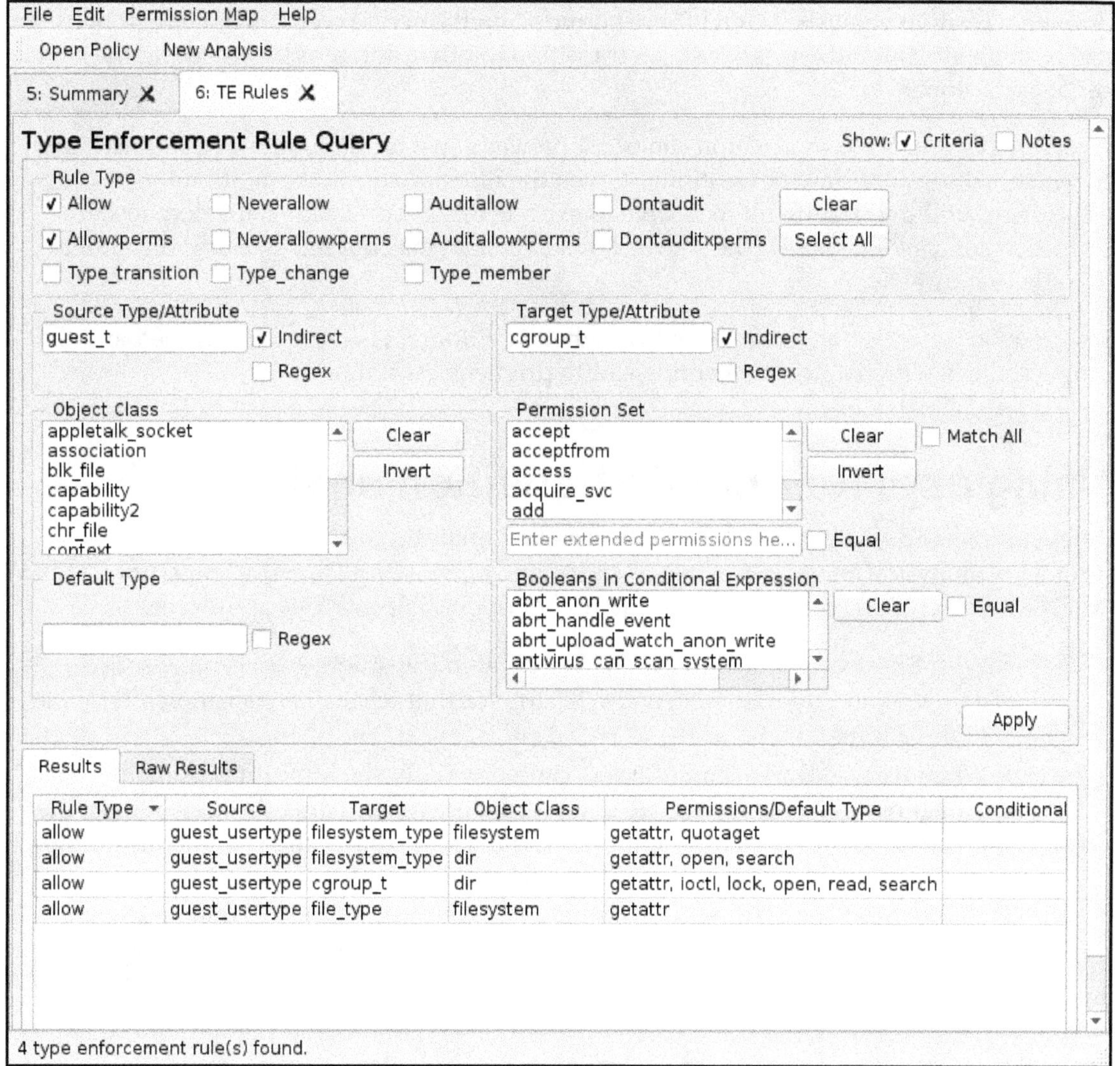

Sample run within apol, querying the type enforcement rules between two types

Domain transition analysis

An important analytical approach when dealing with SELinux policies is to perform a domain transition analysis. Domains are bounded by the access controls that are in place for a given domain, but users (sessions) can transition to other domains by executing the right set of applications.

Analyzing if, and how, a transition can occur between two domains allows administrators to validate the secure state of the policy. Given the mandatory nature of SELinux, adversaries will find it difficult to be able to execute target applications if a domain transition analysis shows that the source domain cannot execute said application, either directly or indirectly.

Use domain transition analysis to confirm whether a domain is correctly confined and that vulnerabilities within a domain cannot lead to privilege escalations.

Using apol for domain transition analysis

After starting `apol`, to perform a domain transition analysis, select **New Analysis**. A number of analytical services are displayed. At the top, we find **Domain Transition Analysis**. The analysis screen shows us a number of possible analysis approaches:

- With **Shortest paths**, `apol` will show domain transitions between the source domain and target domain and will stop for that particular transition after it has found a transition path.
- When using **All paths up to**, `apol` can potentially show multiple domain transitions between the source and target domain, but only through at most the given number of steps. An immediate transition from source to target is a single step (and could easily be deduced using tools such as `sesearch`).
- **Transitions out of the source domain** shows which kind of domain transitions are allowed for a given source domain. The user can then drill down further in the presented tree.

- **Transitions into the target domain** shows which kind of domain transitions result in the given target domain to be reached. This is a reverse domain transition analysis.

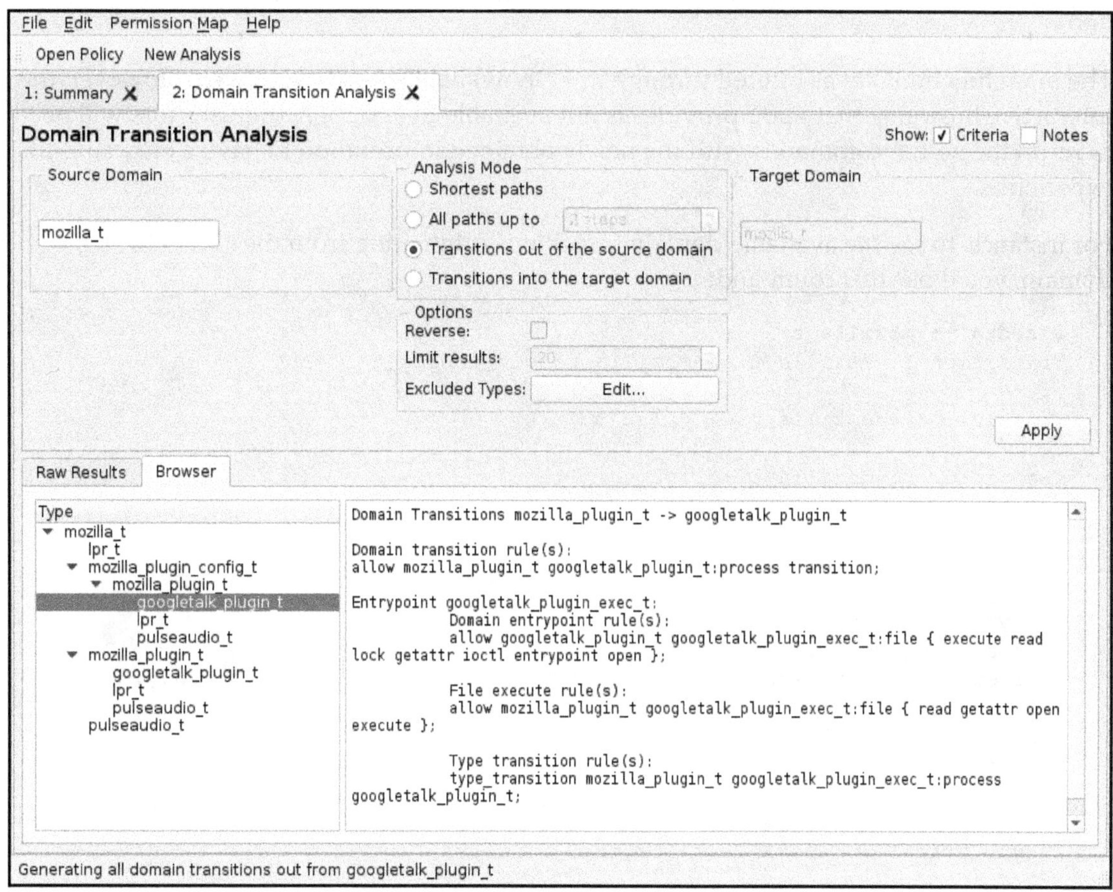

Example output after asking apol to show the transitions out of a source domain

To make analysis more flexible, a number of options can be added as well. For instance, it is possible to exclude certain types from being used in the domain transition analysis. Applications that the administrator holds trustworthy can be excluded from the analysis, such as the `*_sudo_t` domains. These domains would otherwise provide plenty of potential transition steps toward a multitude of application domains.

Using sedta for domain transition analysis

Since `setools` version 4, a command-line application called `sedta` has been available to perform domain transition analysis without relying on a graphical application such as `apol`.

The main functionality as offered through `apol` is available in `sedta` as well. However, the interactive browsing that `apol` provides is not available in `sedta`. Administrators will need to rerun the `sedta` commands with the newly obtained information to have a browsing-like experience.

For instance, to see the available domain transitions originating from the `mozilla_t` domain, you'd use this command:

```
$ sedta -s mozilla_t
Transition 1: mozilla_t -> mozilla_plugin_config_t
...
Transition 2: mozilla_t -> pulseaudio_t
...
Transition 3: mozilla_t -> lpr_t

Domain transition rule(s):
allow mozilla_t lpr_t:process transition;

Entrypoint lpr_exec_t:
  Domain entrypoint rule(s):
  allow lpr_t lpr_exec_t:file { execute read ... entrypoint open };

  File execute rule(s):
  allow mozilla_t lpr_exec_t:file { read getattr open execute };

  Type transition rule(s):
  type_transition mozilla_t lpr_exec_t:process lpr_t;

Transition 4: mozilla_t -> mozilla_plugin_t
...
4 domain transition(s) found.
```

Another example is to analyze if (and how) regular user accounts can execute the **Google Talk** plugin:

```
$ sedta -s user_t -t googletalk_plugin_t -S
Domain transition path 1:
Step 1: user_t -> googletalk_plugin_t

Domain transition rule(s):
allow user_t googletalk_plugin_t:process transition;

Entrypoint googletalk_plugin_exec_t:
  Domain entrypoint rule(s):
  allow googletalk_plugin_t googletalk_plugin_exec_t:file \
      { execute read lock getattr ioctl entrypoint open };

  File execute rule(s):
  allow user_t googletalk_plugin_exec_t:file \
      { read getattr open execute };
  allow user_t application_exec_type:file \
      { execute read lock getattr execute_no_trans ioctl open };

  Type transition rule(s):
  type_transition user_t googletalk_plugin_exec_t:process
googletalk_plugin_t;

1 domain transition path(s) found.
```

Information flow analysis

Another analytical investigation of SELinux policy is information flow analysis. Unlike domain transitions, which look at how one domain can gain a certain set of permissions through transitions toward other domains, information flow analysis looks at how a domain could leak (purposefully or not) information toward another domain.

Information flow analysis is performed by looking at all operations that occur between two types. A source type can be read by a domain, which subsequently can write information to another type. This simple approach is a two-step flow analysis.

However, it is not as simple as just checking read and write operations (although that is of course perfectly possible). Information can be leaked through file names, file descriptors, and more. Information flow analysis must take all these approaches into account.

Using apol for information flow analysis

After loading a SELinux policy, select **Information Flow Analysis** as the analysis method. The following screenshot will look similar to, but not quite like the domain transition analysis screens we have seen before:

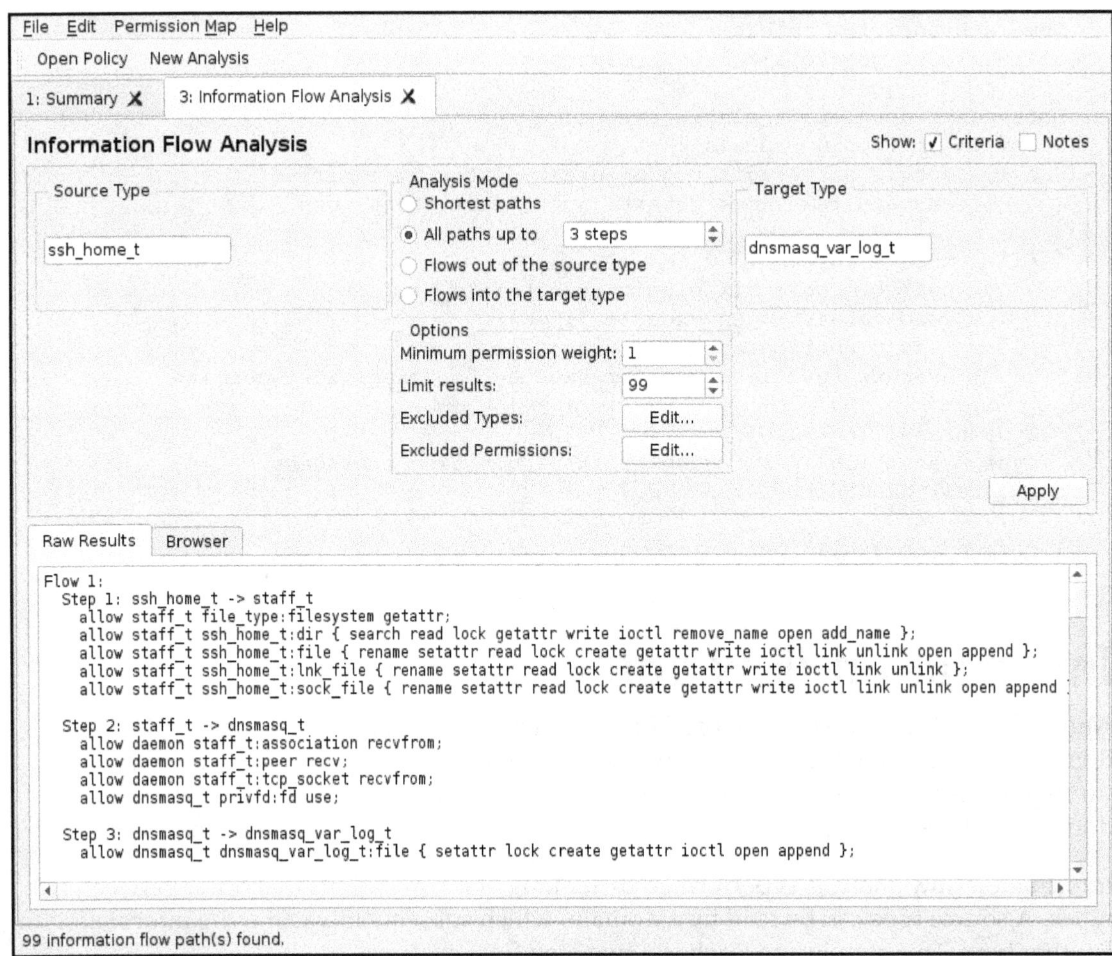

Example information flow analysis without updating the permission map

As you can see from the screenshot, 99 information flow paths were found (after which the tool stopped as the results were limited to 99 in number) between ssh_home_t and dnsmasq_home_t. The first-shown flow informs the user that ssh_home_t content can be read by the staff_t domain. The dnsmasq_t domain is able to receive information from staff_t (due to dnsmasq_t being a daemon domain) and is of course able to append to its log files (dnsmasq_var_log_t).

To perform a decent information flow analysis, it is necessary to fine-tune the search criteria and most likely create a permission map as well.

The analysis mode offers similar options as the domain transition analysis method:

- With **Shortest paths**, the tool will stop processing a particular information flow (one between source and target) when a flow has been found. If there are multiple flows for the same path size, all these flows will be displayed though.
- With **All paths up to**, the tool will find all information flows up to the number of steps (resource read by a domain or a domain writing information to a resource) for a given source and target type.
- **Flows out of the source type** provides a tree-like overview of all communication flows from a given type. Users can then browse through the various domains and types that information can flow to and continue analyzing the flow further.
- **Flows into the target type** provides a reverse information flow analysis, starting from the target type and browsing *upward* to various source domains and types that can be eventually leaked to the target type.

There are a few options that can be set for information flow analysis:

- **Minimum permission weight** allows users to only look at permissions (actions) of a particular weight (and higher). Each action is given a weight in the tool, from a low priority one (such as the lock operation, given the weight 1) to a high priority one (such as the write operation, given the weight 10). The weights are defined in the permission map, which is covered later.
- **Limit results** will have the tool stop after the given number of flows have been found.
- **Excluded Types** allows users to remove particular types and domains from being part of the analysis. Trusted domains or types can as such be removed from the flow analysis, allowing users to focus on the less trusted types.
- **Excluded Permissions** allows users to remove permissions (such as ioctl, lock, and listen) from the analysis.

The last option allows users to manipulate the active permission map. In information flow analysis, creating a trustworthy permission map is an important and not-to-be-underestimated step.

The default permission map is available as `/usr/share/setools/perm_map`. In it, all classes are mentioned with all permissions. For each permission, the map informs the tool whether the permission is a read-like permission, write-like permission, dual channel (so both read and write behavior), or not related to information flows. Next, a weight is given to each of these permissions.

To limit the flow analysis to a particular set of classes, update the permission map (either directly or through the tool) and then rerun the analysis.

Using seinfoflow for information flow analysis

The `seinfoflow` application is a command-line application, offered through `setools` version 4, which offers information flow analysis capabilities like `apol`.

Every invocation of `seinfoflow` requires a permission map to be passed on for its analysis. Although users can point it to the default permission map at `/usr/share/setools/perm_map`, it is advised to use a custom permission map instead.

For instance, when analyzing non-network-related information flows, administrators can create a permission map that excludes all classes related to network communication. As a result, the tool will exclude those permissions from being relevant in an information flow.

As an example, let's look at the information flows between the `ssh_home_t` type and `dnsmasq_var_log_t` type, given a custom map and using the shortest path approach, only using the maximum weighted permissions (`-w 10`). We also exclude a few domains that are either not applicable (such as `nfsd_t` on a system that has no NFS daemon running) or are trusted:

```
$ seinfoflow -m perm_map -s ssh_home_t -t dnsmasq_var_log_t \
  -S -w 10 \
  setfiles_t restorecond_t tmpfiles_t nfsd_t kernel_t
Flow 1:
  Step 1: ssh_home_t -> portage_t
    allow portage_t file_type:dir { read ... write };
    allow portage_t file_type:fifo_file { read ... write };
    allow portage_t file_type:file { read ... write };
    allow portage_t file_type:sock_file { read ... write };
    allow portage_t non_auth_file_type:dir { read ... };
    allow portage_t non_auth_file_type:file { read ... };
```

```
    Step 2: portage_t -> dnsmasq_var_log_t
      allow portage_t file_type:dir { read ... write };
      allow portage_t file_type:fifo_file { read ... write };
      allow portage_t file_type:file { read ... write };
      allow portage_t file_type:sock_file { read ... write };


  Flow 2:
    Step 1: ssh_home_t -> sysadm_t
      allow sysadm_t file_type:dir { read ... };
      allow sysadm_t non_auth_file_type:dir { read ... write };
      allow sysadm_t non_auth_file_type:fifo_file { read ... write };
      allow sysadm_t non_auth_file_type:file { read ... write };
      allow sysadm_t non_auth_file_type:sock_file { read ... write };
      allow sysadm_t ssh_home_t:dir { read ... write };
      allow sysadm_t ssh_home_t:file { read ... write };
      allow sysadm_t ssh_home_t:sock_file { read ... write };

    Step 2: sysadm_t -> dnsmasq_var_log_t
      allow sysadm_t dnsmasq_var_log_t:dir { read ... write };
      allow sysadm_t dnsmasq_var_log_t:fifo_file { read ... write };
      allow sysadm_t dnsmasq_var_log_t:file { read ... write };
      allow sysadm_t dnsmasq_var_log_t:sock_file { read ... write };
      allow sysadm_t non_auth_file_type:dir { read ... write };
      allow sysadm_t non_auth_file_type:fifo_file { read ... write };
      allow sysadm_t non_auth_file_type:file { read ... write };
      allow sysadm_t non_auth_file_type:sock_file { read ... write };

  2 information flow(s) found.
```

Other policy analysis

Two additional tools (`sediff` and `sepolicy`) exist that provide some insight into the current SELinux policy. The next two subsections cover these in more detail.

Comparing policies with sediff

The `sediff` tool, part of the `setools` package, looks at the differences between two policy files and reports the differences to the user. It does not provide patch-like capabilities (which the regular diff does) but is powerful to find and analyze small differences.

A common use case for the `sediff` tool is to validate that a source-built policy file is the same as the distribution-provided binary policy file. Administrators can then be certain that the source code they used to build a policy file is the same as that used by the distribution to generate the provided policy.

Its basic usage is simply to provide the two binary files:

```
$ sediff distro-policy.30 selfbuilt-policy.30
Policy Properties (0 Modified)

Booleans (0 Added, 0 Removed, 1 Modified)
  Modified Booleans: 1
    * mcelog_exec_scripts (Modified default state)
      + True
      - False
```

It is possible to direct `sediff` to only show differences in a particular area (such as available types, roles, booleans, or type enforcement rules).

For instance, to view the difference between a Gentoo Linux policy file and a RHEL policy file on the type level, you'd use this command:

```
$ sediff --type gentoo-policy.29 rhel-policy.29 | grep Types
Types (3220 Added, 269 Removed, 369 Modified)
  Added Types: 3220
  Removed Types: 269
  Modified Types: 369
```

Through this, we notice that the Gentoo policy has far fewer types (`3220`) than Red Hat's policy. This is because Gentoo only deploys SELinux policy modules when a package is installed that uses that policy.

The complete set of supported comparison fields is available in the `sediff` manual page or through the direct help option:

```
$ sediff --help
```

Analyzing policies with sepolicy

Another tool, provided through the `policycoreutils` package, is the `sepolicy` application. We have already seen this application in action as it shows basic information about a SELinux policy, such as boolean information. The utility has a few other tricks up its sleeve, however.

With the sepolicy communicate command, administrators can quickly see whether two domains can communicate with each other through a single intermediate step on the file level. This is similar to the information flow analysis we saw before, but it only focuses on files:

```
$ sepolicy communicate -s mozilla_t -t chrome_sandbox_t
config_home_t
cifs_t
xserver_tmpfs_t
ecryptfs_t
fusefs_t
user_fonts_cache_t
cache_home_t
nfs_t
```

Another analysis that sepolicy offers is a bit like domain transition analysis. It shows which domain transitions can occur in order for one domain to reach another. It does so through the sepolicy transition command:

```
$ sepolicy transition -s user_t -t lpr_t
user_t ... mozilla_plugin_t @ lpr_exec_t --> lpr_t
user_t ... vmtools_helper_t ... vmtools_t ... ifconfig_t \
  ... iptables_t ... insmod_t ... mount_t ... glusterd_t \
  ... initrc_t ... realmd_t ... sshd_t ... unconfined_t \
  ... openshift_initrc_t ... apmd_t ... system_cronjob_t \
  ... munin_t @ lpr_exec_t --> lpr_t
```

Summary

In this chapter, we looked at various methods for analyzing SELinux policies.

We started with single-step analysis, using the sesearch and seinfo tools that we've already used throughout the book. In it, we discovered that those tools have a lot of information to offer to administrators who want to analyze the active SELinux policy.

Next, we used the apol, sedta, and seinfoflow tools to perform more in-depth analysis of the SELinux policy. These tools offered us insight into domain transitions (which domains are reachable from other domains) and information flow analysis (which information can eventually–given the right actions and perhaps vulnerabilities in the software–be made available without SELinux preventing the flows).

We ended the chapter with a few other analytical utilities. One of these was the use of the `sediff` command, which displays the differences between two policy files, allowing administrators to ascertain whether an active policy on one system resembles another.

In the next and final chapter, we will use the knowledge from all these chapters to show how SELinux can be tailored to suit a number of use cases.

10
SELinux Use Cases

The previously described SELinux operational controls need to be aligned to suit administrators' goals and requirements. In this chapter, several cases will be described that will teach administrators to:

- Harden web servers through SELinux category support and proper file labeling
- Secure shell services through the separation of SSH instances and different PAM service usage of the SSH daemon
- Configure the NFS server to deal with different SELinux file contexts and tune applications to use the NFS-exposed files

We'll end the chapter with a small comparison of Samba's SELinux implementation and the NFS configuration documented earlier.

Hardening web servers

Web servers are a common infrastructural service in many architectures. They are also often exposed to the Internet (either directly or behind a reverse proxy, which might enable additional security controls) and as such are more vulnerable to attacks than backend services such as database systems.

Web servers can host various types of content, ranging from static websites to dynamic websites, right on to web services that are used in a microservice architecture. Regardless of their application focus, SELinux is ready to support the web server.

Describing the situation

Before embarking on a SELinux configuration and tuning spree, it is wise to describe the situation properly. By looking at the situation and investigating its various requirements, administrators will be able to get a better view of the architecture and make decisions that benefit the secure state of the system. It often pays off to draw the situation as well, as a schematic is often more powerful than an elaborate description of a particular situation.

When describing such architectures, take several dimensions into account. Each of those has impact on the security-related settings and advises the administrator in a particular direction:

- Look at which user groups are going to connect to the web server. Are all user groups equally trustworthy? Do they all require the same capabilities on the web application(s) they use? Are these user groups connecting from the same locations?
- Consider how the web server will be managed, and by whom. There are two main points here: system and web server administration (which often requires interactive shell access to the system) versus web content administration. The latter does not need highly privileged access to the system.
- Check whether different web applications require different behavior from the web server. If one web application is only hosting static content while another requires connections to databases and other remotely hosted services, then it might be wise to split these web applications and host them on different systems.

Assume that after looking at the hosting requirements, we come up with the following situation: sites are divided across six web server instances, across three website hosting servers. **Public Users** connect to a public-facing reverse proxy, whereas **Internal Users** have their own internal-facing reverse proxy. Depending on the sites that are accessible, the reverse proxies filter out which web server instances they connect to:

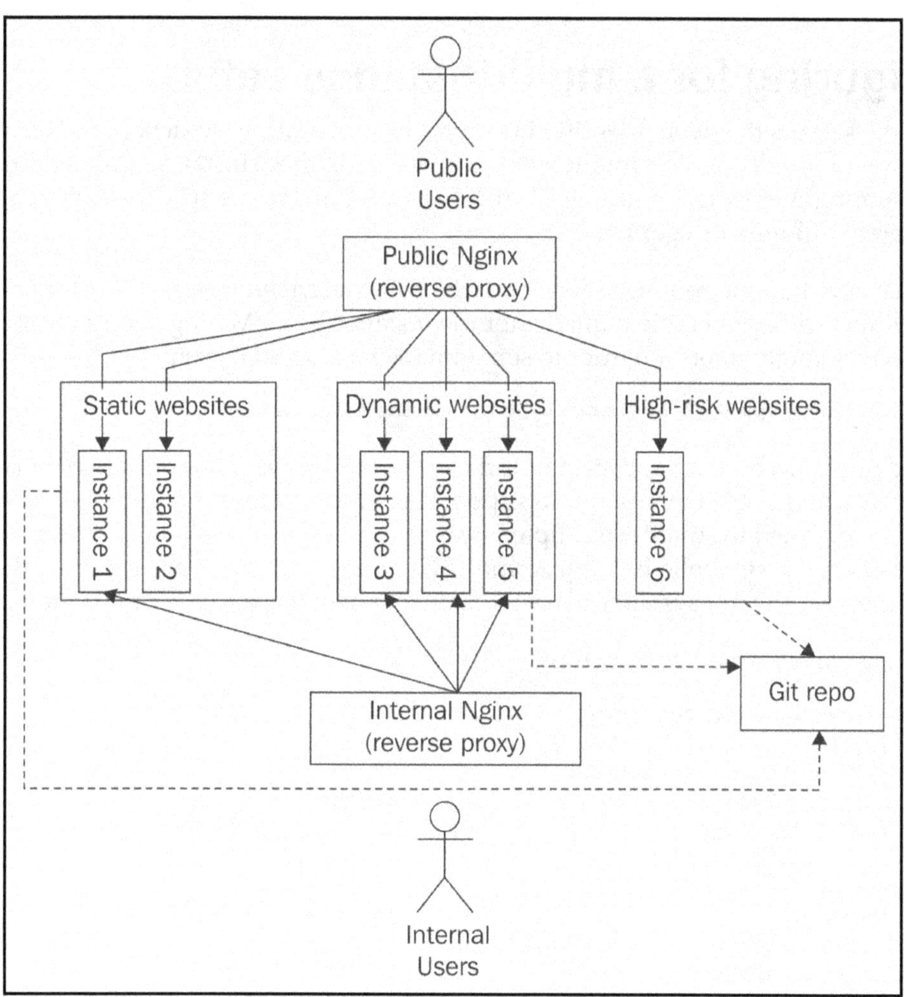

High-level overview of website deployment

For each of the web server hosting components (which includes the Nginx systems), different SELinux configurations and tunings are recommended. We will focus primarily on the instances as those handle the bulk of the workload. However, hardening the reverse proxies should not be forgotten as they are the first line of defense in the suggested architecture.

Configuring for a multi-instance setup

Many of the servers that were identified earlier will run multiple Apache (or other web server software) instances. We might want to ensure that these instances run on different ports (assuming there aren't multiple IP addresses assigned to the server) and even run with different SELinux categories.

First, make sure that the configurations of each of the described instances are located in separate directories, preferably named after the instance itself. Mixing configurations in the same directory might make it harder to separate the instances later on:

```
# mkdir /etc/apache2/instance1 /etc/apache2/instance2 ...
```

Next, update the web server software unit file (when using systemd) or init script (when using a SysV-compatible init system) to support multiple instances. With systemd, the unit file could be updated to support multiple instances. On Gentoo, the init script can be updated to support symbolic-link init scripts. By naming the targets according to the created instances, the init system can easily deduce where the active configuration file is.

For instance, for systemd, we'd do this:

```
# cat /etc/systemd/service/
[Unit]
Description=Apache web server
ConditionPathExists=/etc/apache2/%i/httpd.conf
After=network.target

[Service]
Type=forking
EnvironmentFile=/etc/sysconfig/httpd.%i
PIDFile=/run/apache2/%i.pid
ExecStart=/usr/sbin/apache2 -f /etc/apache2/%i/httpd.conf
ExecReload=/usr/sbin/httpd -k restart -f /etc/apache2/%i/httpd.conf
ExecStop=/usr/sbin/httpd -k stop -f /etc/apache2/%i/httpd.conf
SELinuxContext=system_u:system_r:httpd_t:%i
Restart=always

[Install]
```

```
WantedBy=multi-user.target
```

Through this approach, each instance is assigned its own configuration file as well as its own SELinux category.

Creating the SELinux categories

To support the named categories (for instance, `instance1` and `instance2`) we need to enable the `mcstransd` service and configure the categories in the `setrans.conf` file, as was discussed in `Chapter 3`, *Managing User Logins*:

```
# cat /etc/selinux/targeted/setrans.conf
s0-s0:c0,c101.c106=WebAdmin
s0:c101=instance1
s0:c102=instance2
...
```

This is required since the unit file or init script will refer to the instance name as part of the category. It is not possible to use the actual fields in the unit files and would require some scripting in the init scripts.

Choosing the right contexts

Web servers have a multitude of SELinux contexts at their disposal. Pick the correct context for the website content, as it will ensure that the web server correctly handles the files, even when the discretionary access controls would enable more access patterns:

- The `httpd_sys_content_t` type should be used for read-only, static web content. Consider this for images, CSS files, HTML files, PHP files, and more as long as the web server does not need to modify it.
- The `httpd_sys_rw_content_t` type should be used for read/write web content. For instance, a wiki system that uses a particular `data/` directory for storing the wiki pages would use this type on the `data/` directory, while the rest of the website content (such as the configuration file) remains at `httpd_sys_content_t`.
- The `httpd_sys_ra_content_t` type should be used for content that should only be appended. This can be used for files that are not completely rewritten upon save operations, such as application loggings.

- The `httpd_sys_htaccess_t` type should be assigned to the `.htaccess` and perhaps `.htpasswd` files, which should not be displayed to users, but are read by the web server.
- The `httpd_sys_script_exec_t` type should be used for CGI scripts, allowing the web server to execute the scripts.
- The `httpd_sys_script_rw_t`, `httpd_sys_script_ra_t`, and `httpd_sys_script_t` types are used for files that are only handled by the CGI (and other web server invoked) scripts. These can be read/write, append-only, or read-only.
- The `httpd_user_*_t` types are similar to the `httpd_sys_*_t` scripts, but now meant for user-specific content. Web servers might support user directories (such as through Apache's `UserDir` directive), in which case the `httpd_user_*_t` types are used.
- The `public_content_rw_t` type is a special case. It is assigned to files that are accessed and handled by several services. For instance, if the web server will be hosting content that is uploaded through FTP, it might make sense to use the `public_content_rw_t` type for it (as an FTP server would not have any manage rights on the `httpd_*_content_t` types).
- Several web applications have dedicated policies available. These policies declare the necessary content- and script-related types as well. For instance, for MediaWiki, there is `httpd_mediawiki_content_t` and `httpd_mediawiki_script_exec_t`. The types used for these specific web applications should all follow the same rules, as they are generated through the main web server policy.

Put the right label on the content. Many administrators would probably use the `semanage fcontext` command to associate the right label with the content, like so:

```
# semanage fcontext -a -t httpd_sys_rw_content_t \
  "/srv/web/instance1/htdocs/data(/.*)?"
# semanage fcontext -a -t httpd_sys_content_t \
  "/srv/web/instance1/htdocs(/.*)?"
# semanage fcontext -a -t httpd_mediawiki_content_t \
  "/srv/web/instance3/htdocs/wiki(/.*)?"
```

However, to ensure reproducibility and to benefit from the ordering rules and processing that is used by the SELinux libraries, it might be a better idea to create a (perhaps otherwise empty) SELinux policy module that associates the right context with the locations.

For instance, to create such a policy using SELinux CIL syntax, we'd use the following:

```
# cat custom_mediawiki.cil
(filecon "/srv/web/instance1/htdocs/data(/.*)?" any
  (system_u object_r httpd_sys_rw_content_t ((s0) (s0)))
)
(filecon "/srv/web/instance1/htdocs(/.*)?" any
  (system_u object_r httpd_sys_content_t ((s0) (s0)))
)
(filecon "/srv/web/instance3/htdocs/wiki(/.*)?" any
  (system_u object_r httpd_mediawiki_content_t ((s0) (s0)))
)
```

This module can then be loaded and used directly:

```
# semodule -i custom_mediawiki.cil
# restorecon -RvF /srv/web/instance*
```

Enabling administrative accounts

If the web servers will be managed by different users or teams, it might be a good idea to associate different roles with them. In Chapter 8, *Working with SELinux Policies*, we saw how to create additional roles and user types, whereas Chapter 3, *Managing User Logins*, showed us how to associate users and groups with different SELinux users.

We could create a user group called `webadmins` and then assign the members of this group to the `webadm_u` SELinux user:

```
# semanage login -a -s webadm_u -r WebAdmin %webadmins
```

The website administrators should be associated with the proper security sensitivity and category range. The `WebAdmin` name is defined in the `setrans.conf` file that was created previously.

Handling web server behavior

When the web server is in use, its behavior needs to be properly tuned as well. A static website does not need any of the dynamic access controls that might be enabled otherwise. And even dynamic web application servers do not often require full privileges for both file access and process behavior.

Our design separates the behavior into three areas:

- Static websites will not have any additional behavioral rules active. The web servers will not be able to connect to other systems, for instance.
- Dynamic websites have a common set of behavioral rules active. However, the security-sensitive ones are not enabled.
- High-risk websites have more security-sensitive rules active. These systems are generally more strongly hardened than those hosting regular dynamic websites.

If needed, multiple high-risk website hosting systems can be used. Thanks to virtualization (in which SELinux also plays a role, as we saw in `Chapter 6`, *sVirt and Docker Support*), we can easily create dedicated systems with a particular security mitigation strategy active.

Tuning the behavior access controls is handled mainly through SELinux booleans. There are over 40 SELinux booleans applicable to a web server environment. The following set shows the granularity and sensitivity of the rules nicely:

- The `httpd_can_*` SELinux booleans enable or disable rules related to the action that the SELinux boolean mentions. For instance, `httpd_can_connect_ftp` allows a web server to connect to an FTP server. This might be necessary if one of the web applications is a web-based FTP client. `httpd_can_network_connect` allows the web server to connect to any network-facing service, which should generally not be allowed. A more fine-grained SELinux boolean, `httpd_can_network_connect_db`, allows web servers to connect to network-facing database systems, which is at least a lot less than all possible network services. These SELinux booleans would be disabled on static websites, with fine-grained SELinux booleans used on the dynamic websites and the general SELinux booleans on the high-risk websites.
- The `httpd_anon_write` SELinux boolean allows web servers to write to files that are labeled with `public_content_rw_t`. This type can be in use when the content is managed by a multitude of services, such as a web server, FTP server, and file-share server.
- The `httpd_builtin_scripting` SELinux boolean has to be enabled when dynamic languages such as PHP are to be used. It will generally be disabled for static websites and enabled on dynamic and high-risk websites.
- The `httpd_dbus_*` SELinux booleans (such as `httpd_dbus_sssd`) allows the web server to communicate with other services through D-Bus. It should be disabled for static websites, but could be enabled on dynamic or high-risk websites.

- The `httpd_use_*` SELinux booleans (such as `httpd_use_nfs`) allow the web server to use a particular service or command. The `httpd_use_nfs` example allows the web server to serve content from NFS-mounted locations, whereas `httpd_use_gpg` would allow the web server to call the GnuPG application.
- Some SELinux booleans are very specific. For instance, the `httpd_tmp_exec` SELinux boolean allows the web server to execute content from `/tmp` (or other temporary locations). This is considered a security risk (as attackers might be able to influence temporary content more easily than other content). Many `_exec` booleans (such as `httpd_execmem`) are considered security risks and should only be enabled when the system is otherwise sufficiently hardened.

Toggling the SELinux booleans is done with `setsebool`:

```
# setsebool -P httpd_use_nfs on
```

If the behavior of a SELinux boolean is not certain yet, enable it without persisting its value in the policy store, and then verify whether the changed SELinux boolean influences the supported rules in the expected manner:

```
# setsebool httpd_use_nfs on
```

Dealing with content updates

In the presented architecture, we use a Git repository for the website content. This is, of course, not the only possible content provider. We could be using NFS mounts (as described later on in this chapter) or use interactive shell services to allow users to upload their own content.

The advantage of using a Git repository here is that we can have a locally running batch job responsible for updating the Git repository for each of the websites. Content administrators do not need to log on to the system to update the website, but rather need to push to the right branch in the Git repository. The locally running batch job then pulls in the data while ensuring that the file labels are set correctly.

Suppose we want the `/srv/web/instance1` location to be pulled from `gitserver:/proj/instance1`. In that case, the system administrator (or web service administrator) could create a one-time clone and then create an update script. The one-time clone uses unauthenticated access here (as we do not need any update privileges), which later helps us in automating the Git pull (as no sensitive credentials need to be provided):

```
# cd /srv/web
# git clone https://gitserver/proj/instance1.git instance1
# restorecon -RvF instance1
```

As the `root` user of the site (`./instance1/htdocs`) does not contain the `.git/` folder (`./instance1/.git`), the site content has basic security control over what data is exposed through the website and which content isn't. Of course, this does mean that the directory structure has proper labeling in place.

The locally running job can ensure that the labels (and categories) are properly assigned:

```
# cat /usr/local/bin/update-instance1.sh
#!/bin/sh
cd /srv/web/instance1 || exit 1;
git pull || exit 2;
restorecon -RvF /srv/web/instance1/ || exit 3;
```

The job itself has to run with sufficient privileges to execute these commands. By default, cronjobs run with the `cronjob_t` type, which has basic binary execution rights. The privilege to relabel resources is not granted. This can either be added to the `cronjob_t` type, or a custom domain that contains the right set of permissions can be created for the web content updates.

Tuning the network and firewall rules

Firewalls have long been part of a security approach surrounding systems. Systems that host web servers should also be using a proper firewall setting to ensure that only authorized locations can access the services.

When hosting multiple instances, we might want to restrict access to the instances in a fine-grained manner. The `instance3` web server only needs to be accessible from internal systems, whereas `instance4` is accessible both from the outside world and internally. Given that both websites are first handled through a reverse proxy, the firewall should make sure that only those systems hosting the reverse proxy can connect to the instance.

We can enable SECMARK on the firewall rules as well, ensuring that the web server instances can receive only the right network packets (through category labeling):

```
# iptables -t security -A INPUT -p tcp --dport 8081 -j SECMARK \
    --selctx "system_u:object_r:http_server_packet_t:s0:c101"
# iptables -t security -A INPUT -p tcp --dport 8082 -j SECMARK \
    --selctx "system_u:object_r:http_server_packet_t:s0:c102"
```

The preceding rules only show part of the configuration. More in-depth coverage of using SECMARK was handled in Chapter 5, *Controlling Network Communications*.

As we run the instances on different ports, we also need to configure SELinux to allow the web server to use those ports:

```
# semanage port -a -t http_port_t -p tcp 8081
# semanage port -a -t http_port_t -p tcp 8082
```

Securing shell services

Another infrastructural service that is security sensitive is a shell service. Whereas malicious individuals would be happy to get **remote command execution (RCE)** vulnerabilities on systems to exploit, shell services immediately provide an interactive environment. Of course, securing shell services is an important strategy for administrators.

Splitting SSH over multiple instances

One potential approach to harden a shell-service-providing server is to split the access for administrators and users.

The user-facing SSH server could possibly require just user ID and password authentication or key-based authentication. It'll be running on the default port 22 and perhaps enables chrooted SSH so that the regular users do not have access to the entire file system but only a particular location, such as /var/jail. Additional safeguarding approaches such as enabling a service like fail2ban (which checks the logs for the IP addresses that are trying a brute-force attack against the SSH server and then bans those IP addresses by updating the local firewall) can be enabled on the user-facing SSH server as well. Other similar projects are sshguard, sshblock, and sshit.

The administrative SSH server would be hardened to a greater extent. It would require both password- and key-based authentication or any other chained authorization provider. It runs on a non-default port (such as `4971`) and only allows members of an administrative group to log on through it:

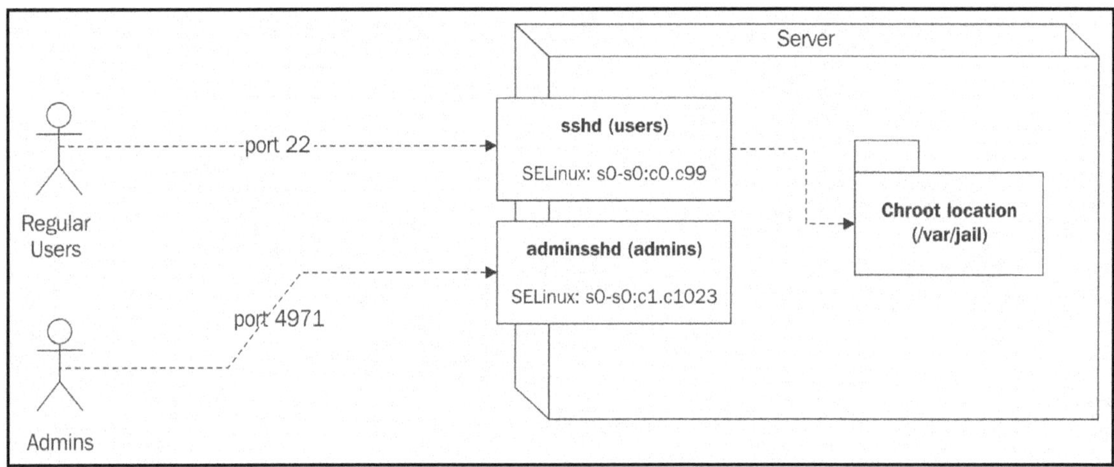

Splitting SSH access based on user role

The SSH daemon configurations can be stored as `/etc/ssh/user/sshd_config` and `/etc/ssh/admin/sshd_config`. The systemd unit files or init scripts are updated to point to the right instance, similar to the approach used with the web server in the previous section.

Using separate instances on SSH has other advantages beyond the security measures and controls. We might want to run the user SSH daemon with a lower sensitivity or restricted category set (`s0-s0:c0.c99`) whereas the administrative SSH daemon either runs with a higher sensitivity (if an MLS SELinux policy is used) or at least with the entire category range (`s0-s0:c0.c1023`). This is different from the multi-instance deployment for web servers, as we did not need a range there.

Here, the users might be split further, with one user having access to category `c7` while another has access to the category range `c8.c10`. Such a separation will be enforced through PAM, but that is only possible if the SSH daemon through which they connect dominates the category range associated with the users.

Separate instances also allow administrators to temporarily lock down the service (by shutting down the user SSH daemon, for instance) while still allowing SSH access for themselves.

Updating the network rules

Similar to the web server tuning, we need to look at the firewall rules. But unlike the web server, we do not intend to use a strongly different `SECMARK` labeling here (unless we use `SECMARK` to differentiate based on the source addresses, ensuring that administrators only log on through a known set of source systems).

Instead, we just enable the `SECMARK` labeling at the packet level (and omitting the category-based labeling). This `SECMARK` labeling is still useful (or even mandatory if another `SECMARK` label was activated already) to ensure that the communication toward the two SSH services are marked as SSH communication:

```
# iptables -t security -A INPUT -p tcp --dport 22 -j SECMARK \
    --selctx "system_u:object_r:ssh_server_packet_t:s0"
# iptables -t security -A INPUT -p tcp --dport 4971 -j SECMARK \
    --selctx "system_u:object_r:ssh_server_packet_t:s0"
```

We need to change the port type declaration in SELinux for the non-default port `4971`. This port will have the `unreserved_port_t` type assigned by default, and this needs to be switched to the `ssh_port_t` type:

```
# semanage port -a -t ssh_port_t -p tcp 4971
```

Usually, administrators log in from a more limited set of systems than customers or regular users of the shell-service-providing system. Limiting this access can be done through multiple settings.

The firewall could be updated to only allow communications to port `4971` from authorized subnets. This will ensure that the service is hidden from other subnets.

If the administrative communication originates from a different network interface, then the SSH daemon can even be configured to only listen on that network interface, while the user SSH daemon listens on all available interfaces.

Configuring for chrooted access

If the user SSH daemon enforces chrooting the users into a sub-location on the file system, we need to tell SELinux that this sub-location should be labeled as if it were a `root` file system itself.

For instance, to have `/var/jail/*` be labeled as if it were at `/`, you'd do this:

```
# semanage fcontext -a -e / /var/jail/
# restorecon -RvF /var/jail
```

The file context equality rules, however, might not be properly addressed for user home directories. As such, it might still be necessary to create custom rules for the individual users. If all users map to the same SELinux user, then this is just a matter of enabling the following rules:

```
# semanage fcontext -a -t user_home_dir_t -f d /var/jail/home/.*
# semanage fcontext -a -t user_home_t /var/jail/home/.*/.*
# restorecon -RvF /var/jail/home
```

The `chroot` jail needs to be built up, of course–an empty directory makes for a bad `chroot` environment if shell services need to be provided. Such jail locations can be filled with tools such as `debootstrap` or `jailkit`.

For instance, to create such a jail environment with `jailkit`, create the basic jail location and pass on a number of environments to `jailkit` to preload the environment with common binaries:

```
# jk_init -v /var/jail netutils basicshell jk_lsh
```

The supported environments (or other binary kits that `jailkit` can introduce in the jail) can be obtained through the `/etc/jailkit/jk_init.ini` file.

When the `chroot` jail is ready, the user SSH daemon can be updated to use chrooted access:

```
# cat /etc/ssh/user/sshd_config
...
Match group sshusers
  ChrootDirectory /var/jail/
  AllowTcpForwarding no
```

A different approach would be to immediately jail the users system-wide (and not only through the SSH daemon). However, this means that any other interaction with the system will either result in the home directories of the jail location being used or all logons to be directly in the jail. As we might want to have different behavior based on which SSH daemon a user logs on through, this is not what we'll look at here.

Associating SELinux mappings based on access

It is recommended that administrators have a different account for administrative tasks than they have for testing the functionality of the services that they run. Test accounts allow them to verify that a service works for a customer or client as it should–testing with administrative accounts is not preferred.

But using test accounts is not always possible, or the situation is such that the same user still needs to connect to both services (for instance, the administrative SSH and the user-directed SSH). With SELinux, we can still associate different SELinux contexts depending on the access context.

We could have the standard `sshd` PAM service used for regular users whereas we use an `adminsshd` PAM service for the administrative SSH daemon. Then, we can use the local customizations discussed in `Chapter 3`, *Managing User Logins*, to differentiate the mappings.

First, configure the administrative SSH daemon to use the `adminsshd` service name, which results in the administrative SSH daemon to using the `/etc/pam.d/adminsshd` configuration instead of the `/etc/pam.d/sshd` one. This allows administrators to even further harden or secure the service on the PAM level.

To accomplish this, we need to make sure that the administrative SSH daemon is launched through an `adminsshd` binary (rather than the default `sshd` one).

Creating a symbolic link is the first step for accomplishing this:

```
# ln -s /usr/sbin/sshd /usr/local/sbin/adminsshd
```

Update the systemd unit file or init script to point to the new binary (well, symbolic link) as the executing process:

```
# cat /etc/systemd/system/adminsshd.service
[Unit]
Description=OpenSSH Server Daemon for Administrators
After=syslog.target network.target auditd.service

[Service]
ExecStart=/usr/local/sbin/adminsshd
ExecReload=/bin/kill -HUP $MAINPID
SELinuxContext=system_u:system_r:sshd_t:s0-s0:c0.c1023

[Install]
WantedBy=multi-user.target
```

Next, edit or create the file for customized mappings in SELinux. For instance, for the user `alice`, you need the following:

```
# cat /etc/selinux/targeted/logins/alice
adminsshd: staff_u: s0-s0:c0.c1023
```

The default mapping for the user, however, is the `user_u` user:

```
# semanage login -l
Login Name    SELinux User  MLS/MCS Range    Service
%users        user_u        s0-s0:c0.c99     *
__default__   user_u        s0-s0:c0.c9      *
root          unconfined_u  s0-s0:c0.c1023   *
system_u      system_u      s0-s0:c0.c1023   *

Local customizations in /etc/selinux/targeted/logins
alice         staff_u       s0-s0:c0.c1023   adminsshd
```

This configuration ensures that `alice`, when logged on through the administrative SSH daemon, is assigned the `staff_u` SELinux user whereas her access through the regular user SSH daemon will use the `user_u` SELinux user.

Tuning SSH SELinux rules

A number of SSH-related SELinux booleans exist that fine-tune the behavior allowed by the SSH daemon. Considering that both the user SSH daemon and administrative SSH daemon run with the `sshd_t` type, these SELinux booleans apply to both domains.

If this is not wanted, then it might be necessary to create a custom domain for one or both SSH daemons. We assume here that this is not needed, as creating custom domains for SSH is a significant endeavor on its own.

The `ssh_chroot_rw_homedirs` SELinux boolean is not applicable when the standard interactive SSH chroot support is used. However, if the SFTP chroot capability of the SSH daemon is used, then the chrooted users will be running with a different context (`chroot_user_t`) rather than their user domain. In this case, the `ssh_chroot_rw_homedirs` SELinux boolean allows those users to read and write to the chrooted home directories.

Similarly, `ssh_chroot_full_access` is toggled when these same chrooted users (running in the `chroot_user_t` domain) need to access various files, even outside their initial home directory (or in their home directory but labeled with other types).

If the required access is toward web server content instead (such as the `httpd_sys_content_t` type as described in the previous section) then full access is too much. Instead, the `ssh_chroot_manage_apache_content` SELinux boolean can be enabled.

To allow users to log in as `sysadm_t`, the `ssh_sysadm_login` SELinux boolean needs to be enabled. Note that in the configuration described earlier, we map administrative users (such as `alice`) to the `staff_u` SELinux user. As a result, these users are assigned the `staff_r` role and `staff_t` domain. These users can then use commands such as `newrole` or `sudo` to switch to the more administrative `sysadm_r` role.

As such, this SELinux boolean does not need to be enabled for our use case.

Enabling multi-tenancy on the user level

Finally, if the shell-service-providing server is shared across multiple user groups, we might want to enable multi-tenancy on that level.

In the preceding instructions, we've mapped regular users to the `s0-s0:c0.c99` range. We could create a more fine-grained set, similar to the instance separation done on the web server systems beforehand:

```
# cat /etc/selinux/targeted/setrans.conf
s0-s0:c1=Customer1
s0-s0:c2=Customer2
...
```

The users can then be grouped into specific groups:

```
# getent group customer1
customer1:x:160348:andreas,bob,chelsea,dana
```

Thanks to SSH's PAM support, all that we need to do is to fine-tune the logins of the groups. The `pam_selinux` module, which is called by the `sshd` PAM service, will do the rest:

```
# semanage login -l
Login Name    SELinux User   MLS/MCS Range    Service
%customer1    user_u         s0-s0:c1         *
%customer2    user_u         s0-s0:c2         *
__default__   user_u         s0-s0:c0.c9      *
root          unconfined_u   s0-s0:c0.c1023   *
system_u      system_u       s0-s0:c0.c1023   *
```

File sharing through NFS

When systems need to share access to the same data set, they commonly use databases when the data is structured or a file server share when the data is unstructured. One of the most popular file-sharing capabilities in Linux is the use of the **Network File System** (**NFS**) service.

However, by default, NFS is not capable of handling extended attributes (needed for keeping track of the SELinux contexts). A number of possible implementations can be followed to enable NFS support on SELinux systems without great difficulty.

Setting up basic NFS

Start with the basic NFS setup to host the content. For instance, we might want to host the content under the `/export` location, with two subdirectories: `instance1` and `instance2`. These subdirectories could then be mounted on web-server-hosting systems.

In the /etc/exports file, put the file system to export through NFS together with the client list (a sort of coarse-grained access control list) and the options:

```
# cat /etc/exports
/export 192.168.1.0/255.255.255.0(ro,sync)
```

Start the NFS services, and then validate that the location is exported:

```
# systemctl start nfs# exportfs
/export  192.168.1.0/255.255.255.0
```

Enabling NFS support

The first and foremost approach used to handle NFS mounts on SELinux systems is to ensure that the services that depend on the NFS-mounted files can deal with the nfs_t type, which is by default associated with all NFS mounts. This is generally accomplished through SELinux booleans that need to be set on the client systems, not on the NFS server itself.

For most services, this is supported through the *_use_nfs SELinux booleans. For instance, cobbler_use_nfs allows the Cobbler software (a Linux installation server that enables quick networked installations) to use NFS-hosted files. Similarly, ftpd_use_nfs allows FTP servers to host and manage NFS-mounted file systems as the user-oriented targets.

A special mention goes to the httpd_use_nfs SELinux boolean. This one allows web server domains to use NFS-exported file systems as the content for the website. If the current NFS server will be used by the previously discussed web server systems, then this SELinux boolean would be a good idea to enable.

A special SELinux boolean is the use_nfs_home_dirs one. When set, several services that handle user home directories are now allowed to have those home directories hosted on an NFS share. Here, the focus is on the target (home directories) rather than the service.

Tuning the NFS SELinux rules

The NFS server itself is also governed through a number of SELinux rules. There are three main NFS-related SELinux booleans to consider on an NFS server:

- The `nfsd_anon_write` SELinux boolean, if set, allows the NFS server to modify files labeled with the `public_content_rw_t` type. This is similar to the `httpd_anon_write` boolean mentioned earlier in this chapter, focusing on resources handled by several otherwise unrelated services.
- The `nfs_export_all_ro` SELinux boolean ensures that the NFS server can only serve the content in a read-only fashion. If a vulnerability exists in the NFS server that allows forced writes or if a misconfiguration would allow writeable mounts, then this setting enforces that the NFS server still cannot write to the exported resources.
- The `nfs_export_all_rw` SELinux boolean allows the NFS server to share files in a read/write fashion, regardless of the SELinux contexts that these files currently hold.

For instance, for exposed web content, the read/write mode should be enabled as the dynamic websites might require writing to the exposed file system:

```
# setsebool -P nfs_export_all_rw on
```

Using context mounts

Whereas the default NFS-mounted locations are exposed as `nfs_t` file systems, administrators can opt to mount shares with different contexts. These contexts are only known on the systems where the NFS mount is active, not on the NFS server itself:

```
# mount nfsserver:/export/web /srv/web/instance1/htdocs \
  -o context="system_u:object_r:httpd_sys_content_t:s0"
```

Sadly, if another location on the same system and from the same NFS server is mounted with a different context, an error occurs:

```
# mount nfsserver:/export/wiki /srv/web/instance3/htdocs/wiki \
  -o context="system_u:object_r:httpd_sys_rw_content_t:s0"
kernel: SELinux: mount invalid. Same superblock,
different security settings for (dev 0:17, type nfs)
```

This is because a metadata cache is used on the system, which prohibits using different contexts for mounts. Luckily, this behavior can be changed through the `nosharecache` option during the mounting process:

```
# mount nfsserver:/export/web /srv/web/instance1/htdocs \
  -o nosharecache,context="system_u:object_r:httpd_sys_content_t:s0"
# mount nfsserver:/export/wiki /srv/web/instance3/htdocs/wiki -o \
   nosharecache,context="system_u:object_r:httpd_sys_rw_content_t:s0"
```

Working with labeled NFS

Recent NFS servers and versions (at least NFS version 4.2) have support for labeled NFS. This enables NFS servers to store and handle SELinux security context information. With labeled NFS enabled, clients can use the NFS mount as if it were a local file system with full extended attribute support.

The use of labeled NFS does require both the NFS server and all the client systems that mount file systems from the NFS server to use the same SELinux policy. When using labeled NFS, the file context of the NFS-server-hosted file system is exposed, and the NFS server will handle and pass through requests for relabeling operations to its local kernel.

To enable labeled NFS, make sure that the NFS daemon is launched with the `-V 4.2` option. For instance, on RHEL, this is handled by updating the `/etc/sysconfig/nfs` file:

```
# cat /etc/sysconfig/nfs
# Optional arguments passed to rpc.nfsd. See rpc.nfsd(8)
RPCNFSDARGS="-V 4.2"
```

On Gentoo, this is handled through the `/etc/conf.d/nfs` file:

```
# cat /etc/conf.d/nfs
# Start with 8 threads, and disable version 2, 3, 4 and 4.1
OPTS_RPC_NFSD="8 -N 2 -N 3 -N 4 -N 4.1 -V 4.2"
```

Restart the NFS service:

```
# systemctl restart nfs
```

On the clients, make sure that the mounts use NFS v4.2:

```
# mount -o v4.2 nfsserver:/export/web /srv/web/instance1/htdocs
```

On the NFS server itself, the exported location has to be properly labeled.

Comparing Samba with NFS

Another popular file sharing service is Samba, a free reimplementation of the **Server Message Block/Common Internet File System** (**SMB/CIFS**) networking protocol. It is positioned similarly to NFS, although the administration of Samba versus NFS is slightly different.

From a SELinux point of view, NFS and Samba have similar considerations.

When we look at the available SELinux booleans, similar SELinux booleans exist for Samba:

- The `allow_smbd_anon_write` SELinux boolean allows the Samba daemon to write to the `public_content_rw_t` type.
- The `samba_create_home_dirs` SELinux boolean allows the Samba daemon to create new home directories. This can be triggered through the Samba PAM modules.
- With `samba_enable_home_dirs`, Samba is allowed to share user home directories.
- The `samba_export_all_ro` and `samba_export_all_rw` SELinux booleans act similarly to the `nfs_export_all_ro` and `nfs_export_all_rw` SELinux booleans. When set, it allows Samba to export any file or directory (regardless of its type) in either a read-only mode or in read/write mode.
- The `samba_share_nfs` SELinux boolean allows Samba to access NFS shares. A better name would be `samba_use_nfs`, but sadly, this (unwritten) convention was not followed by the SELinux policy developers.

Exposed Samba shares are shown with the `cifs_t` type, similar to NFS shares being exposed as `nfs_t`. And to allow applications to access resources labeled with the `cifs_t` type, a number of SELinux booleans exist that generally use the `*_use_samba` syntax.

For instance, the `virt_use_samba` SELinux boolean allows virtual guests to use content (images) stored on Samba shares. Similarly, the `sanlock_use_samba` SELinux boolean allows the `sanlock` application to handle Samba shares.

There is a major difference between NFS and Samba as well, though. Samba shares need to be labeled as `samba_share_t` on the Samba server itself. This dedicated labeling is not a requirement for NFS.

Summary

In this chapter, we looked at a number of SELinux use cases and tuned the system to use SELinux capabilities to enhance the security of the services.

For the web server, we architected the entire setup to manage the different risk profiles of the websites across multiple systems, tuning SELinux on each of those systems. We saw how multiple instances can be started, each with its own category set, and how their content can be managed in a secure manner. We also saw how to differentiate between administrative roles for the same system, and we finished with network-related tunings.

Next, we saw how a shell-service-providing server can be hardened further, splitting the SSH daemon for two different purposes and running both with a different category set. We looked at fine-tuning the file system for chrooted access, and we even used a customized login so that a user receives a different SELinux context based on the SSH instance he (or she) logs in through.

Finally, we looked at an NFS server and discussed the various tuning parameters (handled through SELinux booleans) and mount options that influence the SELinux context of the shared resources. We then moved toward using an NFS server capable of handling extended attributes and showed how it can be used to support SELinux contexts. We finished the section with a small comparison of Samba's SELinux implementation with the NFS SELinux implementation.

Index

A

B

C

D

E

F

G

H

I

J

K

L

M

N

O

T

U

V

W

www.ingramcontent.com/pod-product-compliance
Lightning Source LLC
Chambersburg PA
CBHW061342210326
41598CB00035B/5862

* 9 7 8 1 7 8 7 1 2 6 9 5 4 *